GREENHORN
A Twentieth-Century Childhood

GREENHORN

A Twentieth-Century Childhood

ANNE TIBBLE

Illustrated by
KAREN HEYWOOD

Routledge & Kegan Paul
London and Boston

First published in 1973
by Routledge & Kegan Paul Ltd.
Broadway House, 68–74 Carter Lane,
London EC4V 5EL and
9 Park Street
Boston, Mass. 0218, USA

Printed in Great Britain by
Ebenezer Baylis and Son Ltd.
The Trinity Press, Worcester, and London

ISBN 0 7100 7570 7

Beautifully written, this evocative book
will appeal to anyone interested in the
country, in village life, its personalities
and even today its slow rate of change.
Anne Tibble tells the story of her
childhood in the North Riding of
Yorkshire, where her father was coachman at Rounton and where her ancestors
had farmed for some four hundred
years. She writes: 'This book is about
my up-bringing as a poor man's child
on the remote Cleveland estate of a
millionaire baronet. It is also about the
hamlet which upheld the estate. Most
importantly the book is about village
characters, parents and children, well-
to-do and not well-to-do, and their
trust in each other.'

CONTENTS

1 Father and Mother 1

2 Home 12

3 Facts of Life 52

4 Church Board School 74

5 Country Co-education Grammar School 112

'I'm nobody; who are you?
Are you nobody too?'
                    Emily Dickinson

Such is oft the course of deeds that move the
wheels of the world: small hands do them
because they must, while the eyes of the great
are elsewhere.
          J. R. R. Tolkien, *The Fellowship of the Ring*

1

FATHER AND MOTHER

'Hark that thrush,' my Father ordered. 'T' days is lengthening a cock-stride. But we've nobbut got to January-wi'-two-faces, lassie.'

The morning glittered with frost and sun. Aconites and snowdrops made a yellow and white carpet among tall beech and oak trees. Country silence hummed through the thick surrounding woods.

I was five. I didn't understand about two-faced Janus. But I could tell from the tone of Father's voice that the thrush's song and the lengthening days excited him.

He and I were going for our letters to the Big House. Father was coachman for a baronet, one of Britain's steel magnates : 'a threbble millionaire' Mother called him. In 1876 the millionaire's father had built the Big House for his country home.

The morning my Father and I went for the letters was the last of those sauntering tranquil years of Edward 'Peacemaker's' short reign. The Big House, with its lawns and gardens, was kept up by the labours of the entire village of East Rounton. I may be mistaken because country life changes much more slowly than it is often thought to change, but this particular pattern of community is much less common in England in the 1970s.

Father and I could see the Big House under blue sky at the end of the crooked mossy path through the woods. The five-storeyed mansion was made of yellowstone. It had warm, red-tiled gables and top-heavy chimneys. The date of its building and the entwined initials of its first owners stood out in big figures and capitals on the side of it facing us. Beyond velvet lawns, the Cleveland hills rose steep and greeny-blue, to our right, two miles away, as the crow flies, on the eastern edge of the Vale of York. We could see them through the one gap in the impenetrable green and black-lead of the winter woods.

The thrush stopped singing. Father stopped walking. Father always halted when an arresting thought struck him. 'This earth's round,' he said with a dazzling grin down to me. ''Tisn't flat. An' 't isn't still. No! Some sez we're whizzing along like billy-o.'

He pointed to the hills. His loud, country voice had a dashing disregard of accuracy which I didn't then suspect. Father was not what he himself called 'book-larnt'. He had no more than a holy eye for things big and little in the country. In fact, one part of Father greatly distrusted book-learning. Before we had set out for the letters that very morning he had insisted to my elder sister with three years' schooling behind her – because she was afraid of a newt that had crept into the house : 'Schooling can mek people daft. Tek care it meks you gels wiser; wiser now!'

My eye followed Father's pointing finger as we reached the end of the path. The January sky seemed to be made of bright and dazzling particles. Its blue went rioting down behind the greeny humps across Big Park. 'We're on a round, rolling ball,' Father informed his second daughter next. Hearing an answering thrush further off in the woods, bending to take that in, I rubbed my hand over the last bit of spear-moss that grew between the path's crazy paving. 'An' look you, lassie,' Father added more solemnly, 'beyond them green hills is Infinity.'

'Is Infinity Eternity?' I remembered the word 'Eternity' from my first Church-going last Sunday; and the word 'Infinity' slipped soundily from Father's lips.

'Eternity. Infinity. Heaven. Or – just sky. Call it whichever you like.' Father was already out of his depth but still blithely grinning.

Earth, then, was not a flat pancake. If earth whirls along, I thought, the thrushes and the hills and the trees must all get upside-down sometimes. Yet we always felt solidly, decently, most comfortably right-side-up.

Eternity and Infinity were as puzzling as Heaven. The picture that had come to mind last Sunday in Church when we sang about Heaven with 'streets of shining gold' was of a row of Big Houses and one Palace with yellow, shining towers in streets that led under archways with shimmering pearly gates. Gold streets and palaces lasting in such a Heaven for ever? Suddenly this eternal scene didn't bear thinking about. Sky and stars on and on into what Father had called Infinity then? Infinity made thought boggle.

Coleridge says that children, even very young ones, accept vastness and mystery without difficulty. But an Eternal, Infinite, gaudy, gilt and pearly Heaven was no rival in my mind for the bright living shine and variety of

3

all around, that morning in January-wi'-two-faces about
1910.

My Mother came from that class which still holds three-
quarters of earth's people. Feelings of frugality, of thrift,
of going it the hard way, of starting from scratch, all
derive from Mother. Her father had been, for his whole
life, the cobbler in the next village, West Rounton. He
was six feet four and so thin and kind and straight that he
might have stepped straight out of a Hans Andersen
fairy tale. When I first read about the Little Cobbler, it
was my wraith-like maternal grandfather six feet four
inches tall who took shape before my bedazzled eyes.

Mother didn't spend a night away from the cottage of
her birth — two rooms on top of other two, with the
cobbler's hut at the side — until she married Father when
she was thirty-five. Not in all her life, and she didn't die
until quick, easy travel had long been in, in the 1950s,
did Mother see grey-towered London. She didn't go
outside Yorkshire. At marriage she moved two miles. At
ninety she died.

Some people, thinking in strict terms of plush carpets,
mod. cons., bathrooms, flush lavatories, refrigerators, deep
freezes, washing-machines, might call the cottage of
Mother's birth a hovel or a slum. It wasn't, you know. It
was a warm, neat, clean little house. In it my Mother
nursed my maternal grandmother until granny died of
cancer. What Mother told us about granny was never
about cancer. It was that granny was important in the
village: she had Second Sight. She knew, when somebody's baby was 'pitched' ready to be born, whether it was
going to be a boy or a girl; she could 'see' when somebody
was going to die. Mother didn't explain what good

'seeing' these events beforehand was. Second Sight was a Gift.

Mother didn't think her own life had been dull. Oh no: those A. L. Rowse calls 'idiot people' have a content, often mistaken for stupidity, that helps country people such as Chaucer's ploughman, Langland's immortal Piers, and the millions without names all over the twentieth-century country world, endure. Persecution, war, frantic change, and fanatic hate whirl over their and our heads. But like weeds and some pests, daisies and depredatory wild doves, the country kind endures.

Father's ancestors had been 'men bred to the earth'. This, Father often declared, he knew 'by word of mouth'. 'Word of mouth' meant that Father thought there were other ways of knowing than by written words. During those five hundred years of relative stability in English agriculture between the thirteenth century and the eighteenth, Father's family had not moved from the rich, flat acres between the chalk Wolds and the Yorkshire coast. Before Enclosure, Ns had farmed three thousand acres. When Father was born, they had a thousand acres only. A Georgian farmhouse bears link with them, and their name is still found in Yorkshire at Leven and Withernwick.

North Farm lies near one of the fareways by which our Bronze Age and Iron Age forebears came from the Continent long before the Romans and the Vikings. This fareway was used twice by usurpers in the late Middle Ages. The idea we children got of these earliest forebears of ours was rough and ready; but thanks to Father it wasn't hazy. He said : 'Our early forebears were big men with light-coloured beards down to their waists, and they dressed in skins. They walked in front of their wives to scare away wolves and bears. T' women were heavy-laden carrying bairns on their backs wi' t' pots and pans, see?'

We didn't think of our early forebears doing a great deal of fighting. As a boy ploughing, Father had 'often enough picked up axe-heads, bone mattocks, and shards. An' *they* weren't tools for war,' he said. 'What did you do with the things you found?' we often asked Father. 'Cast 'em back on t' earth where they belonged,' he would reply, as if this careless view of our human past were indisputable.

'There were some ancient mounds in the fields where I was a boy,' he would add. And he spoke about 'a kind of walled ditch' on the east side of the farm; 'For us folk to defend ourselves and keep *free*,' Father said with his knock-me-down trenchancy.

'But mi' grandfather got bit by a bug called Greed. This Greed made him lust and hanker after more money.' Father supposed Greed to have begun to bite men to frenzy only at the beginning of 'modern times'. Later, I knew that the men of Ur started banking with gold from Kush and Ophir. The bug of Greed has been biting men at least since the Neolithic Revolution of about 3000 B.C.

Not having enough interest to consume his fierce energy, Father's grandfather had taken on a sideline to farming. 'This was his method,' said my Father, 'of getting rich quick. Your great-grandad made himself into a moon-raker, a shady buyer and seller of horses. He coined a fortune of some twenty thousand pounds.'

His son, Father's father, was also interested in money and horseflesh, as well as in land and cattle and grain. 'But your grandad had a smart eye for womenflesh, too,'

6

Father would add with a wink. 'He squandered that fortune your great-grandad left, in drink and loose girls.' For some reason, when Father talked of 'squandering that fortune' I remembered a dream I sometimes had – of picking up half-crowns in the grass, coming upon one after another with ever-increasing surprise. 'Loose girls' were clearly girls too soon let loose from home.

Father's many stories painted grandfather and great-grandfather on the cave-walls of our minds. Our tall, fair-bearded, earliest forebears must have got mixed somehow with shorter forebears : for both grandfather and great-grandfather had been small, flaxen-haired, blue-eyed countrymen. Each had an enormous, ringing voice. 'This stamp of voice,' Father was convinced, 'men needed to shout over the sea to each other as they came in their boats' ; grandfather developed his lungs further through years of bellowing at his men across the plain of Holderness. W. H. Hudson says that his father, ranching on the Pampas, possessed such a voice.

'When your grandad had been away for days at Topcliffe gipsy horse-fair, he'd reach home about five of a morning. But he wasn't, as you might have expected, quiet, a bit shamefaced. No fear! He was in a towering, devilish rage. He'd drag his buckskins on, and then his great stinking manure-coated boots, leap astride his Zingari-bought, skewbald pony. And then he'd clatter bareback and roughshod round the farm setting all his men to work. Abuse he flung to left and right. Anybody who was one second late got bell-tinker! Your grandfather was always kittler after a few nights on the tiles. He was sure of being first on the scene. So he had all his words roaring-ready at his little red tongue's end.'

7

'Wasn't he a kind man?'

'Kind? Your grandad was what's called a Tyrant,' Father would roar.

Thus, almost from the first there grew in our minds this idea that some men were tyrants who could threaten continually the freedom and independence of others, and some were too patient and bore the domination of the strong.

'One morning when your granny had waited up all night for him, the old devil actually raised his whip to her. She'd told him off, I expect.'

'Weren't you there?'

'No. But up I comes next minute an' taks her part. Ah clouted me own father's lugs.'

'You never!' we would say in admiring horror.

'He ordered me out of me own home.' Father's grin held remembered outrage undimmed by time.

He was the eldest of seven sons to be ordered from their home. Then grandfather was alone. And soon after, Northgrave's farm was lost, sold away at last. You couldn't, even in Victorian days, farm without sons who would work long hours for no extra pay and precious little leisure. Or could it be that work was, then, somehow nearer pleasure? Last of a long line of stout Yorkshire yeomen, grandfather's farm followed the fate of many such in the early nineteenth-century revolution in farming. By his late middle age he had become one of those disliked interlopers, a mere bailiff. Farm sold and freedom gone, he came to the North Riding to be bailiff-agent in the new rural estate of the millionaire baronet at Rounton Grange in Cleveland.

Grandmother was five feet high. Married at sixteen, she bore her husband seventeen children. One of her two pairs of identical twins died at birth. Eight of granny's seventeen offspring reached eighty years of age. By three minutes my Father was the elder of the pair of identical twins which lived.

The two little fair-haired, blue-eyed boys, Father and his twin, were so alike that only granny could tell one from the other. Fred and Tom shared praise, blame, and punishment. When they were seventeen they quarrelled – 'for the first time in our lives,' Father used to say. 'We were left to finish in the harvest-field when the hired men had gone. We had a battle with our pitchforks.' He could never be brought to remember what the quarrel was about. But his brother's fork pierced Father's thigh. That ended the fight.

The brothers made a pact. 'We linked our little fingers, and we crossed our throats with our left-hand fingers – like this,' he'd demonstrate the solemn-promise ritual with one of us: 'Tom an' me spat our deaths at each other. We swore to let on to nobody what we'd been up to.'

Father's thigh healed of itself. Often we heard him say: 'Some bad weather's about. Tom's fork's giving me jip.'

In her youth granny cannot have been more over-worked in the eighteen-sixties than some of my con-temporaries in the nineteen-sixties with two or three small children and no help except gadgets that save a little labour but no time. Granny had a nursemaid, a henmaid, and a floor-washing woman. Daily she cooked for twelve men and for twenty-two harvesters in September: 'Seven to cut, seven to bind, seven to sheave. And your grandfather too busy telling us all what to do, to do much hisself,' Father would grin.

The ten Irish labourers hired for haytime and harvest slept on straw in the big barns at North Farm. A hundredweight of beef turned and sizzled and roasted each week on granny's hook above her big open fire. She herself made bread, butter, cakes, jams, pickles, sausages, blackpuddings, chitterlings, and brawn. She salted hams, mended the family's shirts and socks and trousers, made rugs and hairpin doilies. She grew thyme, chives, sage, marjoram, basil, rosemary and lemon balm. But what she liked best were 'useless' flowers — violets, lilies, and pinks. When grandfather and granny grew old, they went to live at Croft. And man to man at last, Father and the lively old man were reconciled.

Granny's garden at Croft, their last home, was even more crowded with roses, lilies, lavender, catmint, sweetbriar, pinks, stocks, wallflowers, and jasmin, than her big garden at North Farm had been. At Croft, she had a mania for all the scented flowers she could grow. No other banks of flowers on either side of a winding pebble path have ever come up to my brightly-hued memory of granny's bee-furnished array in the village where Lewis Carroll grew up.

Granny was a little black barrel with clothes on. She waddled among her flowers, nothing like as high as her Michaelmas daisies. On the occasions when she came to stay with us, she wore a cream lace cap on her silver hair and a small white apron round the front of her black taffeta bodice and skirt. Her plump, soda-shiny left hand with the wedding ring hidden in the flesh was forever needlessly smoothing the little apron down. She couldn't have been much more than in her mid-sixties then; but she seemed desperately old. I remember no feeling other than awe, an almost frantic need to escape her piercing eye and sharp tongue. She was more than a grown-up. She was another kind of being, far away, completely fearful, not to be approached for comfort or confidence. Her gimlet eyes were blue as forget-me-nots.

2

HOME

Like his immediate ancestors, my flax-haired Father was small and spare. He took good care, by hard riding and gardening, to remain, as he put it at seventy-five, 'jimp and nimble as a lop'.

When he was twenty-three and had been ordered from his home, Father had become a groom. Later he joined the stables of the 'steel' millionaire for whom grandfather was bailiff. Only a few months after Father began to work for the Bells, their coachman fell drunk off the 'box' one night when driving his Lady home from a New Year's Ball. Next day my Father was installed as coachman and stud-groom; and tactfully old D. was pensioned off.

About 1900, Father's wages under the steel magnate Sir Lothian Bell were fifteen shillings a week. He also had a suit of clothes, a set of blue and silver livery, and a pair of jack-boots every year. When, at thirty-six, Father married Mother, his wages became one pound. The two were given a free cottage, a pint of milk each day, a Christmas goose, a garden in a field corner, and as much manure as Father liked.

Father liked mountains of this powerful syllabub. 'It leavens up our heavy Cleveland clay,' he maintained. A picture which rests behind my eyes is of that twinkle-eyed wizard, my Father, in green breeches and waistcoat, sitting on his five-barred garden rail, stirring manure into his 'meg-tub' with a sycamore stick. His garden humus grew so rich that Father rubbed his horny hands in satisfaction, until they made a sound like wind in bulrushes: 'Soil like this,' he grinned, 'why it'd a'most grow MEN.'

'Begot free, Ah'm now a servant.' Often Father regretfully reminded himself. He clung to certain kinds of simplicity with a pig-headedness that was both admirable and stupid. He and my Mother were sceptical of 'show', 'pomp', ceremony. They despised 'fine' talk. Any parade of feeling that might be 'put on' or 'faked' was wholly distasteful. Ours was a closely knit but very carefully concealed family affection.

Not once did I see my Father kiss Mother, or she him. He rubbed our kisses off, I began to notice, when I was about six. Soon after that, none of his three children kissed Father any more. We shook hands at bedtime or when we were going on a journey. And in our hand-shakes, great warmth, and to the very last, a sense of complete trust, passed from palm to palm. Mother we kissed to the end, of course.

About 1910, our cottage was lighted by electricity from the Big House's new engine. This engine gave light to the estate but not to the village cottages and farms. These had oil lamps until about 1920. And those village cottages to this very day, like streets and streets of factory-workers' houses in some of the finest cities of Britain's Welfare State, have no bathrooms or flush lavatories. The 1951 Census gives 7 or 8 per cent of houses in the rural district of East and West Rounton as having 'indoor conveniences'. Television beat 'indoor conveniences' in rural Britain by decades.

Our earth-closet (Mother mistakenly called it the 'W') was raked out once a week by the home-farm men. The 'W' was an ivy-covered tower with three holes ranging in size like the Three Bears' porridge bowls. A visit to 'Miss Ivy' was a good helter-skelter in rain or snow. We went hatted and coated. The expedition could be a small endurance if one had a feverish cold or a chill. If 'taken short' in the night, we used the pot, which Father called the 'jerry'.

Occasionally 'Miss Ivy' was a refuge. Like most country privies, its whitewashed, brick walls held many fascinations. On their inner sides were designs of bearded gods, pig-tailed Chinamen, lions, snouting pigs, curve-roofed pagodas, Norman castles, and Gothic steeples. Quaintly-shaped islands, whole archipelagos of them, floated on its ceiling. If you had a candle or a storm-lantern with you, fabled animals or strange beings wove themselves out of shadow at your very elbows.

You hadn't to lose your wits in 'Miss Ivy's' world, though. There were real enough, enormous, voluptuous-bellied spiders with silvery skull and crossbones patterned on their grey backs. Green tree-toads were liable to invade and leap wildly across your feet. Black, warty toads squatted, their throats breathing in and out ('Poison — that,' Mother wrongly averred). Or a bronze slow-worm streaked in terror past your eye-corner.

Our cottage was one storey above an archway between an outer courtyard and an inner, glass-domed stableyard.

The whole cottage was remarkably full of draughts. As these were quite incurable, we simply grew used to them and in the end called them fresh air. To warm the big kitchen, my Mother carried coals up two dozen steep steps. She fed our black, insatiable monster of an iron range with logs. It devoured six-foot boughs, whole dead-wood tree trunks ; and then, when Mother had been to the wood and filled up the range's reckless maw until she at least was streaming with heat, that oven was still only warm enough to cook our rice pudding.

On Christmas morning, Mother started at six to feed it up for our goose to be cooked for dinner at noon. By midnight, the perverse thing would, as she angrily said, be hot enough to have roasted a couple of bullocks. But when Mother had cleaned up her hearth, her black-lead shone so that our faces looked back at us quaintly mis-shapen from a dozen little looking-glasses.

Besides the kitchen, our cottage had a parlour, three big bedrooms, a large scullery, and a pantry. The scullery was very dark because of the huge trees outside. Its sink was in a windowless corner under a sloped ceiling not three feet high. The pan-cupboard you had to grovel on your knees before, if you wanted to get a pan out. The pantry basked in the full glare of sun from the south-west. But unlike so many hen-coop houses of twenty years later, the cottage near the Big House was a regular House for Children.

Its three enormous bedrooms each held a double feather-bed and a single hard one. Decked in tablecloths and antimacassars, when we were very young, we danced on our beds in the early mornings. We played 'Going to the Ball' or 'Off to visit Lady Blancmange at Castle Tremayne'. My little sister was the Countess Siggles-

thropple, my elder sister the Indian Princess Zeinab, and
usually I was their groom. We played the same games out
of doors, making Big Houses of fir cones. We rode
hunting, or 'in the Row', ourselves both riders and
prancing horses. Little snobs already, we had half an
imaginary Debrett on our visiting lists. Mother's friends
were the Big House nanny and the lady's-maid. We knew
a little of how the rich lived. Gentry children, for instance,
had brown bread and milk for supper and very plain food
– and so had we.

All the cottage chairs were hard. The advance in
domestic luxury, accelerated in Jane Austen's day, never
reached the cottage. Our only comfortable chair by
twentieth-century lounge standards was the rocking-
chair. This was Father's by divine right. But round it,
with Mother in, whilst Father took his Sunday afternoon
stroll in the fields, we knelt, or sat. Each of us had a
cracket. Mamie's stool was square, Margie's was oblong,
and mine was round.

In our earliest days Mother sang to us from the
rocking-chair :

'Little girl, little girl, where have you been?'
'I've been to London, to see the Queen.'
'What did she give you when you got there?'
'A can of milk.' 'And what did you say?'
              'O thank you, dear Queen.'

The little girl's method of addressing that most bountiful
of countrywomen, the Queen, was 'very sensible', our
Mother said. Other rhymes were felt to have less quality.
The laughingly derisive pawnshop reference of

Half a pound of twopenny rice,
    Half a pound of treacle ;
Mix it up and make it nice ;
    Pop goes the weasel !

escaped us.

Soon we learnt a hymn to say to Mother round the rocking-chair every Sunday afternoon. Mother's favourites were 'All things bright and beautiful', 'Let all the world in every corner sing', 'God moves in a mysterious way', 'Songs of praise the angels sang', and 'Praise to the Holiest'. None of us knew that three of these are by poets. Mirth and praise for being on earth Mother thought very necessary. 'If we'd been in at the Beginning,' she would say, 'when Creation began, we'd have seen the first rose open its petals and the first leaf burst its brown case. We'd have watched Jack Frost make ropes out of twigs like threads for the *first* time. Wouldn't that have been great?'

I spent hours trying to see grass grow and poppies open. Once I did catch an evening primrose, with tiny, noiseless jerks, open its yellow flowers. In the humdrum days which we had reached, eyes evidently had to look with the long patience of ardour for such excitement.

The rest of the cottage furniture was plain and simple and as strong as the rocking-chair. Chairs, tables, and chests of drawers were meant to last a lifetime. They did last. I don't remember any new thing, except the piano, being bought. It isn't true to say that working people like the shoddy and the brightly new. In the kitchen, besides the 'rocker', there were the arm-chair, and four plain ones round a big, square, scrubbed table covered with brown lino. A clean white tablecloth went on for meals ; and when meals were not in progress, the table was covered with a red cloth. A pot of flowers stood in the middle. The parlour had leather chairs; and a basket one gave out eerie squeaks when the red heart of the fire burnt low, late at night. The parlour had also a bamboo table, and a bear-skin rug which was Sir Lothian's wedding present to our parents. Later the parlour held the piano.

For pictures in the kitchen we had a large map of Britain and portraits of our Gentry. Long before I went to school, I could have drawn blindfold the fascinating triangle of our own country. I could have put in the resounding names our ancestors have given to some of our capital cities – York, Canterbury, Norwich, London, Edinburgh; and for years lesser but beautiful names like Dovey, Caernarvon, Aberdeen, Ravenscar, and Glaston-bury said themselves over and over from the map.

Sir Lothian had given Father his portrait. This hung opposite the map. Father had a story about the morning of that gift: 'What's the exact time, Fred?' Sir Lothian asked, having spent a precious minute or two presenting the framed photo of himself before Father took him to catch his train. 'I think,' Father answered, carefully consulting his watch on its wide silver chain across his waistcoat front: 'it's six minutes past eight.'

'Don't just *think*, Fred. Never just *think*,' Sir Lothian returned irritably: 'it pays to *know*.'

There were two pictures in our parlour. One was of a not very lovely, dark-browed lady called Theodora. Theodora sat before a Tarot pack of cards. One plump, dusky arm stole from her almost bare breast and pointed dramatically to the Ace of Hearts. Theodora had been an Egyptian queen, my Mother strangely knew. Actually, Theodora was the emperor Justinian's formidable wife.

She brought a thousand years of Christianity to Meroë on the Nile. But I didn't know that stray item until long afterwards.

The other picture was a cheap reproduction of young Ralegh and his cousin Humphrey Gilbert. With their hands clasped round their knees, the two boys listened to the old seaman's tales of adventure. Our bucolic minds didn't grasp that the old Salt was talking of piracy. I was slower still to learn that love of Britain couldn't be merely to imagine ourselves leaders and governors, or even more intellectual, clean, smart or rational than other nations. At that time Britain led the world. And did we forget it! But soon we must climb down and know ourselves vulnerable as others.

Downstairs, our enormous washhouse looked over the feathery woods. In the washhouse, hairy-kneed spiders lurked, as big as those in the closet, but without skull and crossbones such as the 'diadem' beauties had. There were some nicer little creatures which Mother called 'silver-fish'. One of the earliest lessons Mother taught us was that it was 'silly to be frightened of spiders'. 'Especially when there's some,' she said : 'that can spin far cleverer patterns in silk in the autumn dew than you can yet with your sewing or knitting.' Nor were we allowed to fuss about wasps. 'If you feel something creeping on any part of you, give it a good flick ; but not with a heavy hand,' Mother cautioned us : 'if you thump it, naturally the wasp or bee will dot you one back.'

As a boy, Father had tracked the wild bees to their nests in the fir trees. He and his twin had pinched the honey. Toads gave Mother the shivers, she confessed. And she also agreed that the dusty spinners in her washhouse corners were 'no great shakes at web-weaving'. These spiders she lifted firmly out of the closet or the wash-house, 'about their business', on her broom-end. But she did not forget to chant:

If you want to live and thrive
Let the spider run alive.

Mother was superstitious. She tried hard to outgrow this, having such a practical husband. She thought looking through glass at the new moon unlucky. Spilling salt was, too. To avoid ill-hap, quietly she threw a pinch over her left shoulder, however much Father laughed at her. Putting a shoe on the table was 'mucky' rather than unlucky. But if she forgot something and had to turn back after she had set off somewhere, she would sit down unobtrusively a moment before setting out afresh. If she put her stocking on inside-out, inside-out it stayed all day. Inside-out meant 'luck'; and she just wouldn't forfeit that 'luck' which is still a power in lives not only of working folk. A piece of black soot hanging from the fire-bar meant a welcome visitor for us. If our ears 'burnt', 'Somebody's thinking about you.' Breaking a looking-glass was catastrophic. It meant 'full fifty years' ''Bad'',' Mother said. Falling upstairs foretold a marriage. Falling down-stairs, and fall down occasionally we did, was neither one thing nor another: 'Tuck your fins in and learn to roll,' was both Father's and Mother's advice. 'Let yourselves go.'

The inner and outer courtyards with their big pillars, under the cottage, were great fun for tag, hide-and-seek, and relievo. What places to hide! The cornbin with meal-white spider-webs in its corners was the most secure if you put its lid down on yourself, the hayhouse where you could jump from rafters, the prickly strawhouse, the coachhouse, in the very carriages themselves. Hide-and-seek was the best game of all.

Our toys were few. We had balls, which we threw into the air and caught again after clapping our hands or stamping our feet in a known series of movements. We didn't play hopscotch or hitchy-bay. Kicking a piece of tile wore out our shoe-toes ; at any rate, it took 'the mense off them,' Mother said. We had pieces of rope with which we skipped whilst we sang 'Over the hills and far away' :

Take her by the lily-white hand
    Lead her to the water.
Offer her all that you can give,
    For she's the old man's daughter.

Each of us had a doll – I had three – and we made trousseaux for these dolls with the help of Mother ; and her sewing-machine we used from the age of about five. We begged shoe-boxes to trim with white muslin and blue ribbon from Mother's 'bits-and-pieces bag' for dolls' beds. Occasionally we played dominoes. But we weren't very keen on games in which 'you *have* to win'. And I soon tired of the mere bodily movements of skipping and tag.

There were many hiding places out of doors. Up in a tree was best. You could sit still until birds hopped around as if you weren't there. Gentry would pass underneath and not spy you. The big woods were on every side. A dapple of sunlight, the green and red woodpecker, the red squirrel, the giant yellow fungus, gradually became parts of an extended self that would have been numbskulled if it had grown used to variety such as that which waked us in that remote green place every morning of every year.

The Big House clock chimed melodiously and remorselessly each quarter of an hour. Solemnly it tolled the hours over the summer fields and sage-green woods ; in winter, over brown fields and ruby-black woods. You could hear Time all over the estate, which stretched to the hills. There wasn't a shadow of excuse for any of us being late for meals ; and summer and winter, our breakfasts, dinners, teas and suppers – at eight, twelve, four and eight – were always as punctual as the clock or Time itself. If we were late, we got a ticking off.

Certain other sounds might have passed unnoticed in a quiet less deep. Trains from the London–Edinburgh main line brought echoes of far-away bustle on drowsy, summer afternoons. Doves moaned incessantly through the beeches. Startled pheasants squawked on frostbound winter nights. Mating foxes barked at full moon.

We sisters tramped knee-deep, our arms 'coach-horse' round each other's waists, through November leaves. We balanced on top of railings or in frost-hard ruts, tried to walk on shallow, iced pools without shattering them. We were at the glorious pastime of DOING NOTHING. Absorbed in this pastime I spent most of the first ten years of my life.

The dry rustle of the tawny beech leaves made laughter bubble inconsequently from our lips. Our five peacocks screeched weirdly before rain. Thunderstorms were demonstrations of a glorious Power. Mrs M. and Mrs K., two village women, cowered in their under-stairs cupboards when thunder rumbled along the hills. We Ns rather delighted in thunder and lightning. Even the knock of fear in our ribs that big crashes gave was a thrill we didn't care to miss.

Mrs M. and Mrs K. told their children that the woods were 'haunted' : by men who had been murdered, or by ghosts in white sheets. We knew better. The woods were, as Father put it, 'full of plenty to see and hear'. The woods showered benisons of happiness and beauty. But they could also throw out a sense of wrangling lost ages of indifference. This second influence of the woods provoked a feeling that drove me, at least, near that restlessness christened — by Sartre, later, I think — boredom. Sartre says it 'nauseated' him. But this 'boredom', as well as ambition, must be what drives people from the night-shrouded country to the lights of the town — and back again.

There were times when one longed for the rush and urgency and drama of people. A badger bolting from his sett, a new bird coming out of its egg, made a little excitement. The hornbeam a-dazzle with its green flowers was sometimes enough ; but not always. This relentless slowness of changing time is enlightening to have to live beneath. The opposing sensations, the benison of content and the tough, tyrannous indifference, the sense of peace that is only externally kind, and the sense of quiet that feels changeless and is not, inevitably bring the dawn of the realisation that whilst the woods are beautiful they contain plants that throttle their neighbours and animals that eat theirs. All these fumbling discoveries first cast you back into the cavern of yourself; and then they wash you out to long for human trust, never human grandeur, that venture in the adventurous quest of more and more human wisdom.

But first you have felt the kinship with the bird and the badger, the tree, and the stone. Inarticulately you have found out that there is no absolute division between one kind of earth's inhabitants and another kind. You grasp that your quiescence *and* your sloth are a little like the

c

stone's torpor. You understand without written word or 'word of mouth' the tree's uprightness: the tree is one shade nearer your own quality than the stone. Country-born individuals recognise these elements of homespun philosophy. They are neither commonplace nor sentimental. They glimpse an almost sullen independence that accepts the lonely responsibility of being human among Things; at the same time this independence, though often almost inarticulately glad of human communication, doesn't expect guarantees of any kind to be more than limited, or life to be anything other than under tension and continual threat.

One day in the woods I was wondering what happened to the trees, the paths, the ferns, and the dappled shade when nobody was there to see. Did they disappear? For some time I privately thought they did. Father said not. They were not full of wizards, witches, gnomes and such like. That 1970s' writers still feed our children with such stuff is depressing.

Round some laurels Peter jumped out on me. Peter was fifteen. He was a farmer's son.

He said: 'Come over in those bushes, funny girl.'

I can't remember whether I knew what Peter wanted. Did I? Or didn't I? I think I knew with the kind of knowing that has little to do with one's intelligence. Audacious and curious, I went with him into the darker shadow of the bushes.

As if it was something Peter had known since he was born, he came near and put his knee behind mine. But I knew how to fall as well as he knew how to trip, and the pine carpet was soft. Looking up through green spring leaves I don't recall that during the next few minutes I felt a depraved child. Certainly I didn't think that what Peter did was in any way disgusting. On the contrary, his deed to me aged seven was evidently a clumsily solemn, very intriguing experiment for Peter himself.

When he had helped me shake the leaves out of my hair, straight home I sped through the fan-vaulted beeches. Doubt descended as I ran. I heard myself think : certainly Mother will like to know what Peter did. Up to then I had told Mother everything. I was sure, but I don't know why, that everything had to be confided to her.

How distressed Mother was. But also she was more angry than I had ever seen her. 'I shall go to that boy's father and mother,' she declared : 'he's a dirty brute.'

'But I'm not altered,' I assured her crying : 'I'm not dirtied. Peter wasn't rough. He was quite gentle.'

'You little faggot,' my mother said mournfully. Strangely Credo Mutwa, Zulu writer of *My People*, uses this word of unknown origin for a sexy girl. Could Zulu and British have met in our remote past?

But only the combined tears of her three daughters restrained Mother from marching off in furious indignation to Peter's mother there and then. At last she calmed down enough to promise not to go and make a fuss.

That evening she went out. She didn't say where she was going ; and after about half an hour of her absence, though I trusted her word completely about not going to Peter's parents, I thought : well, she must have had to leave because of the filthy thing I've been and done.

My sisters and I didn't discuss any of this. But each went to two of our neighbours. Perhaps Mother was with one of them? She wasn't. None of us suggested Peter's house. Wildly I set off across the fields towards Arncliffe, where Mother's best friend Minnie lived. Mother wasn't at Minnie's. Back I rushed along the springing corn. It had tiny blue and yellow pansies growing at its roots. The new moon lay in a sky that went clear through into that endlessness that Father had said was Infinity.

When I reached home, there was Mother calmly frying potatoes and cabbage for Father's supper. The ache in my heart was gone in a trice. But that day's happenings drove home a sense of how much couldn't be trusted to be what it seemed. Not only in the woods were matters terribly mixed up. The sureties about ourselves were as hard to come at as Infinity behind the hills.

Some time after that, Father was showing me how to tie 'a knot that'll hold a plunging horse'.

I said : 'It's a very hard knot this, dad,' meaning it was hard to learn.

'An' why, my silly little fout,' Father demanded : 'shouldn't a knot be *hard*. Why should it be simple? Better learn as soon as you like : some things are as simple as muck ; and muck isn't all that simple. And some things are as hard as hell.'

Oh yes, we learnt. Father and Mother had a horror of 'spoiling' us, of 'being soft', and making us 'soft'. All the same we learnt rather slowly.

Our nearest doctor lived five miles away. An awful commotion ensued when any of us got ill. On the rare occasions when we saw that alarming gentleman, Dr Snowdon, he drove a tall dog-cart, wore a high black silk 'shiner', and his white beard, like the beards of our forebears, reached to his waist.

Even when I developed lumps in my throat and a fever, Mother didn't call Dr Snowdon. 'You've sat in them damp woods too long,' she scolded. And of course I *had* been in the woods on the thick fir-moss for hours. Even after experiment and painful result, it seemed difficult to learn that 'sitting in damp gives you chills'. (It doesn't, of course.) But : 'A bit of what it's like to be poorly'll teach you not to be so silly,' Mother asserted.

That winter night of my fever I awoke with the half-pleasant, shivering, burning, far-away-ness of slight delirium. I was in the big feather-bed where I slept with my younger sister. Our elder sister slept in the single bed two yards across the green oilcloth. As it was only about seven in the evening all except me were up enjoying themselves. Murmur of their voices and laughter drifted through the closed kitchen door down the long passage to me in bed. Wind howled with sub-human accents in the woods outside. Now they *did* seem full of the giants, demons and witches of Germanic legend.

'Moth-er !' I tried to call. But an alarming thing had taken place. The voice with which I strove to call was not there. I was ALONE. I had no means of reaching the comfort of her presence. After an age of waiting in the monstrous dark, the kitchen door opened. Smiling and calm, Mother appeared. She bore the brown jug of lemon-and-honey steaming between her fingers. At sight of her fear went away.

Our nearest dentist was further away than Dr Snowdon. A visit to the dentist meant, before buses, a day's travel, an expensive twelve miles. I didn't go to the dentist until I was eighteen. When our second teeth ached, but could not be pulled out, we sat by the fire, wrapped in the brown shawl, and held a bag of hot bran to our cheeks.

Father's standards in the matter of bearing pain were higher than those of his 'women'. He and his twin had performed the service of pulling out loose or aching teeth for each other. They tied the defaulting tooth, still in one of their heads, to a door-knob by a good length of stout linen thread. 'Thread was *thread* in them days,' Father often said. The other twin went behind the door and pulled it sharply. Presto! The tooth dangled from the door-knob on the thread-end.

But we girls could only jostle our loose and aching teeth touchily and bear them in triumphant relief to Mother when at last they were out. She praised us, told us to put the tooth carefully into the flame of the fire. Then she taught us:

Fire, fire, burn a bone;
God send me another tooth again:
A straight one,
A white one,
And in the same place again.

Of course there were one or two villagers whose health was poor; these, Father scornfully said, were 'allus hanging their heads for the auld doctor'. There was another villager who was 'shifty'. That is, he was a rather systematic pilferer of the Gentry's fruit and vegetables entrusted to him. Still another was a toady. Of all these both Father and Mother were deeply contemptuous.

The village community was not traditional, though the Rountons are as old as Domesday Book, and perhaps older. Fresh members had been added in the nineteenth century for the upkeep of the Big House. The forty servants inside the House formed a second, much more artificial, temporary community for the brief flowering of that brilliant family. We Ns had a double link, with the village, and with the Big House.

Soon after my fever had gone, the year I was seven, we were invited to Edie Wright's tea-party. We put clean frocks on. We brushed each other's long yellow hair until it shone. And we washed ourselves so much we all smelt of Knight's Castile soap.

But then Father's new telephone rang. There was an important message. After coming to consult Mother, Father went downstairs again, and began harnessing Priarus the pony into the Swiss trap, which we had for our own use. Mother put on her tight-waisted grey jacket and long, wide skirt. Then she went downstairs, with all three of us chasing inquiringly after her. She climbed up into the trap for Father to take her some mysterious journey. And at the very last moment, leaning from her seat above us, she declared : 'It's not right for you bairns to go to that party. One of you had better run, as soon as we're away, and tell Edie's mother that grandfather's poorly.'

Away went Priarus the pony high-stepping over the cobbles in which sometimes all the colours of the rainbow shone. 'We'll be back before bed,' Mother called as they disappeared round the drive corner.

But here was a predicament. My sister Mamie confessed, once our parents were out of sight, that she daren't go alone through the already shadowy wood. And she wouldn't be left with only little Margie in the house.

We peered out into the January night again. We weren't supposed to be afraid of the dark. Father often insisted : 'Ah've been in them old woods at all hours. Never be soft wi' yoursels. Ah've never met anybody or anything worse than me. An' *you* won't.'

The daffodil moon was hurrying through an indigo sky among torn white clouds when next we looked out that night. Yet oddly the yellow moon remained in the same spot. When the clouds hid her, we couldn't see a hand before our blenching faces. Making a chain by clasping hands, the three of us felt with our feet along the path through the wood to the village, guided by a thread of lighter sky above.

Edie Wright's mother had wispy hair harpooned with enormous hairpins on top of her head. Her cream-coloured cheeks surrounded a large, good-natured, completely toothless mouth. Whenever we saw Mrs Wright this mouth was usually open and laughing, ready with spicy tit-bits of news of what people were up to, in the village, at the Big House, or round about.

Father often declared critically : 'She's Mrs Wrong, not Mrs Wright. She never gets the right end of a story. And she washes and bakes at all the daftest times of the day and night.'

In our house, a necessary, right, and 'proper' order reigned. You could tell by the smell which day of the week it was. Monday was fresh but a little steamy from washday. Tuesday was ironing-day with a smell like lilac. Wednesday was baking-day when the cottage air was appetising with the scent of new bread. Thursday was bedrooms-day. On Friday, 'brasses'-day, we polished the stair-rods, the copper kettle, the pewter teapot, and the silver spoons which belonged to Mother's grandmother. These spoons and some hand-hemmed linen sheets over a hundred years old were our only heirlooms. Saturday was cleaning-through-day.

Mrs Wright let her house go for weeks without any rigorous routine such as this. The house would become shockingly dirty and untidy. It would approach what Mother called 'a terrible look-on'. Then Mrs Wright would have a grand clean-up. This was invariably followed by a birthday party for one of her four children.

That evening, she patted Margie's shoulder as we three stood in our hand-chain, blinking behind our steaming breaths, at her cottage door. We were entranced by her white table spread with jellies, and iced pink cakes, and chocolate ones. A big white cake with silver cachoos and eight candles a-top stood in the middle. Mrs Wright really could do things when she set about them. Except for three empty spaces, her table was wholly surrounded by eager, lamplit faces.

'Don't fret, little souls,' Mrs Wright said kindly to us. 'Your grandad's only been called Home.'

'We're not crying about that,' Margie sobbed, handing in Edie's present: 'we're crying because we can't come to your party.'

But how did Mrs Wright know about our grandfather? 'News travels like wildfire in the country,' Mother often said: 'it doesn't need newspaper or telegraph.' News can move fast in the desert, Gertrude Bell told us too, when she came home from the East and gave us lantern lectures. I knew from Mrs Wright's solemn face, beneath her words, inside my own head, down into my trembling stomach: our last grandad was DEAD.

We three didn't mention this to each other. Back we stumbled through the woods to where our lights were comfortingly on and our door wide open. Nobody bothered to lock doors at Rounton. Why should we think anybody wanted to steal from anybody else?

But worse fell upon us before the next morning broke. There had been, as usual, about six weeks of snow, drifted high and frozen hard, that winter. Sudden thaw had released us from the frost tension only the day before.

Rig and furrow of fields had turned zebra-streaked, dark green and white. Then the wind rose. Swollen, treacherous, the brook in the Barn field below the village was running molten lead. Bank-high, it spread out in waves like sea-tides here and there.

Edie Wright's was a girls' tea-party. Five boys, Willy Drake, Johnny Cruddace, George Tweddall, and two more, all between the ages of about five and seven, had taken the opportunity to go and see the raging Wiske in spate. Four of them went home at nightfall. Johnny didn't go home. An hour or two later, Mrs Cruddace sought Johnny at the others' houses. Each of the terrified children said he didn't know where Johnny was.

By eight o'clock the village had mobilised. Our Father and Mother, back from grandfather's, said that as the Cruddaces were our nearest neighbours: 'We must all help; and thank goodness Anne's fever is better.' Nobody thought of getting the police. The nearest bobby had his beat on the Great North Road two miles away. He rarely came near. Besides, who wanted him?

By the light of storm lanterns the search began. It grew more frantic as we children felt the fell dark on our faces. We gulped mouthfuls of night air. Usually, it was madly exciting to be out in the dark. But that night, a growing sense of mishap seemed to cut us off. Both children and grown-ups, I suspect, felt separate from the rest of the sleeping world. We trekked through the pitchy, streaming woods. The Gentry were in London. There was no blaze of lights from the Big House to help.

Of course Johnny's father had thought of the Wiske. At the beginning of the search, he and another man had started where the stream emerged from the Big House's private grounds. We could see fitful ghost-gleams as their lanterns fanned out over swamped alders and pussy-willows down the winding course of the current.

And at last, about midnight, Willy Drake confessed to his mother that the five had been watching the flood near the bridge. One of them had pushed Johnny. No, he had slipped. Little boys spent their time assaulting each other's persons. Nobody bothered to remember which child Willy named. If anything was to be said to him tomorrow, his parents would say it. For before the long January night had ended, Johnny's father found his body caught by the coat-back in the clutch of a briar, not two yards from the bridge where Willy said the five had been playing.

The next night, we went with Mother to see Johnny. In turn we approached the narrow white bed in the queer-smelling ice-cold bedroom. My spine creaked. This was what had happened to grandfather. Behind the closed lids – no Johnny.

'Now, you touch Johnny's cheek,' Mother said : 'and you wish him well in the Better Land to which he has surely gone.'

Johnny had been a strange, grinning child, with a blob of yellow nearly always below his nose. Mother had said as we came : '*Now* is the time to think about Johnny's good points. He was a clever climber of trees, you remember. Johnny didn't really *see* danger . . . touching him,' she had instructed us further : 'will prevent you being haunted.'

But Margie and I can't get our good wishes out. Mother had to hold our reluctant fingers to Johnny's temple, cold as dew, bruised and blue and scratched by the briar. Not to be alive seemed too dismal to contemplate. And no imagined Better Land could possibly come up to this one.

Swallows had nested in the eaves of their farmhouse all Father's boyhood. The spring after Johnny's death, they began to nest under the archway of the inner courtyard. In spite of the luck Mother said the rose-bibbed visitors would bring, Father became furious when, with wonderfully accurate aim, they began to spatter his silver cockade as he went out to take Sir Hugh to the station, four miles in the carriage-and-pair. The third time this happened, on his return, Father took off his long, pleated livery coat and his top hat. Deliberately he reached for Mother's tallest clothes-prop. Before she could stop him, he had poked the swallows' nest down.

Next morning, when we got up, the birds had almost rebuilt. Surprised, Father dislodged their whole nest a second time. Again the swallows remade the neat, upside-down dome. With one of his spendthrift bursts of rage, Father thrust Mother's clothes-prop into the beak-patterned, ancestral swallow-clay under the green-washed arch a third time. Once again, angrily twittering, the swallows rebuilt. A dozen times in the course of the next few weeks, Father dislodged that swallow nest ; and a dozen times the birds rebuilt it. With cheeky swoops within an inch or two of our noses, their wings bore them in and out of our archway in effortless certainty, their soft twitters as determined and as reasonable-sounding as some of Father's expostulations. After about the thirteenth attempt at destruction, Father gave his great whoop of laughter.

'They're better stuff nor me, lass. Thy clothes-pole's

not a ha'p'orth o'good. Their right to t' place mun be as good as ours, Mother. Eh?' I never heard him call her by her name, which was Elizabeth. He called her usually either 'lass' or 'Mother', or his 'squirrel'.

On another occasion she found a mouses' nest in the washhouse cupboard. Four blind, baby mice were snuggled in the heart of a large ball of brown confetti. Piles of old paper-wrapping, saved by Mother, had been all neatly chewed into small round bits. 'It must have taken that mouse mother and dad days and days to nibble that lot,' Mother said. We put their offspring – idiotically, since they were house-mice – out into the wood.

'Best not tamper with nature,' was Mother's maxim : 'The parents will be sure to smell them out and not let them die.'

But when we told Father he roared : 'Tampering? Of course you were tampering. Who can *help* tampering? Mice are varmint. You'd know if you was me. Bash the whole caboodle on the flagstones next time, and sharp about it.'

Every Boxing-day Father received perhaps ten pounds in gifts. What he valued far more was his employer's equal friendship. Mr Maurice belonged to the third generation of that intellectual and dynamic family of the North. He was not famous as his elder sister, the scholar and explorer, became. He was no inventor like his grand-father the metallurgical chemist of international repute. Nor was Mr Maurice an astute administrator and money-maker as his father was.

Henry James has claimed that nineteenth-century millionaires made themselves rich through 'ferocity'.

This 'ferocity' has its admirable side in vitality, enterprise, and willingness to take risks and responsibility. But such devotion of these Great Ones to hard work, such pressure on themselves, undoubtedly includes a searing contempt for what in anybody else looks like idleness. I never heard that either Sir Lothian or Sir Hugh were beloved, except by their families.

Mr Maurice was beloved. There are more of his kind than we think in the British background. He was shy, tolerant, uncalculating. He was estimable without making himself known either for efficiency or enterprise.

Tall, handsome Mr Maurice was a bachelor. There was sadness sometimes about him. The girl he was going to marry had been thrown from her horse and crippled in the hunting-field. If one peeped through the bushes and he was alone, he sometimes seemed very sad indeed.

But he and my Father would meet three or four times a week. Then they would laugh and blaspheme loudly and heartily together over horse-and-country matters. Father did not scruple to tell the brave Colonel of the Green Howards, who soon was to ride about Flanders battlefields as if they were green, safe, silent Cleveland, his equestrian faults. Mr Maurice took these criticisms with a humour which only really tolerant people can show. True, Father had a store of pithy words, found only in Atkinson's Cleveland dialect dictionary, with which he could equally sincerely applaud Mr Maurice next minute into uproarious laughter.

On Sunday mornings, Mr Maurice would bring his friends — Londonderrys, Fitzwilliams, Zetlands, Southamptons, Peases, Dugdales, and many more with cultured voices, perfumes of Araby and Turkish cigars — to see his horses. Then Father's broadest Yorkshire accent veered to a fair northern tongue. He mimed. He gesticulated. He told hunting anecdotes. He held his audience rocked with glee.

Children of servants were expected to be neither seen nor heard. But I do not remember that our Gentry were ever anything but kind if by mistake we took shape. Once or twice one holiday one of the Grandchildren, Pauline Trevelyan, and I met, stared at each other, approached nearer, smiled, and then ran round the ponds and rock-gardens on the green, mossy stepping-stones as fast as we could go. This was to make ourselves foot-sure. We climbed the biggest trees on the lawn, to strengthen our heads for heights. These initiations were useful. All children like to be able to run and climb without being organised. But no doubt this play with Pauline, Sir George's sister, made me more of a snob than before.

On Sunday evenings another set of beings came to our courtyard. A tremendous thump would resound, out of the dark, on the downstairs door of the flat. We Ns would be sitting round the parlour fire. We might be painting pictures, saying poems, singing 'By the Banks of Allen Water', playing badly on the piano, or brushing our parents' hair.

Because I pretended to have no fears I was sent down to the door at the bottom of the stairs. An uncouth bundle of a figure would step with unnerving suddenness from the lurking shadows. In almost unintelligible language, a croaking voice demanded to see Father. Scarcely daring to turn my back I would make a nightmare retreat upstairs. Father would clatter down to his saddleroom. There he entertained his guests with merry tales and listened to theirs for a couple of hours or more.

These guests were East Riding Tom, Tyneside Geordie, Furness Dick, and many another. Roadsters or tramps, they claimed acquaintance with Father. They said his father had been their 'faythers' best coadie'.

'An now some good hot tea and thy nice cake,' Father would dash upstairs to demand of Mother.

'You surely haven't left that rascally old tramp alone in your saddleroom with all those silver bits and snaffles and tins of leather-soap and Shinio?' Mother exclaimed. 'You'll look well if you find ten or twenty pounds' worth stuff missing after he's gone.'

Father stared at her: 'Ah don't know what makes you think some folks aren't honest, Mother,' he said in amazement. 'For all his bit o' guile, Geordie's as straight as I am. Very few folk's rascals. Anyway, what could Geordie do wi' silver bits and heavy snaffles and leather-soap and Shinio?'

Father did not miss any silver or leather-soap. And I never heard him resent the tramps' begging. Nor did he wonder why they didn't 'set to', as Mother said, 'and earn bread-and-butter by a day's work'. It was not that he was unaware of their squalor. He would hold his nose and say with a frown of laughter: 'That codger, auld Geordie, smelt ranker than a 'possum *this* time.' I think Father admired the tramps' refusal to take to our chimney-corner cautions; just as he would have admired the last little Kalahari Bushman jumping to his death from his precipice outpost when his last poisoned arrow was gone, rather than surrender to the superior equipment-for-murder of the civilised enemy.

There's a great deal of Father's kind of giving still, carefully hidden from commercially organised, publicly known charity and sociological welfare.

Father would press on to these scamps his last year's livery – when he had cut the crested silver buttons off – or his boots, or his trousers. Then he would come stamping upstairs again for five shillings from Mother.

'Five shillings!' Our Mother would lament at such a sum – but only to us when Father had gone down a second time: 'A quarter of our week's money gone!' She would cry a bit. Or the tears would get no further than her eyes but would lie there like pearly drops that didn't fall, and we would take hold of her hands to comfort her. For all his practicalness Father had an unexacting sense of money and possessions. He handed over to Mother all his wages – the whole magnificent pound. She was responsible for our food, clothes, and rare treats; she paid all the insurances; Father had a Life Insurance and we three children had one each at birth for our education; and she paid bills of all kinds. But occasionally she said: 'Dad's all contrairy, giving them tramps more than the few pence he carries in his trouser-pockets. Why, two-pence is ample for gabelunzie-scum like that to throw away on beer.' And she would wring her small, lumpy-knuckled hands until we took hold of them again. But she didn't attempt to withhold the money. She simply 'contrived a bit harder than usual' next week. Father was Father.

At parting, he would clap his guests on the shoulder. He made this gesture exactly as he clapped the shoulders of the countess or the young earl or of Mr Maurice himself. Having no tonsile language, as my Father called Lady Diana 'honey' or Sir M. 'lad', so he usually addressed the tramps as 'sir': 'Now don't forget, sir, to look me up when you're round this way again. Ah'll see you don't go empty-handed.'

And be sure the tramps didn't forget. They sent hosts of their friends as well.

No wonder there was a mystery in our family as to who scratched this √ √ √ and this o o o on the well-painted courtyard doors. These signs were intimations to future comers. The first means that the house in question is not uncharitable. The second means that money (coins) will be forthcoming from the householder. Both signs belong to a very ancient European tramp-code.

Not that, in spite of the single pound a week and of Father's crazy generosity, we were ever the least bit short or deprived. Not a bean, not a buckle, not a button — not a piece of string or brown paper from any parcel we received, if these could be rescued before Father's strong, impatient fingers had ripped or broken them — were in my Mother's cottage ever thrown away. She kept a drawer filled with the most intriguing clutter of sealing-wax, bits of rubber, skewers, thimbles, split-rings, corks, old locks, chains, hooks, spare-parts of all kinds.

If we wanted anything and her jumble-drawer couldn't supply it, Mother was ready with an idea. If we confessed ourselves stuck for a paintbrush, she would say: 'Why, what a duffer! Make one with a twig and ask Dad for a few clippings from Ginger's tail.'

If Mother had any scraps of bread — and there weren't many of these because she made bread-and-butter-and-raisin pudding to use them up — she put the waste scraps aside in the blue enamel bowl. Sometimes, with the quaint reasoning or lack of reason which even then I could see through, she would insist: 'Mustn't waste food. D'you know there are millions on this earth who are still in terrible need of it!' At other times she would chant, in the voice she used for old sayings and rhymes: 'Waste not : want not. Give your crumbs to the birds.' To this day, the sight of good bread in dustbins seems shocking.

We were perpetually hungry. And we lived, I suppose, pretty frugally by today's standards. For breakfast we had porridge, and then egg or bacon, but not both. Our winter weekday teas which might otherwise have been scant were made tasty with parsley. Parsley stayed green in the garden when little else was green. We chopped some parsley with old grated cheese. We added a 'suspicion' of onion and vinegar. Often there were only parsley sandwiches, or bread and jam, for tea. If you had jam, you didn't have butter. Only Father piled jam on butter and was never chidden, being Father and a sort of chief.

I was the 'tiresome' child of the three, Mother said. Sometimes I grumbled. Particularly I groused at my share of one-quarter of an orange. Each week Mother could afford only seven oranges from the travelling fruit-cart. Each day, each orange was divided into four. Father scorned oranges as 'not-British'. He preferred rhubarb. But on our diet of Mother's home-made wheat bread, jacket-potatoes, buttered swedes and carrots, and fresh greens most of the year round, physical security was ample.

We had plenty of eggs, at a ha'penny each. Margarine we didn't taste until the Second World War. We drank milk for supper or it went into junket. If it soured, it became curd or cheese. Our Sunday joint spun out by some spell of Mother's until Thursdays. Then the marrow bone became broth. Our meat was otherwise supplemented by rook-pie, pigeon-pie, giblet-pie, rabbit-pie, jugged hare, black puddings, and chitterlings. Pigeon-pie was 'squab-pie'. We always had it on Whit Sunday.

On Sunday mornings in spring we went to the home-farm to see the new foals, calves, lambs, and chicks. The great attraction was the Black Angus bull. With glaring, bloodshot eyes he snuffed alarmingly through the thin bars of his stall. We always came back home from there with some spare-rib or a can of 'beastling'. An enormous, double-yoked egg stuck out of the top of the can. 'Beastling' is almost solid, but sweet and creamy milk. Mother's reasoning about why cows produce 'beastling' for the first few days after their calves are born was quainter than why we mustn't waste food : 'The cow's milk goes almost solid,' she explained, 'so that her young one can have both food and drink.' Mother baked the 'beastling' with sugar and currants in short pastry. This process resulted in very tasty curd-tart.

As the seasons turned, she strained blackberries, red-currants, and crab-apples, into jelly. Gooseberries and black-currants she made into jam. Parsnips and elder-berries she fermented for wines until her pantry popped with minor explosions from bursting bottles. Fare could occasionally be quite magnificent. Mother's best spread – but only for Sunday tea and if we had visitors – would be brown bread and butter, jam, coconut biscuits, rice cake, fat rascals, maids-of-honour, jam tarts, and fruit-and-jelly-and-cream. There might even be tinned salmon, a great delicacy.

The economy of the hamlet was almost as thrifty as that of our cottage. Rarely were blackberries, mushrooms, crab-apples, watercress, and never bilberries from the hills, left to rot. Frugal sense of ancient food-gathering must have been still strong even after this century, the Age of Plenty, was well in.

Sometimes Mother and I spent whole September days

blackberrying. Dressed comfortably in our oldest clothes, with sandwiches in our pockets, tea cool in a milk-can, we armed ourselves with what she called 'gibbey-sticks'. These were ash-plants made by Father into walking-sticks. They had to have well-curved tops.

We walked three miles across country to the hills. As soon as the hills started, the grass became short, dry, crisp. In the Plain of York, grass was thick, silky, lush. Hill flowers were smaller and fascinatingly different from those of the plain. The hills were a different world. Climbing for the topmost berries, always the finest, occasionally plunged the inexpert head-first into a bramble bush. I emerged torn, scratched, blackberry-less.

'That dashed you!' Mother would be trying not to laugh.

Sometimes I got up alone on a midsummer morning to mushroom. It was best to have a down-to-earth reason such as mushrooming. But really, the errand was altogether different – it was secret, exciting, a little fabulous – to see the earth at three in the morning.

Father had said that button-mushrooms of any night, after a rainbow coating of dew, grew into firm, pink, big ones long before morning. These were the kind Mother would take in her two hands, smooth them delightedly, and say: 'Eh, them's bonny!' They would be perfect before corruption, satin-cold: 'Prime for eating,' said Father. How could they grow in one night?

I decided to get up well before three to find out. Not even Mrs Grimston, the agile old farmer's wife, with her stout, table-legs ending in clogs and her skirt kilted up round her waist, would be earlier than three. Mrs Grimston was reported to be giving her sick husband 'a sorry time'. 'She's killing him by inches with her bad-tempered

45

bullying, that's what. She'd be no help to a strong man, neither,' Mother said. 'But she's a real smart, greedy customer where mushrooms or aught else free are concerned.'

Would new 'buttons' have thrust through the warm, steamy grass that summer night? Would they really have grown by three o'clock in the morning? There was something more: 'Whichever way your eye turns – *if* you're sharp enough,' Father said with a twinkle in his own smalt-blue eye, 'you might catch a mushroom at it.'

'At what?'

'Why, growing,' Father said with a grin.

That mysterious act never loses its lure for the country-man. The old superstition dies hard. Between night and morning, the saying goes, mushrooms can actually be seen pushing up through the green. But this was only half the reason why I stayed awake so as to be out in Big Park well before three that morning.

Sunrise, or earthrise, as it should perhaps be called, is as tricky as mushrooms. Like sunsets, sunrises are the countryman's Turners and Van Goghs. Nobody prates about this. Why should anybody? From start to finish, the best sunrises take an hour or more. Winter ones can be as fine as summer ones. Tree-shapes are etched in fire, charcoal, ink, or silver; and each tree-shape is exquisitely different from every other. We often called each other to come and look at a particularly good 'frolic of crimson'. Though we were usually all busy, perhaps in different parts of the house, we downed tools and rushed out to gasp dumbfounded or stand silent as our daylight little earth 'whirled like billy-o', as Father put it, past the great red sun.

That midsummer morning, having dragged my slothful

bones out of bed by half past two, I sat on the gate in Big Park. I had, or so I thought, the sun to myself. Through the Infinity Father had pointed out behind the hills, the still-unexplained Source of our Being showed himself in one of his most tremendous unforgettable, unruly blazes. At the back of my eyes he is blazing yet. But for once Father was wrong about mushrooms.

Occasionally we filed Mother's broken nails. We put lanoline on the hands whose incessant work made meals and clean frocks appear day by day as if by magic. When Mother's birthday came round we made her a leather oven-holder, or a table-centre. A pocket-handkerchief, or 'a fichu for your blouse neck', tucked round with remnants of lace from her own work-basket, was a better gift. She didn't wear these fichus. But she treasured them carefully. Only much later, when I compared these presents of ours with the kind people send each other so easily from shops, did I realise how crude our gifts were.

One of our Mother's troubles she could not hide from us. This was that she was often upset by Father's bursts of rage. These paroxysms of his occurred when Father was over-pressed by work; they were liable to light on anybody, high or low, within range. At different times he 'ticked off' most of his fellow-servants, the parson and Lady Trevelyan, Sir Hugh's daughter. Sir Hugh said he must come to his study, apologise, and shake hands with Molly Trevelyan: 'Then,' Sir Hugh explained, in his white-whiskered, benign way, 'you can be good friends again.' This shaking hands Father did with laughing alacrity and sincere apology: 'for 'mi foul, rough tongue, Missy'. He couldn't remember, you bet, when Sir Hugh tried to insist on hearing Father's version of the affair, what on earth it was he had been angry about.

But most frequently, of course, Father's rages descended on Mother. We marvelled how, next instant, he could be as sweet as honey to strangers. Occasionally, Mother took the huff. She did not answer his wild words back ; but a tension tightened over the house. Our universe cracked and groaned until anger thawed and a spring of harmony greened over it again. We children begged her, and she often did, forgive. But sometimes she could not quickly surmount his frenzied, silly, brutal words. If she had rounded on him, he might have seen how much he hurt her. Instead, she put on that tiresome, tight-lipped endurance.

One day he demanded something at breakfast and she was slow to comprehend what he wanted. 'Now why the hell,' he grossly shouted, 'was I such a bloody fool as to wed an ignorant lubbert like thee !'

The extraordinary thing was the trice which Father took to forget his rages. He never learnt to stay angry. That day, he came to midday dinner, after his grand outburst at breakfast ; and putting his arm about Mother's waist he tried to waltz her round, while he cried in gay surprise : 'Hey ! What's matter, little squirrel ? Thoo looks worse 'n a wet season !'

She had to give in. She laughed. We children sighed with relief, knowing all was well. Happiness, that ease when you don't stop to think whether you are happy or not, was ours again for weeks or maybe for months. Mother didn't ever try, as some mothers try, to range her children on her side. The sense which remains with me in spite of all Father's rages is of an abiding security in him and in our Mother. But not in all her life did she acquire the least safeguard against her husband's nervous angers ; nor did she gain the least ability not to be hurt by them.

It didn't occur to her that he was too conscientious — if any of us can be that. Their physical love was, I learnt later, interrupted by a 'growth' my Mother developed in middle life. She asked our white-bearded Dr Snowdon about her 'growth' once when he came to 'fetch a baby' for the chauffeur's wife. Without getting down from his high dogcart, Dr Snowdon pronounced oracularly : 'There's probably little wrong with you, Mrs N.' So Mother asked nobody any more. Weathering headaches, sickness, and her 'growth', she lived to be nearly ninety.

For a time, her headaches were terrible. Mother's chief remedy for these was a cloth wrung out in vinegar applied to her temples. She would struggle from 'lying down'. Each side of her brow would be so raw from the vinegar that she could not bear any of us to put a comforting finger on the spot. But she must take her place at the tea-table Mamie had laid. Father could not stand her not to be present. Never did he acquire more than the roughest appreciation of her self-effacing patience, her holiday-less housework. Only in one thing did they match, and that was their love of life in the sun. When both were over eighty and had been together half a century, he was astonished to see her tears at some of his hasty words : 'Ah still have this temper worse 'n auld Harry, haven't Ah, lass ?' he grinned. It was probably the first time in his life he had confessed to being in the wrong.

My Mother was too simple, or else merely too busy, to understand strategy ; but she developed a suspicion — almost an unkindness — towards those less well-off than herself. It is not easy to hold on to identity sure and unbruised. Once I asked a tramp-woman who claimed to be Furness Dick's wife up into our warm kitchen. It smelt that day of apple logs. The walnut-faced young gipsy, with five or six black braids of hair over each shoulder, said she wanted to ask Mother for some bread and sell her some clothes-pegs. How quickly Mother got rid of her ; and without buying clothes-pegs or giving more than one slice of thick bread and butter either. Sharply Mother told her : 'Those pegs of yours are shocking ill-made, my woman.'

But I remember the wink the gipsy gave us. 'Ta-ra, kidlets,' she said : 'Ah'm fed up wi' meself. She sez me pegs aren't no good. She's shoving me out.' (Not 'fed up' with the one who was doing the 'shoving out', but 'fed up' with herself, one noted with surprise.) Gaily she blew us a dusky kiss past Mother's outraged face. Gaily – and gracefully in her long black sateen skirt, broad flat-heeled black boots and emerald-green head shawl – she tripped out of the kitchen and back down our steep staircase into the courtyard.

3

FACTS OF LIFE

IN SPITE of the boy Peter, and like many mothers to this day more enlightened than she, my Mother imagined that we would learn the astounding, physical secret of life 'by instinct'. She left the mystery for each of us to prove in our own way. Between the ages of nine and fourteen, long before we reached the end of childhood that is, we discussed aspects of it frequently among ourselves.

Our talk tended to get vulgar, even bestial. Words slid out of our mouths and, lest they should become sloppy, they became slipshod or, worse still, uncannily debased.

We had a 'Mongol' girl in the village. Eve was the same age as I. She had a yellow slab of a face, soft, black-treacle eyes, and rich, shining hair, coarse as a horse's undocked tail. Evelyn had been overheard praying in their closet: 'Dear God, do let it be a fine day tomorrow. Brother Jonathan and me has to take the calf to market.'

One afternoon, coming home from school, I prompted

Eve : 'Come on now : tell what the boys did to you in the wood last week.'

At first Eve would laugh and deny the story that had gone round us children but had been masonically kept from the grown-ups. 'Now Evie,' I coaxed, 'don't be shy. Tell us. There's a duck.'

'They put their things in my little thing,' Evelyn admitted at last with a giggle.

'They?', I repeated in delicious horror : 'How many, for gracious' sake?'

'All five took turns.'

'Go on !'

'Yes. They did.'

'Whatever for?'

'Just to have a try.'

'Where?'

'On the leaves.'

'No, no . . . Where? How?'

Like the gentle simpleton she was, Eve indicated the most seductive part of her anatomy.

'Didn't you push 'em off? Didn't you fight 'em and get up?' Five began to seem rather many even for pruriency such as mine.

'No.'

'Why not?'

'I liked it.'

'Glory be !' Evie's black, treacle-soft eyes looked at me to see if their owner ought to be ashamed. I took any hint of astonishment or reproof out of my voice : 'And then?'

She returned to giggling.

'And then?' I repeated sternly.

'After a bit of a go each, they took their little things out again.'

'Was it nice, Eve? Didn't five begin to hurt?'

'No.'

'Really?'

'It was nice.'

'How? Nice?'

'They tickled.'

So far, so good; my victimisation of Eve stopped there.

Soon after that, my elder sister and I went to stay the night with Gladys. Gladys's parents were out for the evening. Mamie and Gladys were thirteen; I was nine. Laurie came in from next door. Laurie was thirteen too.

It was winter. Except for the kitchen Gladys's house was dark. We began to play a most exciting hide-and-seek. We three girls hid in the beds and Laurie came to find us. Gladys and Mamie wouldn't let me hide in either of the beds they hid in. Laurie evidently did something very thrilling whenever he found one of them. I judged this from the screams which followed his discoveries.

We went on playing a long time. But he didn't seem to find me. At last he came stealing into the dark back room. Putting his hand under the clothes where I was, he grabbed hold. I struggled a little but not much. Soon his hand reached into my knickers and touched. Screaming, I wrenched free, jumped out of bed, and rushed downstairs.

Laurie followed. The others, having heard my yells, were already there.

'She'll tell,' Laurie said gloomily at once, pointing at me.

'You *dare* let on to Mother!' Mamie said.

I promised I wouldn't, and I was accepted into that guild of reticence of which all children are loyal and lively members. They have to be. But Laurie took care to find me no more that night.

Perhaps I learnt more from watching, and, make no mistake, my friends, thoroughly, if vicariously, enjoying, lovemaking and mating in birds, animals, and insects. No country child, unless blind or daft, can miss this direct source of the senses' primitive, treasured knowledge.

About seven, on fine evenings, the gamekeeper, John Rice, went off to the pub two miles away. Old John walked with a crabwise motion, his shoulders lop-sided from carrying his gun and game-bag. As soon as crooked John was out of sight, one spring evening, I sped for the ponds.

Beside the biggest of the wood ponds, the old wheel which had pumped our water stood in its chill dark house. Spear-moss and grey-green lichen sprouted on the wheel's rungs. Behind the wheel the stream gushed over a waterfall. This wood and pond and waterfall grew more desolate than the rest of the estate was already. Desolation best suited certain moods.

That evening, mad March gales tore at larches and cypresses, beeches and oaks. Singing storm-cocks rode perilously on tree-tops. Fir and yew flowers threw off clouds of pollen. And the golden setting sun lit these clouds to sulphur and yellow colours.

The water-wheel pond's entire surface was dimpled over as if by raindrops. But the dimples weren't rain. They were the glittering eyes of thousands of frogs. Stone-mouthed but slender, some clung with tiny grasping hands to the backs of others twice as big as they. At first I thought the pairs were fighting each other. I spent some time in mistaken mercy trying to separate one couple. But the grip of the topmost frog was extremely tenacious;

and no sooner were they parted than they dashed fren-
ziedly back to each other again. The top frog assumed the
same embrace and the under one the same passivity as
before.

As I was going home I met Father in the fields. When I
explained to him what lots of frogs there were and how
they were situated, he said: 'Now don't be a dulbert.
Surely you tumble to what they're up to: the top ones are
the he's and the under ones are the she's.'

So that was what the frogs were about. Back to the
pond I sneaked behind the next hedge. But Father saw:
'Mind don't neck yersen, that's all,' he called in the strong
Yorkshire he put on for irony. The way I was going was
through swamp, and brambles as high as my head.

When I reached the pond, the orange-rimmed, dew-
drop eyes of the frogs just above the water's surface took
not the slightest notice. I watched a long time but
discerned little.

The next evening that Old John was safely out of the
way was about seven weeks later. Again I stole down to
the water-wheel pond. Baby frogs half-an-inch long were
hopping in thousands up the warm wet grass on the brink.
What happened to all of them after that? Mother Carey
was bewilderingly extravagant and careless.

In the clear light of that same spring evening, a water-
hen had brought off her brood. She led her cortège. Up-
tail, she dipped her head down. She prised some dainty
from the mud. But her prudential, watch-me air was
almost wholly lost. The five balls of fluff were trying new
legs on oily water-lily leaves.

As I stared, there was a splash and a hurly-burly.
Jaws and a curving tail appeared. Monstrous teeth like
Father's saw-edges snapped one of the perky chicks under

water. The sheeny, green-black hen and her remaining four balls of fluff half-scuttered in terror, half-sailed, on. The dame we called Mother Nature, or He we called God, though they revelled in variety and clearly set store on freedom and independence, seemed also not to mind cruelty and havoc. The disorder a Jack pike could set up under their indifference was disturbing.

When I reached home that dusk, the birds were all asleep. Father was watching a dozen or so bats flying in parabolas round our two courtyards.

'Listen,' Father commanded as I came up. 'Can *you* hear anything?'

'The bats?'

It has been put out in more than one scientific magazine that the sound-wave of a bat's cry is of too high a frequency for human ears to catch. But thin, high, piercing little shrieks as of delight – what else could the noise have been but the radar pipistrelles, with wings like bits of umbrella? And many another time I heard the bats scream, softer and more tenuous than the swifts' calling.

That night Father said: 'Dost know, Anny-Pan, Ah can't hear them bats now Ah's gone forty? Not being able to hear 'em squeak is t' first sign,' Father added, smiling ruefully, 'how Ah know Ah mun one day' – his impatient arm with its thick curly hair below his rolled-up shirt-sleeve swung round – 'lie croodled in a black box under all this.' By 'all this' I knew that Father meant the earth on which he and Mother passed on to us that it was joy to be.

The male share in creation was the puzzle, of course: it is for most children. One pouring wet day, tired of flattening my nose and making Os in breath-steam with my lips on the window panes, I sat bursting with inaction on the old blanket chest with the red cover on. Mother came to change her black ribbed stockings. 'Can you tell us, Moth,' said I, 'exactly how the father makes the baby? Gladys said he has something called spunk in his thing.'

Now how could I have been so utterly dim-witted, pin-headed, babyish? How could I not have learnt already our Mother's likely answer to words and rabid curiosity such as that? I was nine. I was going to school. The Peter episode and the Laurie game should have made clear what a transgression it was to try to cross the boundary into grown-up territory.

Our Mother rose from her chair by the blanket-chest with the most indignant swish of her full black skirt. Her black stockings on, she gave a tug at the fresh lace at her throat: 'It's dirty to let yourself think about such-like things, our Anne,' she declared. 'And it's dirtier still to use words like . . . like . . . ' I was alarmed to note that she couldn't get either 'spunk' or 'thing' out, words which up to then had sounded harmless enough.

I didn't try any more questions. The fact that there were no words with which to talk about certain matters freed me from Mother. But I couldn't, or didn't, stop insistent, sensuous thinking.

Soon after that I began to dream a great deal.

In each of my almost nightly dreams I ran through a garden. Always familiar yet always new, this garden was massed high with flowers and glorious with scents. No garden since granny's at Croft has come near that brightly-coloured, nightly vision. At the top of the dream garden path stood 'Miss Ivy' – any country lavatory. But every time I tried to sit on one of 'Miss Ivy's' seats, her whole structure gave way. This disaster plunged me, night after night, to struggle neck-deep below in swirling, smothering ocean sump. Sometimes there was a narrow ledge or plank on which I might clamber up and so balance into safety. Then, below my feet, the water grew blue, clear, sparkling. But it was always deep, unplumbed. And sometimes, even if I managed to climb on to the plank, my foot slipped and I fell off again – to wake struggling.

As I grew bigger, 'Miss Ivy's' dream seats became plush-covered. But they have remained vaguely though radically treacherous to this day. All privy doors in this recurrent dream of mine hang broken-hinged, storm-battered by the raging water outside the garden. Nor can I close my door on the prying eyes above the water which I imagine gleam ready to condemn.

I'm not suggesting that my untaught, country mother, with her busy, chapped hands, her quick step, her tightly-corseted, ankle-skirted black figure, and her cheeks like pink cyclamen, was responsible for my divided mind. It is hard to realise that her and my Father's education had been in the late 1860s. By 1870, Presto! Fourpence a week for each working-class child's schooling was no longer demanded. My parents' generation belonged to the last in Britain which could be called illiterate. It was also the last which lived under the convention of implicit obedience to often violent parental rule.

The 1870 Education Act didn't make either so sudden or so revolutionary a difference as is sometimes imagined, though. Father and Mother were both what might be called illiterate, but both could read and write a little. In each of her daughter's autograph books, pretending it was her best spelling, Mother inscribed:

59

2 ys u r,
2 ys u b,
I c u r
2 ys for me.

But how many times did Father observe: '*We* had too much rod. Tom and me and Sarah and Jane and the younger lot weren't allowed to eat a bite until our parents had risen from table. We stood behind their chairs. An' we daren't speak for our lives, not even if we heard t'auld uns making all sorts of bloomers. Now what good could *that* do?'

So he and Mother brought us up without severity, with a kind of rough gentleness. They insisted that we pushed common-sense to the limits of which we were capable. 'You're to learn to use your own judgments.' Both said this over and over again. Not once did Father, for all his quick furies, lay a finger on us in punishment. Eagerly, though neither cared about money beyond the essentials of security or independence it could buy, both wanted one thing: 'You lasses must know more than we did. Aye, and be wiser.'

Knowledge, then, was an aid to judgment and judgment was connected with wisdom. But how could knowledge and judgment both mean no more than that commonest of all things which Father so oddly prized — common-sense?

Half-instinctively children know that there are many contradictions in life and that sometimes the same subjects can be looked at from directly opposite points of view. But almost without the child's knowing it, a desperate search sets in to put the humpty-dumpty divisions together again in one splendid whole.

Mr Maurice took great pleasure in breeding foals to show at the Yorkshire shows. After elaborate checking of 'points', he and Father would choose the finest thorough-breds for sires. One shining black 'Arab' horse had nostrils lined with scarlet. Its eyes flashed white fire. The electric wires of this stallion's legs no more than touched the ground, as he pranced into the courtyard on his visits to the mares.

The 'Arab's' keeper was a little paper-faced man in grey-green, groom-cloth breeches and shining, brown leather leggings. He was a scarcely more astonishing creature than his horse. How did so small and insignificant a being control the fiery dancer at his heels? The 'entire horse' (my Father said that this was the polite name, not 'stallion') could any minute have snapped the fine thong which held him. Here was another matter to puzzle over.

The stallion's groom was the person who made me aware of what now seems a common but still unacknow-ledged complication. The groom would catch hold as soon as I went near him, lift me in his arms, swing me high over his head. For a long time I liked that. If he were sitting down he would draw me softly close, smooth my arms or my bare legs. Mother saw him and she looked daggers. 'You keep far out of the way of that wicked man's hands,' she commanded as soon as we were alone. 'You are too big to be pawed and slimed over.' The sensation of Jock's hands hadn't felt slimy, only sensuous.

A length of grass behind a row of loose boxes was the stallions' meeting place with the mares. It was assumed that my sisters and I would never peep. As far as I know they never did. But the whinny of Tomboy, my Father's favourite mare, as she was let out to meet the black 'Arab' stallion, rings in my avid ears to this day. Tomboy trotted to him. They knapped each other, neck on shining neck. Quicksilver streamed from her tail. Her second whinny echoed with all the delighted anticipation that I knew then belonged to what would take place. But how those creatures, armed with hard hooves and inaccessible parts, performed their rite so aptly, has remained another permanently fascinating cause for wonder. Birds and butterflies, so much more fragile, are also, in this respect, too quick for greedy seeing.

When the wobbly, gate-legged foals came, my Father would discuss matters without any reference to the detail I still craved for : as if one knew as much as he. He would laugh at the mare's whinny for the stallion as if it were some rich, powerful joke. I laughed too – when he and I were alone. When he laughed over this kind of subject before Mother, none of her children dared laugh. But alone with Father, the matter seemed at least natural.

We begged to see Tomboy's new coddy immediately it was born. At about nine o'clock one February night, we go down to the stable – mother, my two sisters and I. When we get there, I can see, stealing a glance at Mother's face, that she is appalled for us. Triumphantly Father explains – his eye on her, too, I note – that the frightful, blood-stained tatter hanging from top to heel behind Tomboy is an excessively thick caul in which the foal had been wrapped. 'I had to slit it, to let the coddy out,' Father says. The foal is standing up, half an hour after its birth, seeking for the milk. 'An' sitha,' Father nudged me chuckling, 'it's staggering by instinct straight to the very spot it needs.'

The foal's colour was unusual : a particularly pale

chestnut. It had a white star on its forehead and a pair of superlatively clean white socks. 'To be born in a caul's luck,' Father next explained, artfully pandering to Mother's superstitions. 'The caul will come away from Tomboy of its own accord in a short while, with no difficulty at all.' The caul then seemed to me not only bloody but excellent. The beautiful and the beastly coalesced for a little time in natural triumph.

My parents' only son had been born about a year before my birth. I don't think he was a weak baby. He weighed eight pounds. But Dr Snowdon, driving five miles in snowy January, wasn't there, and something went wrong. In haste they sent for the parson two and a half miles away. And too late the parson arrived.

This High Anglican did not, of course, enter Mother's bedroom. He explained matters shouting chastely from the kitchen : 'You must not hope to see your unblessed child in Heaven, my dear Mrs N.'

'But oh sir –' my Mother's voice had sounded, as Father later recorded with his hardy sympathy, 'like a weasel's trapped in a sink-hole.' 'Oh sir – '

'Unbaptised infants cannot look upon the face of our Lord,' the parson called.

Tearfully shouting back, Mother besought the parson : 'But can't he be buried in hallowed ground? I had his name ready, sir. It's Charles Frederick Lonzer. Frederick Lonzer didn't miss getting baptised through his own fault.' She daren't do more than hint that the parson had been slow in coming with only two and a half miles to walk.

'Behind the Church is where we lay the ungiven,' the parson returned, shouting gently now, but adamant.

Behind the Church was the rubbish-tip of dead flowers and broken jars.

Disbelievingly my Father hooted at the parson's bleakness – once he had shown him out: 'You don't need to mind, lass. Holy folk can often be grudgers.'

'Dad meant to comfort me,' Mother often said. But bitterly disappointed Father – and, I think, Mother – had been when their next child was a girl.

Not by word or deed did Father ever wittingly betray his disappointment. How then did I, their next child, know? But I did know. There was a continual sense in our house that it would have been so much better in all ways if there had been a boy.

Father, therefore, sought to teach at least one of his three daughters the manly attribute he called 'guts'. If Mother were by, he called this characteristic 'pluck' or 'gumption'. His task was vain, but he was not one to give up easily.

One of Mr Maurice's hunters, called The Grey, not bred by Father, was so treacherous that only Father dared mount him for a time. Without warning The Grey would buck. Then he would rear. In a trice his back-end flew in the air. It came down. His front end went up. His head, down in a buck, would rise so quickly and violently that it would catch Father on the nose. The nose would stream with blood. But Father at the age of four had been slung on to Clydesdale cart horses' backs to ride to the horsepond and back. Father took some unseating. After a tussle lasting twenty minutes or so – as suddenly as he began his bucking and rearing – The Grey would give in. With extraordinary calm he would walk amicably forward.

'He throws these tantrums becoz he's been ill-tret as a young 'un,' Father would sagely and tolerantly explain.

64

And then, sadly, since Father didn't like admitting impossibilities even with horses : 'Ah'll *never* cure him ; just have to lump it.'

In the field with the other horses, The Grey scorned all offers of corn shaken in feeders. When Father wanted to bring them into their stables — in wild and reckless gallops — The Grey would lead the others round and round forty-acre Big Park.

One August day, when the under-grooms were a little late from their dinners, Father came to the stair foot.

'Sharp ! Sharp ! Sharp, our Anne !' Wanting things done Father used the voice and tone he had inherited from his father : 'I'm going to get t' horses. Ah' need help.'

One learnt to hurry. One must avoid the terrible impatience. Downstairs I raced.

I was placed at a vantage point in the Park. 'Now hold hard,' Father warned me : 'You mustn't let that devil of a Grey past you. But you needn't be frit. No horse will ever run a man down.'

He left me at my post, looking as he did when I knew he was regretting his lack of sons. How could a child with even the small amount of 'pluck' that I had, a child fed also on Gertrude Bell's stories of her wanderings in the wilderness among Kura'ish and Amarer tribes, show fear of a mere dozen, very civilised, horses ? Yet instead of the desired courage, only a ridiculous burning need to excel, at all costs not to let Father down, was born in me.

His word about horses being of so heroic and friendly a nature was not to be doubted, of course. Would they know the difference between running a man down and running a useless little girl down was all I wondered.

Led by the rebel Grey, they come thundering along the Park side. Railings are not near. In any case, Father's scorn and disappointment if I turn tail, or do not succeed in turning The Grey, seem far worse than mere possibility of being stamped into grass and mud by forty-eight galloping hooves.

There is a sound of somebody's heart bumping like a distant drum . . . Yet it is exhilarating to see the furious, wide, red-lined nostrils of The Grey approach. I keep my eyes from his hooves. The Grey pauses – within two yards of me . . . What Father said is coming true. The Grey and the rest aren't going to gallop over me. Snorting and excited, the creatures have drawn back on quivering haunches. I spread my own inadequate four limbs, flippers or scarecrow-ends; I shout wildly. Swerving madly, the horses about-face in the utmost limits of space. But no sooner have they turned than they find small, jimp Father at their very noses. Nimble as the lop he so often talked about, he has run up behind them.

'Co-ep, Co-ep.' With horses Father could use the most coaxing, winning murmur of a voice you ever heard.

And why do they halt at sight of a figure quite absurdly dwarfed among the acres of Big Park? Father's favourites – Tomboy or her half-brother Boyard – suffer themselves to be approached. They are patted. They are talked to as if they could comprehend. Perhaps they can. The appetising oats are shaken and both are allowed a munch or two. A halter slips unobtrusively over each head in turn. Tomboy and Boyard walk away at Father's heels. Like lambs the rest follow, the rebellious Grey last.

My Father trained Mr Maurice's young hunters for him. When they were yearlings they were given names, Carthusian, Ginger, The Nun. A snaffle was put on them. Getting a young horse to 'accept' the bit in what Father called the 'right' spirit often took whole days. Next a saddle and fake rider (Father's jacket stretched over two wooden arms) had to be accepted equally 'rightly'. For weeks the young horse trotted, walked, cantered round Father in a ring at the end of a rope – until he knew and obeyed Father's every command. More important still, he learnt from Father's tones whether Father was pleased or displeased, urgent or leisured, commanding or permissive. Only then was he taken on to the highway to learn road sense. And only at the end of some further months' training did Father mount.

Three or four days a week, throughout the winter, Father on the young horse and Mr Maurice on a fully trained one, hunted. The Meet might be at Eiryholme, Urlay Neuk, Osmotherly, Thimbleby, or Skutterskelfe. Even before one had any knowledge that our Cleveland dialect is rich in Norse-Irish sprinklings, one knew that Eiryholme must mean a summer refuge up in the green hills. Most of 'the pleasant names of places' around seemed to tell of a game of naming which Cleveland Hob and Lob long before ourselves had played.

Neither Mr Maurice nor Father had anything but admiration for the fox's superior cunning. They were also quite realistic concerning the battle-odds against him.

'Rennie's varmint! He's cruel enough hissen to kill ten hens for the fun of the thing, when one would mek him a meal,' Father laughed. 'Serve 'im right if he has t' whole pack at his brush-end!' At other times he would actually contend: 'Garn! Red Rennie *likes* being hunted. It's his nature to like being tried out.'

And to watch Red Rennie elude fifty-six pairs of snapping jaws and sniffing noses in an acre of not very thick gorse is to be convinced that Father was right about Red Rennie's cunning at least.

This cunning Father seemed to identify with our human commercial cunning, spine-chilling cruelty, as well as with our qualities of endurance and adaptability. 'Craftiness, like pluck, is a damn' good thing when you're up against bloomin' great odds,' paradoxically he would assert. What he meant by craftiness was in no sense guile or mean cunning (though all three words, craft, craftiness, and cunning, must be allied). This craftiness operated best, Father seemed to think, in the wordless area below speech where all creatures including ourselves approach the potential threat or infringement of others. In this labyrinthine jungle we prepare ourselves for our eventual rendezvous with death. But for all Father's admiration of cunning, not once did I hear him tell a lie himself; nor did we hear Mother ever deliberately indulge in one either.

Sitting on a tar-fence one frosty morning at a November Meet, I watched a big dog-fox break covert at my feet. Like Yellow Dog Dingo he pirouetted one gay moment under the silly noses of fifty-six hounds. As I opened my lips for a 'tally-ho', he glanced up. Neither cringing nor swerving, admirably indifferent to the red-scarfed enemy squatting on the fence, he swung off. My lips closed without a sound.

Four hours later, that same fox, recognisable by his yellowish hue and the black tip to his now bedraggled brush, sought refuge in our courtyard. I happened to be alone there; and again the betraying shout died on my lips.

But what folly or fatigue had induced him to sanctuary here? The pack rushed howling in. Next came the tall, red-coated, black-silk-hatted huntsman, glowering through a painful-looking monocle held in by the screwing

69

up of the other side of his Lordly face. He jumped off his gaunt bay. With a cool haste, his eyes on the fox safely cornered by the pack, he made water. Then, buttoning his fly, he strode into the mêlée. Cleverly he seized the dying but unvanquished fox. His First Whip handed him the open knife. Expertly the 'mask' was slit off while still it snarled; next the Whip caught the orange-black brush as it fell. The rest was hurled into the midst of fifty pairs of jaws. Beauty, courage and cunning changed into blood-stained tatters in less than two twos . . .

But the real glory for Mr Maurice and Father, with their mettlesome horses, was charging over the rich, heavy clay of Cleveland. Splendid Mr Maurice weighed sixteen stones. Father was nine, took care not to put on more, and sat a horse as if he had grown there.

Both knew every field, spinney, green lane, and moor-path in Hurworth. Father especially was alert on the question of right-of-way across once Common Land. He was always having to apologise for being in the forepart of the hunt, when, as he confessed to Mr Maurice, 'I ought to ha' kept behind, following you Gentry like a runty recklin.' For reply Mr Maurice would hand him a pull from his wine-flask.

Father rose at three in the mornings to go cubbing. He came home long after he had promised. Time passed. Other hunting men returned. The grooms left for the night. Mists of evening curled low in each earthy hollow.

Margie and I would give the horses their supper. Finally, in the celadon near-dark that made one's blood race and tingle, Mother and we would go to Big Park gates facing the blue hills. 'Infinity' and 'Eternity' were dropping, as usual, behind them. Each pair of far-sighted eyes strove to spot the distance-tiny figure first. Then we could all get relief. In black coat, white breeks shockingly mud-bedaubed, scarlet waistcoat, and morning-white gloves, Father would be walking his young horse home. He would walk it twelve miles without a trot. 'If it breks into a sweat after a good day, it might tek a chill an' then colic,' he would explain after Mother's 'Well thank goodness, Dad, you're home safe at last!'

Most of Father's fingers were at one time or another knocked out of joint and blithely pulled in again in the heat of the chase. One evening his half-trained mare arrived home alone. She was breathless, lathered in sweat, and shaking with fear. We put her in her box, gave her a warm linseed drink, threw a rug over her, and turned to each other's blanching face, asking what to do next. Half an hour later, Father himself arrived, bloody, collarless, hatless and gloveless. The young mare, experiencing her first rough hill-scramble, had fallen when coming down Scarth's Nick, after they had killed the fox. Her fall in a precipitous place had tipped Father neatly over her head. Whilst he pulled his middle and third fingers back into joint and probably swore at her for being clumsy, she had panicked. She had stumbled on alone down an almost perpendicular gully. In vain Father called. She wouldn't heed. Down on the plain, a couple of men let her go by. Father set out to overtake her by a short-cut, since he was almost certain she would go home. 'But like a fool,' he explained to us in an angry bellow, 'I stopped to waste wind cursing those other two fools for not holding her. She beat me at the short-cut.'

His box-hat had been sliced open. But for its crash-helmet efficiency, when he pitched over the mare's head, his own head might have cracked on the rocks. Instead, he had only a cut eyebrow. He had hung the wrecked hat which had saved him on a bush, torn off his white stock, and thrown it and his gloves away, for ease in running.

When any of the horses was sick, Father himself became careless about eating and sleeping. He would spend the night on a rug in the invalid's box. One evening, he found Tomboy's caul-born offspring, then a fine two-year-old, with head drooping and his whole body stiff and hard. Since the horse was not in pain, Father went to his own bed, though he was puzzled and anxious. At about two in the morning we were all wakened up. 'Tetanus,' Father roared.

Thrusting on his trousers and coat and boots, he literally flew downstairs. His heels scarcely touched the steps. Rushing to the newly installed telephone in his saddleroom, he rang and rang until the butler answered. Father demanded that the vet be summoned. Rattled from sleep, the butler was justly angry. But in less than an hour the shrunken little vet arrived in the October night, injected serum, and saved the 'lucky' caul-born colt. It lived to get lock-jaw twice more. By then he whom Father called 'a little sot' was in a home for dipsomaniacs. Father injected the serum and saved the horse himself.

That telephone was a great thorn in my Mother's flesh for years. Perkins the butler complained that Father shouted so loudly that 'the wires cracked and spluttered'; he couldn't hear a word usually, he said.

Mr Maurice came to instruct my Father. They practised, Mr Maurice going back to the Big House end, Father at our end. But soon Father grew impatient. He dropped the receiver, left it swinging, and came out of the saddleroom. Cupping his lips with his hands and turning in the direction of the Big House, he shouted:

'Ah'm out in the courtyard ... can you hear me better now, sir?'

'Yes,' Mr Maurice's voice came faintly back.

'Ah told you a proper voice is more serviceable than that mechanical contraption,' Father shouted triumphantly.

By then Mr Maurice was in the courtyard and Father was coaxed to another try with the telephone. Temporarily he was convinced after more practice that what Mr Maurice and he both called his 'horse-whisper' could occasionally answer almost as well in long-distance communications as a vociferous roar. Further than that Father could not admit.

But whenever a horse fell sick or any of the orders from the Big House displeased him, his voice rose again to its most alarming bull-bellow. Mr Maurice amusedly humoured him. But in the next few years our telephone extension was as often out of order as in.

More and more frequently, the Gentry's victoria, landeaux, dog-carts, and tub-traps stood idle in their coach-house. A big garage spread, first for three and then for six cars, next to the stable-yard. Father never ceased to hate the usurping cars.

All Mr Maurice's adult horses went to the First War. All except Tomboy were lost. Mr Maurice kept two breeding mares long after the slump of the 1920s when the family lost its millions. He and Father couldn't give up breeding good horses.

But the world was different by then. Or did this seem so only because one was growing up and could view it from a wider angle?

4

CHURCH BOARD SCHOOL

BEFORE THE Norman Conquest, men who owned land
at the Rountons also farmed it. In 'Domesday' 'Tor and
Carle' had '8 Carucates' of land apiece. By 1086 the area
became 'Crown Land'. In the thirteenth century, the
owners were no longer the men who worked the land ; and
since then, land has passed through many different
owner-hands and worker-hands. Sir Lothian bought the
'manor' in the nineteenth century. Between the 1841
census and the present day, the number of Rounton's
working families has remained curiously stable. There are
still too few books about the ownership of earth.

When as a child I knew it, it had a social scale – and
yet it had no social scale. As soon would Father have
thought of himself on a list with bulls and stallions as
'graded' among human beings. The place was full of what
he called 'characters'.

There was Tommy Farrell. At thirty-three, Tommy
wore petticoats and a bib. He had spindly whiskers. He
'couldn't keep himself clean'. He dribbled helplessly and
laughed with continual, good-natured inanity. Yet his

mother did not dream of Tommy's being cared for by anybody but herself; and the rest of us accepted him without comment.

There was a tough, hunch-backed farmer with a more gently spoken wife. He 'took his pleasure', as Father put it, with somebody else's wife. Occasionally Father and Mother wondered 'how either his la-di-dah lady or his woman could fancy John Thomas who smelt so of cow-muck'. But there was no further criticism. Private lives were the business of those most concerned.

One of Father's frequent assertions was: 'Folk everywhere are as various as the kings and queens of England, y'know.' And the slightly boastful assumption on which he himself usually acted was one which genial Mr Maurice did little to discourage. This was that in some prime element of manhood, Father, or anybody else for that matter, might draw level with the Gentry if they cared to set about it.

Mother was much less sure. She separated, without realising that she did so, human distinctions from social ones. Privately she hoped that socially we drew level with the head gardener, the head keeper, the head chauffeur, the schoolmaster, the private secretary. But the 'lerned clerk of Christes gospel' was no brother to us all, as Chaucer's 'good man of religioun' had been the plough-man's brother back in the fourteenth century.

'We're all equal in the sense that we're all souls, surely?' Occasionally Mother ventured this in her most tentative tones. The sense she meant was not a mystic one, but plainly human.

'Rot,' Father would crisply reply, dictatorial as usual. 'What thoo means is that nobody can ever tell how much more equal we might have been if odds against every

75

jack man of us could ever be totted up. An' that's but half the "ifs". All we can do is ho'd together.'

Socialism was introduced to us in that first decade of the twentieth century. And from whom did we first hear the word but our brilliant Gentry? Their children and grandchildren were brought up in what the old nanny confided to Mother with some dubiousness was the 'New Freedom'. They were allowed to answer grown-ups back. They ran barefoot. They played with us. Thanks to our Gentry, Father's belief, and hence ours, in freedom, initiative, independence, even a kind of equality, remained unmolested.

As for Socialism, he stoutly voted Conservative. Mother favoured the Liberals. Yet neither of them paid allegiance to any heroes, of battle, exploration, or politics. They would never have agreed that postman or bricklayer were less 'valuable' than postmaster-general, master-builder, peer, professor, or poet. 'We can't get on without one and t'other,' Father insisted. He would have hooted at phrases like 'the squint-eyed, vulgar herd', 'idiot people', 'the slobbering brutishness of the poor'; William Morris's 'degraded' class, Samuel Butler's 'dull, vacant ploughboys, uncomely and apathetic', would have astonished him. Virginia Woolf's 'working-man' ... 'egoistic', 'raw', 'nauseating', like Rowse's 'idiot people', would have left him staggering but eloquent with anger. I am almost sure that Mr Maurice felt as my Father did. I hope I am not romanticising or falsely deluding myself in this matter; but I didn't hear these phrases about working people until I was nearly grown up. Their inaccuracy is surely because they are based on insufficient knowledge: 'ignorance', as Samuel Johnson might have said, 'pure ignorance'.

'Still, if we go on levelling,' occasionally Father contradicted himself to prophesy, 'some Toms, Dicks, and Harrys of working folk'll be bound to imitate the fancy wants of a lot of gold-toothed fools I could name.'

'East' was a favoured village. Our Gentry, in 1906, built it its village hall. This had a stage for plays and concerts, and a polished floor for dancing : its walls were lined with kudu heads. There were also a billiard-room, a women's room, and a library.

But it was an artificial village in that it had no pub. The neighbouring village made up by having two pubs. Children came from both villages to the one school. There were about forty children between the ages of five and fourteen at school in 1914.

Little of the 'New Freedom' seeped into that school. Its nineteenth-century building and its atmosphere were as bleak as those of Blake's or Cowper's schools in the eighteenth century. The Big room was gaunt and full of fine, sizzling draughts. It had a sour, dusty smell. It was built to Jeremy Bentham's plan for schools ; its windows were so high that we couldn't see anything outside that might be thought to take our attention from the delights that went on within.

In winter the Big room was heated – or not heated – by a very small coal fire. At this, the headmaster, by standing directly in front and lifting his black coat-tails, kept warm his bony rump. There was a smaller room in which a young girl taught the five-year-olds.

The backless benches of the Big room were fixed to the floor. On these, we pupils spent most of our time in silence and some of it in dire dismay. When we were not using our country hands they were required to be folded away behind our backs. This Yoga position induced a slowing down of physical energy.

By 1960 that rural Church-school had electricity instead of paraffin lamps, a more efficient stove, and hot dinners were supplied daily at a shilling a head. In 1960, the piano, bought fifty years before, was still in use, its candle-brackets and most of its tune gone. Up to 1960 there was still but one enamel wash-bowl, filled from a water-butt. The closets are, to this day, emptied once a week.

Our master was tall, bespectacled, skeleton-thin. Long, narrow-trousered shanks gave him the appearance of a daddy-long-legs. Usually he arrived in shocking ill-humour on the stroke of nine. At sight of him we rushed into two lines. Like soldiers or convicts, we were marched into school from the yard.

At once, to call the register, our master sat down on the piano. He was so tall that the piano lid was just the right height for his seat. Chairs were far too low. But if, by some mischance, the piano lid was already up, and our master did not notice, an anguished cacophony issued instantly from his bottom. Purple to his stiff, tight, white collar, he would spring up. He banged the lid down – to warn us. He seized his cane from its place on the desk top. Words streamed from his mouth.

'If you bumpkins don't watch out, the Germans will be on your doorsteps one of these days. Then you'll be slaves as well as bumpkins. Meanwhile, I'll *make it hard* for you, if you dare to sit there grinning.'

With giant strides he leapt about the room. Down came his cane, here, there, anywhere, on backs, shoulders, or legs, of anybody whose face dared to show the least glimmer of anything except due solemnity. Soon we

78

were all slavishly dithering. Dust flew. Tears rained:
except in those heroes who took pride in complete
physical and mental stoicism.

And thus our master whacked his way back to prestige.
Without prestige he didn't seem able to begin the first
lesson. This lesson was about God's good works.

After daily scripture every morning of school brought
an hour's grammar. Then came an hour's arithmetic.
Grammar was a splendid eighteen-seventy legacy from a
thousand years of Graeco-Romano-British education for
the few. Arithmetic was our share of the new enlighten-
ment, the modern literate and scientific outlook.

The first ten minutes of every arithmetic lesson was
devoted to 'mental'. Madly our minds blurred, the
moment the master's chalk-dry finger began darting
sternly at us for answers. Surely, one thought, it is
fascinating to know how much hay there is in a stack,
what weight of potatoes a sack will hold, even what
that perishing nine-times-seven are. By whose power our
democratic lives are run, in the matter – say – of fixing
the prices of everyday essentials, is still, in the 1970s, a
dark mystery. But why was our master so determined to
take away the joy of knowledge?

After 'mental' hard at it we went with long-multiplica-
tion, or long-division, or HCFs and LCMs, or recurring
decimals, or compound interest, or weights and measures,
or square-roots. Few gleams of the amazing story of
Hindu-Arabic number, no hint of Pythagoras, or of
Platonic order permeating our lives shone through.
Three of our branches of arithmetic were certainly
'distraction', 'uglification' and 'derision': so that suspicion
was set up in more than one immature mind what a
quite admirable world we might have without so much of

this base money-lenders' emphasis on profit, quantity, number, and the fear of loss.

Pages of spellings followed arithmetic. Then came history – about wars, generals, kings, parliaments. Never was history, as my friend W. G. Hoskins has spent his life trying to make clear, about ordinary people such as ourselves. At the Church school forty years ago what seemed important was how Britain had won wars, how we had bossed and got more than so many others. There was never the slightest hint that there could, if only we all tackled the problem, be a sufficiency of good things for the whole earth.

In geography we repeated lists of headlands, bays, and rivers. Facts! Gradgrind facts were dinned into us with little or no relation to each other. 'Stretch those intellectual muscles,' our master ordered. This phrase 'intellectual muscles' contains a misconception at least two thousand years out-of-date about the mind's invisible rhythms. About the unity of peoples and of knowledge, at the Church school at East Rounton, never a glimmer.

Gradually a certain dismal process became evident in our school. We children knew the spellings, tables, lists of battles, at the end of each particular lesson. By the next lesson we *didn't* know them. What went wrong? Obviously we all meant to remember. If we didn't there was the stick.

Our master knew the answer to this abominable educational mystery of our forgetfulness. 'The class to which you yokels belong,' he repeatedly shouted, 'isn't capable of more than a very low standard of education.' Some in the 1970s still believe that myth.

One day a small collection of books was sent from the Big House to school. This was to form our first school library. Not until I was ten did I read a book complete. Much later was it before I owned one.

The afternoon of the books' arrival, the donors were to come to school. Mr Maurice's stepmother, my Lady, was interested in us and school. She, some of her friends, and the parson, were to come that day. There was to be a speech from my Lady about reading, and one from our master of thanks for the books. After the speeches, we children were to march past the Gentry. Girls would curtsey, and boys would bow.

'Make specially deep obediences,' our master cautioned us. 'Woe betide any of you tomorrow morning who has performed this respectful observance in a slovenly, half-hearted manner.' Already he had warned us about the matter of the 'obediences' many times: 'Six of the best any bad performer shall have tomorrow.'

That morning, lessons had to be got through in just the same quantity, but quickly. Hurry, however, was fatal for our 'Mongol', Evie.

'How many pennies to a shilling?' Cranefly demanded this of Evelyn, now eleven years old.

Alas, she had forgotten again.

She was made to count: 'One penny, twopence, threepence . . .' But just as Evelyn should have reached 'one shilling', the attendance officer arrived.

The kid-catcher, as he was more generally called, was a mauve-visaged man, singularly like the new advertisements for Michelin tyres. He wore green cycling knicker-bockers, a green jacket and handsome green, turned-down stockings. All these stretched over the sections of him between his joints, as if the whole of him was squeezed like sausage-meat into green skins. But it was abundantly clear from the kid-catcher's demeanour that he felt himself a very efficient man. The big boys had a coarse joke among themselves about his bulk and self-sufficiency : If the kid-catcher lets a fart he'll split.

Sergeant-major Herringbottom's purplish cheeks were shaken by percussive blinks. Father did not appreciate the RSM tactics by which the kid-catcher sought to induce our attendance at school during a scarlet-fever epidemic. Father had already threatened to hurl 'Fatty' down our stairs. But on the whole, the attendance officer was as feared as was our schoolmaster.

Instead, therefore, of Evelyn's continuing safely, after the kid-catcher's entry that morning, to '. . . one shilling,' in her nervousness she ended with '. . . twelvepence.'

Angrily our master bellowed : 'Start afresh, idiot. And mind your ps and qs. Use that sawdust you've got in place of brains.'

Again she counted. In vain I sought to send the right words across the horns of dust-particles from the high windows. Already I suspected that any efforts of mine at this kind of ESP, or of prayer, were singularly in-effective. '. . . elevenpence . . . twelvepence,' came once more from Evie's quivering lips.

Our master took one of his long-legged, lightning rushes. He beat Evelyn on both sides of her head with his fists. Her blue-black horse-tail fell all about her streaming face. Her cream complexion grew mottled, red, green, purple, and streaked with grey. Again she was made to start from the beginning : 'One penny, twopence . . .' and again the silly girl stammered '. . . twelvepence.' Yet we all knew that Evelyn, eldest of eight, was no idiot. Hadn't she shopped quite satisfactorily for her mother since she was five?

After my useless efforts to send Eve the right answer in

soundless words I had retired into a ridiculous preparation
of real words. These were to denounce Cranefly's harshness. He was not harsh to me, though that fact made
defence of Eve more necessary rather than less. I imagined
myself rising. In the silence somehow commanded, the
wisdom that lay hid in books must be boldly said out loud.
Then all the other children would rise too. Cranefly
would be ashamed. He would be kind to Evelyn.

A particular quotation I had had ready for weeks for
just such an occasion was from our *Standard Seven
Graphic Reader*. It was out of a poem by one Samuel
Taylor Coleridge. Why I thought this quotation applicable
to our master I don't know. I would shout :

> *There's no philosopher but sees*
> *That rage and fear are one disease.*

But Father's training in pluck had been conspicuously
wasted. My heroine Gertrude Bell's example when she
was faced with the spears of Beni Hassan tribesmen
proved unavailing. I was too big a coward. And though we
were thirty to one – to two if we counted the kid-catcher
our master's ally that morning, none of us had ever risen
to champion poor Eve against Daddy-long-legs' whisky
rages.

We weren't solid enough in our sense of his stupid
torture. Some of the boys had already divided this world
into Craneflies and themselves. They took a silly delight
in running risks from his anger. When they were beaten,
their pride was not to wince or flinch or bat an eyelid.
Others among us simply didn't think about Cranefly's
harshness beyond saying with a grin : 'The old gaffer's
in a bit of a tear this morning, i'n't he?'

Knowing that I would never rise on Eve's behalf, that morning I skulked further. I had taken one of the new books. It was open under my desk. Striving to shut out the horrible noise of sobs, I also wanted to forget my cowardice. The story I was reading seemed the rumour of a serener universe borne through a cloud :

And there at last he found the three Grey Sisters by the shore of the freezing sea, nodding upon a white log of driftwood beneath the cold white winter moon ; and they chanted a low song together : 'Why the old times were better than the new'.

The master had retreated to the kid-catcher's side to hear Evelyn's third try. When it came it was still that stupid, mesmerised 'twelvepence'. He made yet another of his giant lunges up the gangway between the desks towards her.

But Bob, the biggest boy in the school, tall as Amyas Leigh, was rising to his feet. As the master passed, expertly Bob bent forward. His curly brown head met the gaunt, black-waistcoated midriff. There was a crash, a wallop. Sprawling, Cranefly went right over Bob's head and hit the floor. A half-laughing Bob straightened himself. 'That's for you, you old bugger. Now I'm off!' And evading the kid-catcher's advancing bulk, Bob made for the door and disappeared. Youthful rebellion is nearly as old as the hills.

Stifled gasps of relief, delight, horror, burst from the tame rest of us. Our tall and dusty master picked himself up. The kid-catcher and he both dashed to the door. But Bob was far away ; they must have decided that pursuit was useless.

Bob came no more to school. That morning Evelyn and her 'twelvepence' were mercifully forgotten. Our day went on and the ceremony of the 'obediences' for the books was concluded without further hitch.

As it was a rural school, in time the movement to link country schools more to their surroundings reached it. We were ordered to keep 'nature diaries'. The stalwarts who didn't mind being whacked occasionally scrawled across a whole page : 'SAW NOTHING'. Sometimes it seemed as if the chief thing bawdy, sharp, rustic, early-twentieth-century schoolchildren learnt from the advantages of nation-wide literacy was the wilful, vital, necessary strength of their own individualities.

'SAW NOTHING' was such a joke. If you hadn't seen anything how could you write about it? The entry was sometimes but not always whack-proof. Yet what continually bemused both Father and me was how many of those country boys and girls did not, as Father put it, 'know a peewit from a 'pie'. To many children both were 'just birds'. Actually the place teemed with creature-happenings which the more interested among us set down docilely and inadequately in our diaries.

Beneath the very school windows, for instance, high above our repining heads, lambs ran races up and down a steep slope. When Margie and I tried running *up* a steep slope we found it difficult. Running *down* steep places with any speed, we sometimes ended in heaps at the bottom.

'As legs, you see,' both Mother and Father often agreed laughing, 'you children's shanks are nothing like as good as the lambs'.'

In spring, too, lapwings burst into their 'peewit' calls. The first aeroplane we had ever seen came over and looped the loop among the lapwings tumbling head over heels in air. In winter the black-and-white peewits all faced into the north wind on the grape-bloom sillion of the plough-land. The birds disliked the strong gale blowing their cockades the wrong way.

Small birds mobbed the many owls which screeched from cedars, oaks and elms. In spring, we had wild daffodils as well as snowdrops. We were as rich as Three Mile Cross in our scented violets. White scented violets grew with snake's head fritillary beyond the rubbish-tip behind the Church where my only brother lay. In autumn again, beech leaves grew picot-edged and golden-brown ; and then they fell into hollows in the wood above which white mist curled each morning. One of these hollows, feet-deep in leaf mould, produced a strange flower : 'It's a bird's nest orchid,' Father told me. And in autumn, too, coral-pink spindle berries contrasted with the vivid orange of their seeds. Nobody but the dame we vaguely called Nature or He the parson called God could have put two such colours as orange and pink together and made the combination work.

One moonlit February night, Father said that he would give his wife and three little girls a treat. He led us to Big Park. A hollow old lightning-struck ash tree stood in the far corner. 'Hist,' he bade us. We stole up in a line behind him. By full moon, five baby-foxes were playing with their mother's tail. 'You can see t' mothering smile on t' auld vixen's face,' Father whispered gleefully. And so we could.

He taught me how to mimic a rabbit's squeal ; and sometimes the competent head of a stoat would pop inquiringly out of totter-grass when I made the sound. The foxes' and the stoats' eyes were so bright that, years later, when I read : 'The creature hath a purpose and its eyes are bright with it,' the stoat and the vixen and the mating frogs were what I remembered.

Besides all these dramas, there were next year's buds in place long before the autumn leaves fell. It was a relief to see them so soon. God, the person whose name conjured up in my mind an amalgam of the schoolmaster Cranefly, Dr Snowdon, and Father, at least intended one more spring. So I was happy. I wanted another spring.

But not all the country secrets lay open for us to see, read, or write down so easily. Some had to be searched for ; and searched for over the high, barbed railings which separated the private grounds from the outer woods. Father's children — or any others — weren't supposed to go into the private grounds.

The head gardener, Old H., was a grey-bearded, well-read Scotsman. His grown-up son was already a bank-manager in the city. After fifty years of Yorkshire, Old H. talked with the most fascinating Highland Scottish accent. But he was very severe.

If one of us was needed for secret 'reiving', as our Mother called it, into the private grounds, my sisters and I had a 'Tell' :

Eena meena mina mo,
Catch a rabbit by its toe
If it squeals, let it go :
Eena meena mina mo.
OUT GOES SHE.

We went on chanting the 'Tell' until the last one left 'in' was the one of us to do the required job.

On this occasion the task fell to me. I was to climb

the high railings which surrounded the private grounds to look at a nest on the other side. Unfortunately, my cotton frock caught on a barb at the rail top just as the head gardener sighted us through his field-glasses.

When Old H. reached me, disingenuously I pointed down: 'Look, Mr H., at that nest near the earth-nut.' Old H.'s frowning feet were nearly on it: 'Please is it a chiff-chaff's or a willow-wren's?' Already, warned by the song of its mate, the small, greenish willow-wren had flitted noiselessly as a snowflake from its tiny dome.

The willow-wren has a very pure, delicate stave for its song. About fifteen notes soften and descend, as if, I read later, in W. H. Hudson's *Birds and Man*, a laughing child were calling a remark whilst running off into the depth of a wood. Years before, Father had taught me to distinguish the willow-wren's song from the 'chiff-chaff-cheff' of the chiff-chaff, the willow-wren's first cousin.

But Old H. would not be coaxed to look at the nest. He minded his foot just in time, however. He said: 'Ye're TRESPASSING. Ah mun tell yer feyther.'

The suspense of waiting for him to tell was so bad that I got round to confessing to Father about the willow-wren's nest myself. 'Old H. caught me on the rail,' I added: 'he's coming to you.'

What surprised us all was that the Big Un laughed uproariously: 'The auld rascal,' he bellowed; 'he's allus hockering about prying into what doesn't concern him. Yorkshire clay's softer to his foot-soles than his own rocky muck.'

But next time I met Old H., another surprising thing happened. He said: 'Come into the Arboretum.' He had collected some leaves. He spent half an hour writing their names : a Big Un doing this for a child – for me! Wellingtonia, Californian redwood, cedar of Lebanon, deodar, sequoia, hornbeam, wayfaring tree, black and silver poplars – many more besides the great oaks and beeches filled the glorious woods of Rounton Grange.

And as Old H. held up each green design between him and the sun for me to see, he scratched his chin. His grizzled beard rasped and waggled. And every time this happened, out like an owl from the dove-cot behind our house flew a great Latin name. But I was hopeless at remembering these, though Old H. thought them so important. Only the English names which he told me stuck.

As well as giving us books, my Lady came regularly to school and taught us singing. This was a blessed relief from Cranefly ; though he contrived to become almost human whilst she was with us. Even with my Lady's singing lessons, though, from the first I didn't like school. School was prison. But Mother was adamant. To school we must go ; and for years we didn't miss a day, and there was no point in whining.

My Lady was always exquisite in rustling grey silks and innumerable, Botticelli scarves. These veil-like adornments were the fashion among very rich, ageing ladies. She always wore palest grey, or fawn, or white, suede gloves. The knobs under her gloves were her many rings. In these rings, diamonds, amethysts, and rubies shone dully when occasionally she took off her gloves. Never, never, I used to think staring, had those white, dryish, oh-so-delicate fingers scrubbed or cleaned or polished, as Mother's hands had. Who kept my Lady's gloves so clean for her? How many pairs had she?

Twenty? I had two, a woollen pair and a white cotton pair, both darned.

'Shakespeare,' her Ladyship taught us, 'knew that "music and sweet poetry agree". But this harmony, though it was there in Shakespeare's songs, is not always achieved. Some songs and much opera have very trivial words.'

My Lady taught us 'Where the bee sucks', Ben Jonson's 'To Celia', 'Drink to me only with thine eyes', and Keats's 'Shed no tear'. 'In all these,' her Ladyship said, 'music and poetry harmonise as they should.' So they do in :

> Thrub, thrub, scrub, scrub, rub, rub away.
>> There is nae luck aboot the hoos
>>> Upon a weshing-day.

Two folk-songs that we enjoyed for some reason were more sensuously connected with far-away-and-long-ago than my Lady's lessons : 'One man came to mow my meadow' and

> O there was a woman and she was a widow.
>> Fair are the Flowers in the Valley :
> With a daughter as fair as a fresh sunny meadow ;
>> Fair are the Flowers in the Valley.

> The harp, the lute, the pipe, the flute, the cymbal.
>> Sweet goes the treble violin :
> With blushes red, 'I come,' she said.
>> Fair are the Flowers in the Valley.

My Lady also taught us a quatrain called 'Summer'. She said we must remember that this was written, not so long

ago as the previous folk-song was, but more than two
hundred years, in 1704:

> Where'er you walk, cool gales shall fan the glade:
> Trees, where you sit, shall crowd into a shade;
> Where'er you tread, the blushing flowers shall rise,
> And all things flourish where you turn your eyes.

But we knew in our country marrows that 'gales' don't
'fan'; flowers don't 'blush'. The whole verse, we whispered to each other, was 'pretty blown up'. 'Pope was
imitating the Greek court poet from Syracuse,' my Lady
explained. Cleverly she sensed our reaction to it. 'Yet
Pope was only sixteen, not much older than some of you,'
she went on, 'when he wrote "Summer". And though he
came to be a despiser of the country, the great poet in
him shines through those formalised lines.'

Her Ladyship never talked down to us; and for her
sake we sang 'Where'er you walk' with raucous attempt at
feeling. Yet our singing of it was no more than an insur-
rection against silence. With her little white baton in her
gloved hand, she strove to reduce us to pianissimo. Never
once did she betray the slightest horror at our uncouth
noise.

It was easy to be top, in all subjects other than singing,
of a class of musical, practical-minded children. But a
cookery van came to the school. Eight of us, all those girls
between the ages of ten and fourteen, were to receive three
weeks' 'housewifery'. We were scornful among ourselves.
'Whose mother would send her out not knowing how to
keep a house clean?' we said.

The mistress of the van was a grey-haired, plump little
bosser. The first day she set us to clean all the pans. When

she inquired why I wasn't cleaning mine, I tried to explain, reasonably as I thought, that at home we didn't clean our pans when they didn't *need* cleaning ; and these pans were so clean that it was a pity to waste time when I could not possibly improve them. This angered her very much. Next we were set to polish the windows. I looked at the lilac outside in the sun, and when she came to inspect, explained again that the windows were so beautifully bright that it was silly to soil the nice clean cloths, and then have to wash them.

The small shrew was speechless. Long before the end of the three weeks, down I had siled to the class bottom : and there at the bottom I stayed. Being at the class bottom gave a good knock to my growing vanity.

There were three social events in our village year. These were all presided over by our Gentry. Other than these, events of the country were not such as would be regarded as absorbing forty years later. Finding the first snowdrop and first violet and hearing the cuckoo were not less important than saving sweets during Lent. For six weeks we ate no sweets but saved all we were given, until Easter Day.

This was not self-sacrifice. Father made that clear : 'It gi'es nobody a lift.'

'What's the good of saving up then ?'

'Teaches you a bit of self-control, that's all,' Mother said.

For Easter we dyed eggs with gorse, onion-skins, or quassia. Onion-skins produced a marbled greenish-yellow. Quassia made the eggs anything from a rich Tyrian purple to a mauve as delicate as that of bog violets.

'Tid, Mid, Miseray. Carling, Palm, and Paced-egg

Day,' Mother sang. In the blessed freedom which holidays from school always meant, we ate our saved sweets. We paced our eggs, one a day, all Easter week. For a long time I thought that 'paced-eggs' had something to do with paste or dough. Mother said: 'No, silly. Children have always paced eggs down hills at Easter. Then the eggs crack and they can eat 'em.'

The best place for pacing eggs was the Barn field. Here a skirmish of the Battle of the Standard had been fought. Our Northern long-bow men beat back King David and his Scots on their grey ponies. This Barn field skirmish story was probably no more than one of our many battle-legends. These survive, but only overtly, much longer than stories of people's courage or endurance.

The Barn field ran steeply down to Kemp's wizzen and Dead Man's Hollow. Our yellow and purple eggs bounced down green hillocks. A surprising number of times they arrived unbroken in Dead Man's roomy dip.

There were also pancake day, April fool's day, hot-cross-bun day, oak-apple day, Hallowe'en (the Pagan New Year), and bonfire night. On the twenty-ninth of May, the boys came to school armed with the longest stinging-nettles they could find. Nobody remembered much about King Charles hiding in the oak. Paleozoic oak, and nettle, symbolised daring and danger. The boys' hands, secure in red handkerchiefs, carried nettles. Girls who had oak twigs with oak-apples on were supposed to be let alone. But if we girls didn't pluck the nettle danger from the boys, we were well and truly stung, oak-apples or no oak-apples.

In summer holidays, Mother arranged picnics. We carried our kettle, matches, and picnic basket across the fields to the nearest spring-head. Though this pool

94

swarmed with tiddlers, sticklebacks, water-boatmen, and spider-skaters, 'It's good water out of the clean earth,' Mother said. At it we filled our kettle. Then we gathered dry sticks ; and Mother helped us to make a 'real gipsy fire'. After tea we played 'testing fortunes' by means of couch-grass :

Tinker?
Tailor?
Soldier?
Sailor?
Rich man?
Poor man?
Beggar man?
Thief?

By looking ahead and pulling the seeds off if necessary in the wrong order, you could always finish at 'rich man'; at all costs avoid 'beggar man' or 'thief' for a future husband. Of course we knew the game was all nonsense. But a shred of feminine superstition stuck obstinately.

After 'testing fortunes' we played 'Cowboys and Indians'. We had carried one each of Father's horse-blankets with us, and feathers which the five peacocks dropped from their tails. We crayoned ourselves for 'war-paint', and ranged through the woods armed with bows and arrows which we made from willow-withy.

In all my childhood we had only two holidays away. One of these was a week which we spent with my Father's youngest brother in The Shambles at York. Uncle Harry was a fat, red-cheeked butcher. His ears, nose, and hands were all fascinating in their bigness, redness, and fleshiness ; and the amount of meat he and his family consumed was astonishing to my Mother.

The only other holiday of my childhood was a week-end by Teesside. The aunt whom we visited was Mother's only sister, a widow with three grown-up children. Her son was a dark, oily young man, a steel-worker earning six pounds a week. He divided all girls into either 'tarts' or '*nice* tarts'; my aunt's younger daughter had had a baby coming when she got married; my aunt's elder daughter was a teacher of infants. 'Maud's a cut above them other two,' Mother often whispered.

My aunt's house was one of those built by Liberal and Quaker millionaires in the heyday of British world-leadership. Cramped, dark, bathroomless, it had an ash-pan closet down a sunless back-yard. With thousands of other ash-pan closets, this was emptied by 'Padden-can men' at night because the stench was so bad. And with thousands of other dark, bathroomless houses, my aunt's was wedged in a drab street among scores of other streets equally drab and ugly. This kind of dwelling still secretes the throbbing lives of tens of thousands of colliers, steel-workers, industrial workers of many kinds in the Automation–Welfare State of the 1970s.

The district round Middlesbrough and Teesside to the sea was so caked with grime that you couldn't put a finger or any other part of you anywhere without getting blackened. For twenty miles the air smelt of chemical and ash and soot, as the crowded houses smelt of old cabbage, cheese, and cat. Pavements round my aunt's were covered with black, gluey mud whenever it rained. There wasn't a speck of green grass or a tree with which to refresh your eyes for miles.

How could Sir Lothian have allowed crowded, grim streets and houses such as these for people to live in? Where had his liberal kindness been? Did the people see

97

their houses and surroundings as so blindingly, filthily ugly? Soon I knew they did. No doubt most of the dwellings, like my aunt's, were relatively neat inside, once you got over the dark, and the impure smell. But I was glad we went only once to Teesside.

Sundays at home were holidays, trying ones. We wore our Sunday frocks. Black woollen stockings pricked our knee-backs. I had been born with an extra toe, so my shoe pinched my 'witch' foot. Sunday clothes were the means by which girls learnt to put up with discomfort.

We mightn't sew or play with our dolls or balls or skipping-ropes in the bland order of the Sabbath to which Mother paid heed. We might read; but other than the *Bible* there was only the *Prayer-book*, Father's *Live Stock Annual* and *The Lady's Companion* which Mother took.

Frocks must be kept clean. We didn't wear pinafores except for school. But either the cat or one of the young hounds was sure to jump up and leave a paw-mark on my Sunday white muslin.

Saying collects and hymns round Mother's chair had given place to going to Church. Dressing for Church was a long-drawn-out ritual. Something approaching obsession with personal cleanliness was already sweeping over our working classes. With our 'Sunday best' for Church we had to have specklessly shining shoes, freshly washed gloves, clean handkerchiefs, and best hair-ribbons under our hats. One foundered in a rising sea of material details. It was utterly depressing to keep one's attention on neat hair, tied shoe-laces, and clean finger-nails.

Father did not go with us to Church. For all the quick ending of his angers, evidently he found it hard to forgive the parson who consigned his only son to the rubbish-tip. The parson, moreover, suffered from what Father called a 'puzzimus'. This was a speech defect which made him difficult to comprehend. An impediment I think Father meant.

Christmas being the time when we forgave wrongs and forgot griefs, one Christmas, at our combined persuasions, Father consented to go to a service. But he couldn't sit still. Finally, having grunted audibly many times whilst we hung our heads for him, he actually interrupted Parson W.'s sapless sermon on the 'values of childlike humility'. A vehement, scornful 'No!' burst from Father's lips. Without knowing that he was quoting, he added more loudly still: 'A man's a *man*. God wants nobody kow-towing.' And up got Father and marched out of Church regardless of our shamed blushes. I longed to follow but meekly stayed with Mother.

After that there was relief among his family over Father's resumed absence from Church. We met him after evening service; and he took us along green lanes, down ancient paths, and by winding rights of way. 'These bridle ways,' he asserted, 'have to be used by us folk oursens to keep 'em open. If we don't use 'em, t' clever auld farmers'll soon sow clover and vetch all over. Then these bridle-paths'll be lost to folk for good.' It was like a holiday to be out on those long walks with Father and Mother peaceful and happy.

Sometimes one of our five or six sailor cousins came to see us. He was on leave from HMS *Dreadnought*. He told us stories about places like the Andaman Islands: 'There,' Fred number two said, 'everything's backside-first. Water runs up-hill. The men are little and the women big. And the women, if they put on any clothes at all, it's the trousers.' We liked listening to grown-up talk when it was as entertaining as our sailor cousin's.

99

The first of our three social events came a few days after each Christmas. Christmas belonged to a world of carollers with banjos, sooty-faced, beribboned, Cleveland sword-dancers from Skelton, candles, bells, the holly and the ivy, and the ancient comfort of logs blazing on the parlour fire. We celebrated the turn of our bitter Northern winter as well as Bethlehem and tenderness for the Child without knowing that we were remembering the pre-Christian Feast of Hope when life sprang green and strong again from limp, grey 'death'.

Into this other-world of Christmas came the first event of our social year, the New Year Concert. My sisters' long, thick, flaxen hair, and my own, was washed. Usually our hair was washed only once a month. It had an extra wash for events such as the Concert. Mother boiled bucket after bucket of water in the big copper kettle for our weekly bath by the kitchen fire. We had a screen round us on which she had pasted pictures. Mother didn't know that she had put a print of Breughel's 'The Blind leading the Blind' next to one of dead-looking dogs guarding dead grouse and a doll-faced lady mounted side-saddle before a handsome castle.

When Mother was sweating with washing three heads of long yellow hair, we put on flannel nightgowns that wrapped cosily round our toes. In a row on the hearthrug we sat hair-drying and eating our suppers of brown bread with milk. Then Mother plaited us five or six braids each, to form the desired Concert frizz.

For the Christmas Concert we had new frocks. Mother made all our clothes until we were fourteen or so, including our topcoats. In 1914, the material for three silk frocks cost twelve shillings. Feeling gorgeous in our white silk, wrapped up in coats, scarves, gloves, and tams, we still shivered. When we shivered, we didn't feel that being cold was anything but a thrill. Through black velvet shadows in the eerie light of the snow-laden wood, we went with Mother carrying candle-lanterns, to the village hall. Father scorned the Concert as 'daftness'.

At the Concert, the Baronet's daughter and her husband sang 'The Keys of Heaven'. The son of that Richmond family which knows so much about Britain's sea-battles recited in ringing child-tones:

Admirals all, in England's name
  Honour be yours, and fame . . .

We schoolchildren performed one of my Lady's fairy play translations such as 'Rumpelstiltskin'.

Other talent for the Concert was usually plentiful. Never were we short of offers to sing, dance, or recite. One of Father's grooms was particularly in demand. Frankie was an ape-like dwarf of a man who always smelt rankly of horse. Father didn't smell like that. Why did Frankie? He also blew his nose between his forefinger and his thumb: 'Vulgar oit,' Mother said. Frankie's relatives were circus acrobats, tap-dancers, and ventriloquists. He had a repertoire of songs such as 'The raggletaggle gipsies', 'The foggy, foggy dew', or 'The everlasting tree'. The frenzy of the chorus of 'The green grass growing all around, all around' usually brought the Concert-house down. But the applause, though wild, was usually, for some reason, slightly shamefaced. We knew the song was sexy. Another favourite of Frankie's was 'Champagne Charlie is me name, ha ha'.

The second social event of our year was the Tenants' New Year Ball. I can't remember that my Father and

Mother took baths even for this important occasion. They washed parts of themselves daily, of course. They used neither toothpaste nor toothbrushes; but they rinsed their mouths often. I recall them as being always sweet-smelling, pleasant-breath'd. Not so long before their time, Queen Caroline, it seems, stank. Though they were born to inherit the century of British luxury, and though Mother bathed us children in the round tin bath filled from kettles to the end of our childhood, bathing remained superfluous to my parents themselves. They liked a kettle of warm water when they were tired or grubby. But usually they preferred cold water. Far more people, as Bergen Evans has pointed out, have died untimely from the effects of hot baths than from lack of them.

For the Ball my Mother put on her foulard gown with guimpe trimming. The gown was the colour of October beech leaves. I don't recall that she ever bought a new Ball gown. Only twice a year did she wash her long hair. After its summer wash, she walked up and down the paddock to dry it. Its second washing was for the Ball. This time she curled its brown strands round the front with the hot poker. She looked pretty but strange. Beauty has so many forms. She brought tangerines, small crackers, and candied figs for us from the Ball, in the pockets of her voluminous skirt. Smell of tangerines always limns behind my eyes a picture of Mother in her beech-leaf dress with wasp waist. And the stories she and Father told when they came back at two in the morning and we wakened up always made us think we had been to the Ball ourselves.

The third social event of our year was our Show. This 'horticultural exhibition' was begun by our Gentry. Nearby, Osmotherly's Summer Games were of medieval folk-origin. It took two World Wars to kill Osmotherly's Summer Games. But our Show fizzled out after about a score of years. Osmotherly's great event was the chasing of a greased pig. A pig race was asked for at Rounton; but the idea was turned down as 'unseemly', 'noisy', 'vulgar', 'uncivilised'.

On the first Saturday each August, in a field near our house, a big marquee smelling of bruised grass and tarpaulin had gone up by eight o'clock. All morning we carried in our exhibits. At half past two, my Lady or one of her titled friends declared the exhibition open.

Our brass band played 'Rule Britannia', 'The British Grenadiers', 'Men of Harlech', 'Annie Laurie', and other stirring tunes. The band also played mournful ballads such as 'Barbary Allen', and the one made poignant because my Lady had told us it was by an unknown Scot who lost his Stuart cause at Culloden and his life by hanging a few days later at Carlisle:

The wee birdies sing and the wild flowers spring,
    And in sunshine the waters are sleepin';
But a broken heart it kens nae second spring,
    Though the waeful may cease frae their greetin'.

There was a cricket match against a neighbouring village team and a quoits match against another team. We children sang songs and danced round a maypole, with red, white and blue ribbons. There was a sweet-stall, a lemonade stall, and an ice-cream man, on the Show field. Our customary, weekly ha'pennies rose for that one Saturday to the exorbitant sums of threepence apiece.

Inside the dimness of the Show tent, apples, plums, pears, fat gold corn, and vegetables of many kinds, were banked on trestle tables. Butter varied from palest cream to rich marigold in colour. Pounds of it, long and round, were decorated with basket-weave, rope-twist, and lozenge patterns. These patterns were seen in Egypt, Crete, and Mesopotamia, five thousand years ago. The brownness of brown eggs and whiteness of white ones made choice between them almost impossible, though we all followed the experts to judge for ourselves. Roses and pansy-faces peered blithely from cardboard slits. Needlework, embroidery, tatting, crocheted quilts, patchwork quilts, loom-cloth that would have delighted Penelope — all were piled in the profusion of that marquee in a shady green field at the foot of the Cleveland hills.

Mother usually won the prize for cooked potatoes and the prize for brown bread. She steamed the potatoes in their jackets. The jackets cracked just sufficiently to reveal the 'floury' insides. We often ate this kind of potato with butter and salt. Mother also won first prize for darning and patching. To this day, when few of us darn, I cannot help thinking that a well-woven darn, an invisible or even a feather-stitched patch, can enhance rather than degrade stockings, jerseys, and coat-elbows.

My sisters dressed dolls. I wrote muddled essays and offered old H.'s collection of leaves, and my own of wild flowers : wild flowers such as harebell, moneywort, pimpernel, and honeysuckle are so much more delicate than man-made tulip and blousy dahlia. Rounton flowers were so rich that one had gathered them since one could walk. To Mother's dismay, Margaret and I had once stuffed violets up our noses : 'to keep the smell there for good'. Even on that occasion Mother didn't ask the butler to ring for Dr Snowdon. 'Keep on blowing : and you'll blow the violets down where they belong,' was all she said. But I think she was a bit bothered until she saw the violets come down.

Father, of course, bore off many prizes at the Show. He won the biggest prize of all, for the neatest and most well-filled garden. All summer he fed his onions with 'meg' until they were as far round as cheese-plates. Vegetable marrows grew bloated like over-eating, middle-aged men and women. Gooseberries – if a disastrous shower just before the important day didn't crack them – swelled to the size of bantams' eggs. Flowers were 'women's toys'. It was beneath Father's manly dignity to spend time growing flowers.

On Show day he was usually to be found, surrounded by a large group of listeners, laying down the law about everything that concerned the growing of fruit and vegetables, and often about what did not. How persuasive he was over the occasional fraud practised : 'You didn't need to swipe Jack's beetroot on Thursday night,' he would say : 'Your own's pretty near as good.'

Yet I don't think that competition at the Show was virulent. Certainly the individuality which everybody's different efforts produced was rich.

By about nine in the evening of Show day, the marquee was taken down. Gentry and Big Uns had gone home. Paired lovers wandered off along the innumerable little green paths the country keeps for centuries. Boys and girls of between the ages of about ten and eighteen were left. And a completely new excitement descended over the darkening, deserted Show field.

There was a pause, a waiting on some edge. Then the older boys and girls in a cluster struck up :

Oats and beans and barley,
Oats and beans and barley,
You nor I nor nobody knows
How oats and beans and barley grows.

But we didn't want tame, daytime songs such as 'Oats and beans and barley' and 'Here we come gathering nuts and may' on Show night. Boys and girls began to make two lines. Alternately the lines danced forward and then away from each other. First the boys sang :

Here's three old Jews
Just come from Spain
To ask you for
Your daughter Jane.

The line of girls replied :

Our daughter Jane
Is far too young
To understand
Your flattering tongue.

Boys :

Stand back, stand back
To the cottage wall
We'll pick the fairest
Of you all.
The fairest one
That I can see
Is pretty Jenny. (or another name arrived at by
                              unspoken accord)
Come to me.

Then the girl named joined the 'Jews'.

But this game, too, was really only a warming up. A bigger thrill lay in store.

Boys and girls formed a ring round three girls. Covering their faces, these knelt and sang.

> Poor Mary sits a-weeping,
> > a-weeping,
> > a-weeping,
> Poor Mary sits a-weeping,
> > > On a bright summer's day.

Then the ring sang:

> Pray tell us what you're weeping for,
> > you're weeping for,
> > you're weeping for?
> Pray tell us why you're weeping,
> > > On a bright summer's day?

Then the girls replied:

> We're weeping for our true loves,
> > our true loves,
> > our true loves,
> We're weeping for our true loves,
> > > On a bright summer's day.

And briskly the ring chanted:

> Stand up and choose your lovers,
> > your lovers,
> > your lovers,
> Stand up and choose your lovers,
> > > On a bright summer's day.

The girls then each chose a boy from the outer ring. The six made an inner ring of their own. Hand in hand these danced round and round. The tune of the outer ring changed completely. It rose. Quicker and quicker it went; it ended on a frantic climax and fandango:

Now you're married you must obey,
You must be true to all you say;
You must be kind; you must be good;
And help your wife to chop the wood.
Chop the wood and carry it in,
And kiss the girl that's in the ring.

Seizing the girl who had chosen him, each boy in the inner ring kissed her. There was some slight conflict between the publicity and privacy of kissing but the conflict made the thrill bigger. Then the three girls came out and the three boys were left in the middle. The boys had a shorter song:

I wrote a letter to my love
    And on the way I lost it;
One of you has picked it up
    And put it in your pocket.

Each boy threw his handkerchief at a girl. He pulled, carried, or bore her willing into the ring. After that, 'Now you're married you must obey' began again, to end, as before, with its scramble of kisses.

I don't remember any ring-leader for these games. Nobody dictated orders. There was no disorder. Some boys were too shy to grab girls or to kiss them. Some girls broke out of the ring and had to be brought back by a number of boys. That was all.

That August night, for the first time I noticed how few older boys there were at our Show-night games. I saw, too, how often my elder sister, with gold hair that waved round her face, and blue eyes that changed colour as the light changed, was chosen.

I noticed another thing: I wasn't chosen at all. Desperately I wanted to be and wasn't. Why wasn't I? I was skinny. My hair was straight. My lips were thin as string. My most terrible Roman nose (wherever did I get it? 'Certainly not from *my* forebears,' Father assured us) was freckled. 'And you have a shifty look,' Mother had been heard to admit.

The Show field darkened. The tremendous whirr of kissing echoed in my stomach and nether parts. I grew miserable. Laurie was about to choose me when suddenly he drew back. 'No,' he said, 'you're a telly-pie-tit.'

Still I only half grasped how telling about Peter four years ago must have approached the breaking of an age-group loyalty.

The Big House's private grounds were still open. I wandered off down the bee-drive. Beyond the conservatory, a stream ran underground and bubbled out again like Kubla Khan's at Zanadu. Round the pond through which the stream passed was Miss Bell's noted rock garden.

Beyond the bee-drive a carved stone font stood; Gertrude Bell had brought this font from the Ancient East. Near it was a sundial with a motto round it:

How small a part of Time they share
That are so wondrous sweet and fair.

But on that particular evening, moonlight shone on some

words I hadn't seen before. These were carved on a stone sill :

A time to watch what Time's next step may be.

Even at my unripe age, peasant sense hinted that thus to pry over Time's shoulder wasn't possible.

Beyond the stone sill a heron stilted gravely on one leg towards the stream. The kingfisher shot, a steel-blue arrow, down the length of water his ancestors had most likely fished for hundreds of years. But a gulf was widening before me which words and explanations would not bridge. Frequently of late, at housework, Mother complained, 'Our Anne, you don't frame.' In that workaday world of practical intelligences I was almost stupidly unpractical. When I read *The Water Babies*, *Hereward the Wake*, *Rob Roy*, or *Lamb's Tales from Shakespeare*, an unspoken opinion grew in the house that reading was 'as bad as doing nothing'. And doing nothing, now that we were growing up, was the worst of all possible faults.

The Gentry's lawn had diamond-shaped patches of thyme : Mother said : 'for ladies to trail their ball-gowns over.' I pressed my ear to the thyme, imagining earth breathed ; but of course 'inanimate' earth doesn't breathe in any rhythm like ours.

Our Gentry were so rich. We were so poor. Yet anyone could have lived at the Big House without being awed by its spacious beauty. With the utmost strength of mind that I could summon, I determined to escape from the meanness for which I thought Father's servitude stood.

And what was the next step for that Edwardian mansion with its paradisal grounds and supporting village? What was almost the next step for a Britain with gardens, Satanic mills, and smoke-black cities? Already the standard of living for her people was the highest in the world.

That summer night all seemed as permanent as the figures carved on Miss Bell's font from ancient Babylon. But the next step had been taken. Europe's bloodiest war to date, the First World War, had begun.

New financiers, prospective millionaires from a fresh set of middle-class families, were appearing. Talented scholars from working-class parents were reaching high positions. George Orwell's 'general post', as later he called it, was being stepped up. Change, more rapid than ever before, was hurtling over us.

The dynamic of our liberal Gentry would fall back before more cunning and shrewder new men of high-finance and urban industry. Ordinary people would work to gain luxury unknown before, but not much more freedom. What would we make of these complexities? Britain would be hurled from her banking and trading eminence in the world. But what worthwhile wisdom would we have to put in the place of new, civilised eminences?

5

COUNTRY CO-EDUCATION
GRAMMAR SCHOOL

When the First World War had broken over our heads, people at Rounton, like working people anywhere, hadn't shown up as enthusiastic patriots and fighters. Still, we gave five lives. The Zeppelin raid on Hartlepool brought war nearest to us. When Earl Haig could think of nothing but hurling men into trenches to die in millions – though such tragedy seemed far away, we prayed as best we knew how to pray: 'O God, let our soldiers and sailors not die *only* for us.'

Otherwise the warning, the words carved on the stone sill, altered life at Rounton astonishingly little. Father and Mother remained determined that their children should continue their education in spite of all difficulties. 'I had hard words and knocks and no schooling worth speaking of,' Father repeated. 'You three must all do better than that.' None of Father's daughters got one of the new free places. But we were among the first to go to a Grammar school from those remote villages.

By 1917, there was only one train to the town in the morning, and one train back at night. The town was ten miles away. If one missed the train in the morning, one missed a whole day's school. If one missed the train home at night – well, one didn't miss the train night or morning.

It was four and a half miles to our station at the home end of the journey. Before I could start the Grammar school my elder sister had to finish her two years. Then I could inherit her bike. This ancient machine had brakes and tyres and lamps ; these essentials were all that could be said for it as a bike.

On summer country mornings larks' and cuckoos' and throstles' songs echo as down church aisles. But in January, the year I began the Grammar school, day after day, before I had gone a mile, I was soaked to the skin. Morning after morning my bike was beaten to a stand by the crazy wind that sweeps the Vale of York. Only the plan of shouting the poetry which I had to learn could make me forget the clammy dejection and the frustration of being knocked sideways by a tearing blast round every corner. Fortunately the driver of the train soon grew to expect me. Waving his black rag as he leaned from his cab, he would keep his train a minute or two whilst I panted up the last bit of lane. If I had been heard shouting poetry to the wind, I would have been pronounced simple, 'off it', 'not all there'.

North Yorkshire usually has plenty of snow in February. Then the wind whips the top of it into curves like those of the Greek acanthus. Often the snow was four feet deep by the roadsides. The snow-plough didn't get out much before half past seven. Tommy Norman the postman with his horse Dick and his red two-wheeled mail cart made the first wheel-track. I rode in Tommy's track. But one little wobble – and off I came, plump into the cold, white glory. I'm not 'putting it over' that this was hardship. It was fun. It made me notice the patterns of 'the secret ministry of frost' which otherwise I should have missed. But it was necessary to keep one's attention fixed on the job in hand and leave poetry alone when Cleveland February roads were solid sheets of frozen, grey slush.

Coming home tired through the dark made me sleepy. Once I found myself so comfortable in the gutter among dry cat-ice that oblivion must have clapped down the instant I skidded off my bike. It was under the bridge by Dead Man's Hollow. A tramp, his nose in a white plaster bag and a lump of cotton-wool in one ear, holding a flickering match above my head, waked me.

'Arl reet, lassie?' And he dropped the spent match to crack his finger-joints loudly in an uneasy concern.

'Quite all right – sir.' Just in time as I hastily rose did I remember my Father's injunctions as to the respectful form of address for these Independents of the road. The tramp faded back politely into the black velvet of the night as I gathered myself together.

I was even a little rested to renew the battle with the dark and the wind and the ice. Today, sounds of storm give me a restless sense of being over-protected if I happen to be in a town-dwelling. And most hotels, cinemas, theatres, and centrally-heated houses, by the 1970s, seem hermetically sealed, hot and unbearably airless.

The L.s kept a small-holding near the station. They let me leave my bike in their shed for nothing. This meant

one of Mother's precious shillings saved each week. Mrs L. was plump, waddling, rosy-cheeked. Her hair had the bluey-black sheen of a swallow's breast. She wore a print frock all through the winter, a pink sunbonnet, and elastic-sided black boots. 'Sandy and me eloped when we were both not much older than you,' she told me.

Sandy was another of those unambitious country characters whose minds brim with information that is almost wholly unformalised. He had a creamy-white ferret with pink eyes which nestled within his shirt and black cardigan.

'Now suppose that ferret gives your chest a good nip?' I couldn't help asking. The chest in question had thick black hair in magpie contrast to the cream of the ferret-fur.

Sandy retorted with most persuasive confidence: 'Contrary to what folks think, ferrets are loyal enough little beasts: once they trust you, of course . . . They keep to one mate, too. Did you know that?' And Sandy gave me one of his cheerful winks.

I would have liked to give him a wink back. But though I had spent long enough trying, I hadn't mastered the art of these symbols of mutual understanding. Mother said: 'Don't try. Winking's laddish.'

Sandy had, too, a young vixen, nearly tame. 'An' yet,' he said, stroking her so that I would stroke her too: 'I can't keep her shut up. Sooner or later she'll hear the call.' He turned her pointed nose, and mouth with its gleaming sharp teeth, up to us: 'Won't you, lass? You'll be off with a mate in the woods.' And of course, one morning, the little vixen's nest of hay in Sandy's shed was empty of her curled shape. She'd gone all right.

Sandy's wife used to give me a glass of milk warm from the cow before I set off on my dark rides home.

Once, whilst she was getting the milk, Sandy did a strange thing. He seized hold. His big fingers fumbled for two breasts rising not very perceptibly beneath my green stuff tunic. He kissed my lips, chance-met and therefore blankly bungling with surprise.

There was no time to think what to do. A few seconds I stood gaping at the mystery of him. And Sandy gaped, I suppose, at mine. Then he drew back.

'Took leave of my senses,' he said sombrely. 'Hope what I've done'll make no difference, lassie.'

'I don't see why it need. Do you, please?' I whispered the words a little frantically because I was so frightened Mrs L. would hear : 'There's a lot of things yet for you to tell me about, anyway.'

He smiled and said 'Yes.' I pitied him a little then. But I had no business with pity. He was admirable in so many ways. Later, I grew more used to men's sudden kisses behind doors. I have always found human guile and cunning amusing, as Father found Rennie's : even likeable, when it harms nobody. These quick, gentle, friendly, yet sensuous kisses never fail to take me by surprise. Usually they are given when we are talking about something of absorbing interest. But they also never fail to make me grateful for a moment's encounter at some earlier, candid depth involving no faithlessness or sensuality worth getting fluffed about.

An encampment of gipsies accused Sandy, quite mistakenly I am sure, of poisoning their curs. Sandy warned Pink Sunbonnet : 'Gippos can be brutal when their danders are up.' He was a little nervous of some reprisal. That night I passed the swarthy men grouped surly and wrathful, gazing down at five stiff-stretched mongrels. Their women, their black braids of hair hanging down the fronts of their shoulders, were cooking stew on tripods over curly, blue wood-smoke. One of them asked: 'Tell's the time, missie.' I got off my bike to tell them with best care and ventured to add: 'Y'know, Sandy L. would never do such a dirty trick as poison your dogs.' The gipsy faces remained impassive. Nobody made any reply. I couldn't tell whether they believed me or not. I said 'Goodnight, see you tomorrow,' and got on my bike again. It was from the gipsies that I learnt how little trust there is in words alone.

Those rag-tents were too nicely denuded of clutter. They were so empty of comfort or beauty as to be unbearable for more than a short time. But I may be being materialistic. That gipsy cavalcade, packed for itinerary, is still vividly colour-printed among the other booty which I keep behind my eyes.

The headman of the twenty or so individuals had a face tanned as dark as the bark of an alder tree. He drove the first, top-heavy, wooden caravan. This vehicle was semi-spherical. Garish red and yellow paint adorned its sides and its enormously thick old wooden wheels. It must have been heavy: but one horse drew it. Another piebald was reined to its side. The second flat-cart had a home-made, tarpaulin-covered top. Stretched over semi-circular withies, this could be taken off and used for a roof on the ground. The second cart held the four women and perhaps a dozen black-haired children. This was driven by the grandmother of the tribe. Third and last came a flat-cart without a top, driven by one of the younger men. Three or four other men sat beside him; and behind the men, their wolfish, half-breed dogs travelled. (The gipsies soon acquired more dogs after the poisoning episode.) With alert dignity the dogs sat on sacks or other baggage. No gipsy's prized cur ever pants, tongue lolling, behind his master.

After the three carts, piebald colts and yearlings trotted loose. Such a cavalcade is rarer now. But occasionally one may be seen along Fairy Glen near Bettws-y-Coed, at Kirby Ferrers in the Vale of Belvoir, by Helpston Heath in John Clare's Northamptonshire, by the Queen's Highway on Fosse Road South, or on Kentish commons. The gated road near Sandy's, where I used to pass them as a schoolgirl, is still a gipsy haunt. Real gipsies are as obstinate as some primitive tribes over bartering their independence. *Vive* men's differences! Gipsies, Dinka, Nuer, Masai – most of us in fact, in varying degrees – in spite of dismal prophesies about urbanism, communism, socialism, and other -isms, will take a good long time to toe the same line.

Gipsies in the 1970s are blamed for leaving rubbish about. But of course we blame others for what we ourselves feel guilty about. A few more dustbins at lay-bys would help enormously.

The Grammar school at Northallerton had been endowed in 1349 as a 'School for Song and Grammar'. It had decayed under Edward the Sixth, revived, shut down again, and, after nearly six hundred years, it was having a third good lease of life.

It had one or two scholars of note, Erasmus, and Thomas Rymer, the first English literary critic who, in 1692, pronounced *Othello* 'a horrible progress beyond any human imagination'. But during the nineteenth century the school's most learned headmaster taught 'blind' in prolonged bouts of drunkenness. Boys' fathers paid this inspired alcoholic thirty shillings a year. Then the school got a soberer master and new buildings, and for the first time in its long history it began to educate girls as well as boys.

In 1920 it had about two hundred scholars between the ages of eight and eighteen. A strong idea flew in that school air at this time that most children were good at something. We heard nothing about leadership, little about gentlemen and ladies, nothing either about competition or 'streaming'. There was no question of cribbing or copying. We were expected to help each other if anybody got stuck.

The Head was a small thin man with a neck like three thin twisted ropes, and ears and eyebrows he could move at will. His gift as a teacher was that usually he knew what was going on in our minds better than we knew ourselves. He wasn't stern or cranky or fanatical. He hadn't any standards of perfection ; and he didn't think, as the great Arnold did, that the Devil pops a double dose of wickedness into boys when God isn't looking. He managed boys quite well without a cane.

At morning or evening assembly he would come striding in. Instead of a prayer, he would read us a little of Goëthe, or Mill, or Tolstoy, or Swift, or even Hugh Lofting. Once he brought us Hopkins's 'The Windhover' (my Father called this bird 'our little red hawk'), from Bridges' edition. On another occasion he read us, from a book published in 1920 :

> I love at early morn from new-mown swath
>   To see the startled frog his rout pursue
> And mark while leaping o'er the dripping path
>   His bright sides scatter dew
>   And early lark that from its bustle flyes

To hail his mattin new
    And watch him to the skyes

And note on hedgerow baulks in moisture sprent
    The jetty snail creep from the mossy thorn
With earnest heed and tremulous intent
    Frail brother of the morn
        That from the tiny bents and misted leaves
Withdraws his timid horn
        And fearful vision weaves

Ah . . . so the snail *was* our brother?

The Head then read the notices for the day. As usual he ended with that piece from Paul to the Philippians :

> Finally, brethren, whatsoever things are true, whatso-
> ever things are honourable, whatsoever things are just,
> whatsoever things are pure, whatsoever things are
> lovely, whatsoever things are of good report ; if there
> be any virtue, and if there be any praise, *think* on these
> things.

The world had reached the stage when Bertrand Russell was writing of the tyrannies Cartesian man can impose in the name of liberty. America was the richest country. Russia had not emerged from bloodshed and revolution to impose new tyrannies in the name of democratic communism. Germany was facing economic and other sorts of disaster, and slithering out of war-debts. China, Africa, Asia, South America hadn't waked. Britain had lost the lead to the USA.

Our Head summed the situation up thus : 'The bles-sings of civilisation are paid for with bloodshed and misery. You rarely get something for nothing.' He called this process 'the eternal conflict between understanding and force ... You are children of those who have worked and died to interpret the mysteries of the universe,' he would say. 'There have been Lao Tsze, Buddha, Socrates, Plato, Jesus, Mohammed.' These names he usually put in a list like this. And then he would add: 'There are countless teachers, doctors, and scientists besides. Ethic, medicine, music, poetry, art, and science – all are above nations.'

After he had been insisting on such as this, he would slap his high forehead: 'But don't take too much heed of my opinions,' he would end: 'That is, never let other people do your thinking for you. Don't take anything for granted. And don't ever forget the wonder of the world. It's a tall order. But that's it.'

He had another favourite piece with which he sometimes dismissed us. This was what Paul said to the people of Corinth:

' ... now abideth faith, hope, love.' (Here the Head would add off his own bat: 'hate and fear as well'.) 'And the greatest of these is love.'

One of his eyebrows would shoot up into his forehead. Frowning, he drew the other down. He gave his crooked nose a clockwise twist with his thumb and forefinger. Descending from his rostrum, he would hurry away along the sun-spattered corridor, tatters from his ragged gown flying out behind him. The glass doors swung to, glug, glug.

Lessons were maths, history, geography, English, French, Latin, science – all the subjects which at that time were being crammed into school timetables. Yet lumber was more kindly loaded on us than at the village board school. Our science master, who smelt of Harris tweed, delighted us writing as nattily with his left hand as his right. Another would inscribe the whole of the Lord's Prayer on paper the size of a threepenny-bit, for our amusement. When we couldn't do a 'rider' the fat, black-haired, black-whiskered maths master solemnly exhorted us : 'Now watch this board while I go through it.' He seemed not to understand why this was every time greeted with a roar of laughter. Strange that one so clever could be so dim. Then there was that complicated business of how winds rise. The geography master would explain with exquisitely careful diagrams. But invariably little Dodsworth, a midget of a boy with a long white face, rabbit teeth and too-long shorts, rose and said with polite plaintiveness : 'Pleathe thir, I can't underthtand.' And the whole intricate explanation began again.

Day after day I rode my bike through sun, wind, mist, snow and rain, to the Grammar school. 'Book-larnin',' as Father both admiringly and critically called it, as well as vulgar ambition which I hadn't learnt to beware of, buzzed in the back of my head like bees. The six years at Grammar school were so hectic that my sexual senses quite went to sleep. I avoided talking to boys except at cricket, tennis, or in the children's committee. That school was among the very first to practise 'self-government', persuasively giving us children a bit of a voice. I had a girl-friend and she was all I needed.

At fifteen I became a woman, as Mother called it ; she improved the shining hour by impressing on me : 'Your bad temper had better improve now, our Anne ; women have a goodish deal to put up with.' This rather gloomy injunction reduced me to tears.

I was confirmed in a white frock three years old, and veil. The Bishop's words induced piety – for a time. I read the Bible, twice, without understanding much. Mother was nearly through her third reading.

When a more eloquent parson followed the one with the 'puzzimus' I went to Church morning and evening and taught Sunday school. In duller sermons the fancy would not stay at home. It roamed. Renouncing all idea of romance and marriage, at the end of a life of service for others, I would be taken to heaven. Amid the watching congregation I imagined myself wafted into the rafters, to perch there like St Joseph. Then through the Church roof newly sprouted wings would flap me high into the air. Tree-tops and cloud-hid steeples must be cleared. Nothing should bring the budding saint down.

If anyone had done evil it was hell for ever for him or her at the Judgment Day. Christ said so. If we have done well – pink-fleshed and almond-shaped, in perennial dawns above the clouds, our souls will live happily in perfect ease. No details of this over-crowded heaven or of so unforgiven a swarming hell, troubled my crudely embryonic imagination. No problems arising from ever-lastingly mirthful idleness emerged. Nor was it clear to female stupidity what eternal, individual life, or per-petually punishing hell, can purposively solve. I was too dumb to glimpse these myths in relation to the whole of man and to earlier religions arising from the mystery of the glorious earth and our being here. Grateful to One who 'gave his life', I was a believer.

But my Father had said so often : 'Use the sense you've been given. It was meant to be used or it wouldn't be there.' Dr B. at the Grammar school said : 'The amazing story of Life is far more spiritually humbling than any

Holy Book, than all the "Inspired Books", or than all man's present very imperfect knowledge, can tell.' These statements, often repeated, shook me; as 'Infinity' and 'Eternity' pointed out by Father beyond the blue hills had shaken the invisible imagination awake at five. But the pleasant fog of mental sloth settled again.

By this time I had two quite opposing sets, inner and outer, of values, and two kinds of speech. With unconscious snobbery I imitated the Gentry's way of saying certain words, such as 'girl'. None of them pronounced this 'gurl'. *Their* way was preferable. I could even mimic tolerably the self-confident tones of some of the rich. I tried, even more spuriously, to 'air profundity in a comment'. But I kept ready not a few pithy turns of phrase which belong to dialect. These prevented the family of accusing me of 'putting it on'. To be thought 'stuck up' would be shameful indeed.

Like many another family, mine had felt the pinch of the lean years that for the quiet and unenterprising always follow wars. Mr Maurice raised Father's wages to twenty-two shillings a week. Yet I was Friday's child. I must earn a living without more delay. There was never any doubt as to how I should do this. From what Dr B. called 'the common heritage of human knowledge' I was to offer children the glorious story that, if offered cleverly enough, they would be bound to crave more of.

No longer did I deal in the little affairs of home: keeping Mother's work-basket tidy with a fierce zeal for its petty but necessary order; making salad – of which we all-year ate much – from cabbage, swede, parsley, chives and mint. My sisters forgave me housework so that scholarship work could get done. Without a scholarship I should get nowhere.

But henceforward I must live in cities, and deal in words — subtle, fabulous, far more ferocious than pike, fox, hawk or weasel. I should be an outcast, against much of what cities stand for — but never, never against people who live in them, of course.

Th
Publish

CW01023558

Printed by John Breare Printers Ltd.
Storpoint House, Tickhill Street,
Bradford, West Yorkshire
BD3 9RY
Tel: (01274) 725078, Fax: (01274) 308147

Paper Supplied by Rothera & Brereton Ltd.
Fairfield House, Armley Road,
Leeds LS12 2QH
Tel: 0113 263 2541

Bookbinding by Woods (Print Finishers)
Unit 3, Sheibarg Industrial Estate,
Cutler Heights Lane, Bradford,
BD4 9HZ
Tel: (01274) 656755

Laminating by UK Laminators PLC
Ventnor Street, Bradford, BD3 9JP
Tel: (01274) 737384

Cover Design by Opus Design
500 Leeds Road, Bradford BD3 9RU
Tel: (01274) 737781

Pages set in 12pt Garamont by
Arcadia Desk Top Publishing
Storpoint House, Tickhill Street,
Bradford, West Yorkshire,
BD3 9RY
Tel: (0831) 450063, Fax: (01274) 308147

ISBN 0 9528548 0 5

Acknowledgements

ALL MY FAMILY
TERRY LARKIN
ROTHERA & BRERETON LTD.
JOHN ROSE
H.M. ROYAL NAVY
JOHN BREARE PRINTERS LTD.
ARCADIA DESK TOP PUBLISHING
UK LAMINATORS PLC.

ROY TINSLEY'S AUTOBIOGRAPHY

"TYPES & FACES"

Dedicated to my beloved wife
Shirley

To Gary, Happy 60th, All The Best, Roy

FIRST PUBLISHED JULY 1996
REPRINT DECEMBER 1996

INDEX

Chapter 1	The Early Years	3
Chapter 2	Roy The Apprentice Printer	19
Chapter 3	Too Young For A Tot Of Rum	27
Chapter 4	Far Eastern Promise	49
Chapter 5	Bombay - City of Schemes & Dreams	71
Chapter 6	Speed Trials & Home Prospects	85
Chapter 7	Goodbye Bushwood - I Belong To Glasgow	95
Chapter 8	Home At Last	113
Chapter 9	Demob Time	117
Chapter 10	Brahney & Tinsley - Printers	125
Chapter 11	Moving Above The Bread Line	139
Chapter 12	Moving In	153
Chapter 13	Moving Up The Ladder	165
Chapter 14	A New Salesman On The Road	175
Chapter 15	New & Second Hand - The Market	179
Chapter 16	Roy W Tinsley Ltd	185
Chapter 17	Tom & Roy Link Up Again	191
Chapter 18	Moving On	205
Chapter 19	The Tinsley-Robor Experience	213
Chapter 20	The Hanson Intervention	223
Chapter 21	Picking Up The Pieces	233
Chapter 21 (A)	I Left my Husband in San Francisco	241
Chapter 22	Who Wants To Be A Millionaire?	249
Chapter 23	The Sting	253
Chapter 24	What The Hell Have I Done?	267
Chapter 25	The Final Chapter	283

— CHAPTER 1 —

THE EARLY YEARS

My first memories of life go back to 1930/31 - and of my father as the "bringer of light". It was a two and a half mile walk from where he worked to our home in Fartown near Huddersfield but every night when he finished work at 6.30pm, he walked it to save one penny. There was no electricity in the back-to-back houses in our street then, and one of my earliest memories was sitting in the house by the light of a candle - mother, me and my baby brother Donald. Eventually we would hear the front door open and dad would come in, give mother a kiss and go to a cupboard under the stairs and put that penny he had saved into the gas meter. He would then light the gas mantle and we would have light.

My parents, Bill and Gertrude Tinsley, married in Crewe in Cheshire after a two year courtship. Dad

was 23 and mother was 20. They had been married about three months when Dad got a note in his wage packet saying: 'Your services are no longer required.' Just married - no money - no job! Mother's eldest brother, Arthur, had moved to Huddersfield to take a job as an assistant manager at the '50 Shilling Tailors'. He heard of their plight and made enquiries about work in Yorkshire. Dad at least had a trade - he was a fitter. Arthur wrote and told them about a company called Carriers in Lockwood, who were setting on fitters. I think the wage was about £1 10s for a 54 hour week. In 1926 Arthur assisted them in obtaining a back-to-back house in Mount Street, Lockwood at 4s a week and my parents made the big move to Yorkshire. A year later they had their first child (me!). Dad held that job for about three years when Carriers announced they were to move lock, stock and barrel to Luton. We had just moved to another back-to-back house in Bradford Road, Fartown, and my parents decided against going to Luton. Instead dad managed to get a better job, this time at ICI and he was to remain there for the rest of his working life.

Our new house was a slight improvement on that in Lockwood for there were only two families sharing the toilet at the bottom of the garden! We had the front of that house looking onto a busy main road. I remember the old couple who shared the toilet with us. Horace and Maude Bell lived in the back house. They must have been in their 70's then. They had no family but really liked children - so we were well received when we went round

the back. My very early childhood memory was refusing to have my toe-nails cut. Instead I told my parents to take me to the Bell's and let them do it.

We had a very, very small front garden with a wall and a gate to keep me away from the busy road. When I was about four I used to stand by the gate for long periods watching the trams and buses go past as well as the bicycles, horses and carts. The most interesting though were the motor cars. Then one day I noticed the gate could be unlocked. I had this burning desire to touch one of those motor cars and decided that when the next car came along I would open the gate, dash out into the road and touch it! Bradford Road was very straight so you could see a car approaching about a quarter of a mile away. When I saw one coming I opened the gate and ran into the road and touched it as it went past. God I found it exciting! When I touched it I heard one or two loud blasts on the horn and the car jammed on its brakes. I quickly went in and closed the gate. My mother came out carrying Donald and couldn't believe what people were saying. 'This kid's just tried to kill himself,' a man shouted. 'I saw him run out in front of that car,' cried someone else. 'Three cars had to brake to avoid hitting him.' To me it seemed a lot of commotion over nothing. Whilst this was going on I looked up the road - saw another car coming and did exactly the same again. My mother screamed. I just missed a horse and cart and as I ran out the car driver jammed on his brakes. Soon we seemed to be surrounded by

a lot of angry people. I could not understand it. Eventually a policeman came and had a long talk with my mother. She then explained to me that I could have been killed. She had to tell my father too that evening - and even worse, the policeman returned. He and my father chatted for a while and then the policeman came over and gave me a long lecture. Finally he put his hand on my shoulder and threatened to take me to prison. 'Oh no - don't take him away,' my dad exclaimed. 'He won't do it again.' I certainly never did - I was so terrified that the policeman would take me away.

A year later, when I started school, I had to cross that road four times a day. Mother took me the half a mile to school morning and afternoon but I had to come back by myself. The arrangement was to get to the edge of the road and then shout for my mother to see me across. Although I was only five I cannot remember mother ever being there. I always had to shout - sometimes for a heck of a long time! At school I marvelled at the electric lights and I told my mother about them. She said we would have a house one day with electric lights.

One morning about September 1932, I remember the postman calling and leaving a letter which I took to my mother. On opening it she let out a wild cheer: 'Hooray! Hooray! We've got a new house.' 'With electric lights?' I asked. 'With electric lights and a bathroom,' she replied. I didn't know houses had bathrooms! In fact, I didn't know what a bathroom was. A zinc tub in front of the

fire on a Friday night was all we had. Mother was so excited - she spent the day watching out of the window for Dad. When she saw him coming she rushed out. 'We've got it - we've got it,' she cried. 'Got what?' asked dad. 'Our new house, of course,' she laughed. It's not surprising they were so excited. From our little back-to-back with just one room upstairs and one downstairs we moved to a brand new corporation house with two bedrooms, kitchen, living room and bathroom. It even had a garden at the front and back. Address - 13 Nether Crescent, Rawthorpe. It was a marvellous place to grow up for it was surrounded by trees and open fields. The Huddersfield Town Football Club was only a mile away. I soon had a lot of friends at school and I enjoyed my childhood there. By the time I was eight I had joined the church choir and on Sundays went to church morning, afternoon and evening! By the time I was ten, mother found me a job as a paper boy. I delivered seven dozen papers morning and evening and a hundred on a Sunday - so I had to drop my Sunday mornings in the choir. The paper boy wage was 4s a week (20p at today's prices).

One of the worst times in my life occurred during the winter of 1937. I was 11 and Donald was 8. We had noticed mother was getting very fat but I had no idea how children were born and didn't realise mother was expecting another baby. Dad came to school with Don and I one day in October and asked to see Mr Gill, the headmaster. I had no idea what was going to happen. In those days there were some very, very poor families. There

was a sort of workhouse for children too. It was called Honley Home. To me that seemed a wonderful place where the children played football most of the time in a stadium similar to the Huddersfield Town Football ground, complete with proper referees, goalposts and nets. Dad explained to Mr Gill that mother was expecting a baby and he had no one to take care of Don and me. He had heard of Honley Home and wondered if we could go there for a couple of weeks. The same day Mr Gill sent for me and said he had made arrangements for us to go to Honley Home. 'When sir?' I asked quietly. 'Tomorrow' he said.

When we got home mother had gone to hospital. Dad said she wasn't very well. He still mentioned nothing about having a baby. We packed our worldly possessions into a brown carrier bag the next morning and Dad took Don and me to school. There we said goodbye to him. Mr Gill sent for one of the older boys and gave him the bus fare so he could take us to the Home. I have never felt so miserable in all my life. It was six weeks of hell. Don was very young and very brave but he also hated every moment there. We were literally thrown into a large cold home with about fifty of the roughest, toughest lads anywhere in England. Usually children were sent there for two weeks at a time, arriving in groups of twenty on a Monday morning. Don and I arrived in the middle of a week just as one group were about to complete their two-week 'sentence'. They lost no time in telling us what a hell-hole it was. Many kids ran away. I wanted to but knew that, with mother in

hospital, there was nowhere to go. To make matters worse both of my legs were covered in boils, huge ones that had to have hot dressings put on twice a day. We slept in a large dormitory and had to be in bed every night by 7pm. The lights were out at 7.05pm. The master was a man called Mr Oates who had a big long cane which he seemed to like using at every opportunity. It used to get very hot in the communal room where we went after tea each day. I remember once asking for a drink of water from Mr Oates but he refused. There was one toilet in the room and I figured out that if I flushed it I could get my hands in and get a drink before the water hit the bottom of the pan. I used this method for about a week until one evening Mr Oates came in and caught me drinking this way. I expected to get beaten about the head and back with his cane. But no - he looked shocked. 'Don't do that Tinsley - please don't do that,' he said. 'Come with me.' He took me to his quarters and gave me a big pot of barley water. 'Do any of the other boys drink that way?' he asked me. 'Yes sir - all of them,' I replied. He looked very concerned. He went back with me to the communal room with two huge enamel jugs full of barley water. 'From now on there will always be barley water after tea,' he announced. 'Nobody must drink water from the toilet.' Looking back he probably thought he could have a typhoid epidemic on his hands. That six weeks seemed like six years. It was dreadful - constant fights and plenty of cane. God we were miserable. Then one day Mr Oates sent for Don and me. We went down to his office and there was dad. We ran to him

and Don started crying: 'Take us home Dad - please take us home...' I dare not say that in case Mr Oates gave me the cane! Dad promised to take us home for Christmas, but said we might have to come back afterwards. You know I hadn't realised it was nearly Christmas. By then Don and I were the only two kids in the home. All the other boarders had been sent home for Christmas. We were overjoyed when Dad took us home. We had to take three buses and when we got to Nether Crescent mother was there to greet us. It was one of the happiest re-unions of all time. Don immediately started to plead with mother not to send us back to Honley Home and she eventually promised she wouldn't. We went on to spend probably the happiest Christmas I can ever remember while I lived at home. We received at least three presents each and my prize possession was a small steam engine. When I put water in it and lit some methylated spirits inside, it produced steam that drove the engine. It was fantastic. I never let it out of my sight for the next couple of years.

Once Christmas was over I was fearful that we might be sent back to Honley Home again but thank goodness it didn't happen. On the night of January 3rd 1938, Don and I were woken up by the most terrible screaming in the next room. 'That's mum!' I exclaimed. 'Is someone killing her?' cried Don. 'I don't know - shall we go and see?' But it took a while before Don and I finally found the courage to get up and knock on our parents' bedroom door. Dad barred the way, urging us to go back to bed. 'It's alright - don't worry - your

mum's poorly - I've sent for the doctor.' At that point there was a heavy knocking on the door and Mrs Beaumont, our next door neighbour had come to help. Don and I spent the rest of the night laid in our room listening to all the comings and goings plus all the screaming - it was dreadful.

When dawn broke and it was light in our bedroom things seemed to calm down and eventually dad came in and asked us to go see mother as she had a surprise to show us. We went into the bedroom and there was mother - looking absolutely terrible, but at least giving us both a smile. I asked if she was better. She said 'Yes' and then held up a shawl - in it was a baby. She proudly announced: 'Look - you both have a brand new baby brother. Say hello.' We went round the bed, had a look at our new brother, David Malcolm, had a few words with mother and dad together, then went back to bed. We were still wondering what all the screaming had been going on for. It would have been an ideal time to explain the 'birds and the bees' to Don and I.

I enjoyed living in Rawthorpe. We went to a school about a mile or so away called Moldgreen Church School. We had to walk there and back twice a day - no school dinners in those days! The bus fare was a half-penny each way but we rarely had the money to use the bus - maybe if it was raining heavy! It was also at this time I started going to woodwork class and I really enjoyed that. The woodwork class was at Spring-Grove School in town. I was glad it wasn't my regular school for it

had one of the most sadistic headmasters I could ever remember. It seemed he had to cane at least ten a day - it was a sort of magical figure he had to attain. You would receive a brutal thrash on each hand for the mildest misdemeanor, like if you didn't have your apron on straight. Or he would line up six at the start of the class and say the caning was for causing a noise at the bus stop when we left the previous week! For about six weeks at that time I had been working on a buffet. It was my pride and joy. It had fully interlocking joints and was beautifully stained. It looked marvellous. When we completed anything we took it to our class teacher to pass it and give it a mark. I will never forget the day it was finished. My teacher looked at it, turned it round a few times and said: 'It's not half bad Tinsley. I didn't know you had it in you.' He marked it inside with a nine. No one had ever seen him give above a seven before. Was I proud. I couldn't wait to get home. I dashed into the house, showed it to my mother who said: 'That's nice. I told Mrs Beaumont you were making one.' Hard to believe, I know, but before my dad got home my mother had sold the buffet to Mrs Beaumont for 2s. Talk about being hurt - and she didn't want me to tell dad she had sold it! I didn't tell him even though it took quite a while to repair the hurt.

As a family we were finding it a bit overcrowded living in a two-bedroomed house with mum, dad and three sons and my parents had applied for a three-bedroomed council house. Eventually this was granted and we were allocated a house in one

of the roughest, toughest parts of Huddersfield. It was known as a slum-clearance estate called Brackenhall. When I told the headmaster at Spring-Grove I would be leaving he asked where I was going to live. When I said Brackenhall he just started shaking his head from side to side and tut-tutting. Not a word - just that. I was pleased to get away from the sadistic big headed snob anyway but to be honest I did not like Brackenhall at all except for one thing - the church. It played a very significant part in my life and Mr Wade, one of the Sunday School Teachers there, was responsible for me entering the printing trade. A chapel in the middle of a rough council estate didn't have much support from the locals. I was 13 when I started attending and really enjoyed it. I went to morning service at 10.30am, Sunday School at 2.15pm and Evensong at 6.30pm. The vicar was Mr Wardle who was a wonderful man. He had a great head of black curly hair and his wife had one of the worst wigs I have ever seen. They were a devoted couple who worked hard in the Parish but had a thankless task. They had a very able helper in Mr Wade. He and his wife put in hours of unpaid work trying to convert people in Brackenhall but it was difficult. There were seldom more than 12 of us in the the church each Sunday - Mr and Mrs Wardle, Mr and Mrs Wade, Arthur Longbottom the organist, seven of us in the choir and perhaps two in the congregation. Not a very good turn up I'm afraid but Mr Wardle still prepared his sermons in much the same way as the Archbishop of Canterbury would have done.

I suggested to Mr Wade that we start a youth club one night a week and then perhaps a football team. I believed it might help us get a few more people into the church. He thought it was a good idea and put it into practice. It proved an enormous success. In fact, membership of the youth club started with about ten and inside the first month had grown to sixty! You had to come to church to be a member. We had darts, table tennis and draughts. As it was a mixed youth club it gave us an opportunity to meet girls. I may not have liked Brackenhall district but our move gave me the chance to attend an all-boys school called Hillhouse Central. I feel I learnt more there in two years than the previous seven years at Moldgreen.

Life was good for me as a 13-year-old. The paper rounds didn't seem as hard to do. I was enjoying school, including the cricket. Through the youth club I met and played table tennis with a girl I liked - Marjorie Seater. I enjoyed all the times at the church and Mr Wade arranged quite a few football matches for us. We didn't have a very good team - in fact the best performance was losing to the team at the top of the league 15-3. I decided that if only we could get a few lads from the bottom end of the estate to play we could be a good team. They were rough lads but played for the school team and were good. Mr Wade insisted everyone who played for our team had to go to church and it would have been easier to get Adolf Hitler to preach to the local synagogue than get those lads to do that. Eventually I persuaded Mr Wade to allow these three lads to come only to the

youth club. This they did and were duly picked for the team. Their first match with us was against a good team from Moldgreen and we turned out on a dreadful Saturday morning. The new lads played very well and we were holding them to a 1-1 draw at half time. My father had also come to watch and was stood next to Mr Wade when we trooped off at half time. We all made over to Mr Wade and my dad to receive instructions for the second half and as we gathered around one of the new lads exclaimed: 'Fecking good performance but we're not hard enough. Let's give 'em some feckin pasty in the second half.' I could have died. I had obviously never heard Mr Wade swear and as for dad - I never heard him utter one swear word in his life. Dad played hell with the lad and told him to 'wash his mouth out'. Mr Wade went just a bit whiter than I did and said we were a church team and he could not do with any of the team talking like that. To be fair the lad accepted the criticism very well. He said he was sorry and after that played the game of his life. We won 3-2. He continued to come to the youth club for the next three years and joined the Royal Navy on the same day as me. He also teamed up with my 'girlfriend', Marjorie Seater, although I didn't mind too much about that.

When I was 13 years and 11 months old I left school and took a job in an engineering company as an apprentice turner. I worked 51 hours a week -five and a half days - for 13s. My mother was frantically trying to find me a job that paid more and every Saturday afternoon arranged for me to

attend various interviews. There was one for a porter at Huddersfield Station, and others included apprenticeships in painting and decorating or chicken farming. I didn't fancy any. Yet I hated the job I was doing. So I decided to leave and look for a job myself. The next day I went to see the foreman and told him I was leaving. He played hell and said: 'Don't you know there is a war on? We're making munitions and you're not allowed to leave'.

During the war if you were an engineer on munitions you were exempt from the Services but you had to stay in that employment. I put on a brave face and said to the foreman: 'That only applies if you are 16 and I'm only 14.' 'Well you look 16,' he replied. 'Come back tomorrow and see me. I'll tell you then if you can go.' I duly went back next morning. He called me into the office, gave me an envelope with 6s in it and told me 'Good riddance!'. When I got home at 10.30 in the morning mother was a little worried for I had no job and would not be bringing in any wage. She was pleased though to get the 6s.

It was youth club night and Mr Wade asked me how I was getting on in the engineering trade. I told him I had left and didn't have a job. He asked me what I wanted to do but to be honest I didn't know. It was then he mentioned that he might - just might - be able to get me into the printing trade if I was interested. English was one of my best subjects at school and I immediately said 'Yes'. Two days later he called at our house and said he had arranged for me to see a Mr Green who had a

printing company called Swindlehurst & Nicholson in Huddersfield. They wanted an apprentice printer and Mr Green would give me a job if he liked me. The next day I went to see Mr Green, who was a strong church-going man himself. He did like me and offered me the job at 12s 6d for a 50-hour week. I said 'Yes' without consulting my parents and went home feeling very happy. My dad was delighted his son was going to be a printer. My mother had mixed feelings. She suggested I should only have taken it if they paid me 15s a week. I explained I didn't fancy going back and asking for that much and was finally able to take the job with her blessing. I loved it from day one - it was as though printing was the trade made just for me. The day I started Mr Green took me to meet the foreman - Arnold Booth. He had a face like thunder and a heart of gold. He was one of the kindest gentlemen I ever met in my life and the training he gave me was excellent. He also went on to save my life within six months of working there.

— CHAPTER 2 —

ROY THE APPRENTICE PRINTER

It was 1941. The war in Europe was digging deep into the lives of us all. France had capitulated and Britain stood alone. We were being asked to sacrifice in every way. Food rationing was giving everyone a balanced diet but not a very tasty one. Fruit was non-existent and so were sweets and chocolates. One bright spot was my job - I loved it. One of the conditions of employment was that I attended a practical printer course at Technical College, three evenings a week. On my first evening there I felt a bit strange but I needn't have been, for I was met by Gordon Brahney and Syd Gronow. They had been in the same class at school as me although they were a year older. They made me welcome and we became very close friends over the next 40 odd years. I seemed to take to the printing trade like a duck to water. Although I was supposed to be an apprentice machine-minder I asked the teacher at Technical College if I could take the compositor courses

and he agreed. So five and a half days a week I was working on machines and three evenings a week learning to be a compositor. It was marvellous. One day at work I watched how Arnold ran a big flat bed machine and convinced him I could also work it. It was mainly used for printing posters and the motor had to be switched on in the cellar. Through a system of pulleys this machine was connected to a huge motor, the latter being driven by a large leather belt. The belt and pulleys ran above the flat bed machine.

One day while the press was working the leather belt slipped off and the press stopped. Arnold said that when that happened I would have to go into the cellar and switch off the motor and then come back and loop the belt back onto the two pulleys. Only then could I go back down and switch on again. After the belt had come off three times in one morning Arnold became a bit fed up of it. When it came off again he turned the handle on the machine to off, stood on the flat bed of the machine and with a side stick (a piece of wood) eventually managed to loop the belt back onto the running pulley. He went round the side of the machine, put the handle to on and it was running. I was very impressed. It saved going down to the cellar to turn the motor off and on. After a few weeks I was working the big machine myself. When the belt came off I always turned the motor off - until the day when I decided that if it did it again I would try that trick with the side stick. I did one fatal thing, however - I did not turn the handle of the machine to off. I took the side stick,

stood on the machine and tried to loop the belt on. After a while it took hold but what a shock for me. Once it was looped on, the bed of the machine moved backwards. I fell and dropped into all the huge gears. I was trapped and with the machine in reverse it was moving back on to me. Then - from absolutely nowhere - I felt these powerful hands grab me under the arms and pull me out. As the machine came back it just caught my ankles and gave them an almighty crack. I fell backwards on top of Arnold - but I was safe. He had obviously been watching me even though he had no reason to be there. But for him I would have met a terrible death. Arnold laid me down on the floor and put a blanket over me. I was absolutely petrified. Myra, one of the girls in the machine room had gone to fetch Mr Green. 'I thought he was going to die,' Myra told Mr Green as they hurried over to me. Arnold gave him a full report. He could never explain why he had left his own work and come to see what I was doing but thank God he had. Mr Green was obviously worried about the consequences and gave me sixpence to take the bus and go home, it was only 2d fare, the 4d must have been compensation. Within a couple of days I was back on the machine printing the posters and ensuring that, if the belt came off, I turned off the motor before putting it back on.

After about two years as an apprentice machine minder the last compositor was called up for the Navy. This left Alf Curry (81) and Bob Hartley (74) in the comp-room. Mr Green asked me one day if I had any idea how to compose text (comp).

I told him I had picked up a lot of useful points at Technical College and felt confident I could comp a few simple jobs. He had a word with Arnold, my boss, and said he would like to give me a chance in the comp-room. The next day I joined Alf and Bob in the comp-room and Mr Green gave me a simple letterhead to comp. I did it in about half an hour, tied it up, pulled a proof and took a copy to him. He was amazed - so were Bob and Alf. From that day onwards I had a job as a compositor as far as Mr Green was concerned. He seemed to give me all the rush jobs and I responded by completing them quickly and efficiently. He was always telling me how valuable I was to him but I was still on only £1 5s a week. In fact, in those days you could qualify as a doctor in six years and yet to become a printer you had to complete a seven year apprenticeship! I had joined the Sea Cadets at 16-years-old and enjoyed the comradeship. In a short while I had enough qualifications to be a leading seaman except for one thing - I couldn't swim. No, I could not swim! I was desperate to become a leading hand so started going to Ramsden Street Baths two or three times a week. Learning to swim at 16 and a half was not easy, but I was determined. With the great help of the instructor there I accomplished it and managed two lengths of the baths which was the minimum qualification for promotion.

About a couple of months after promotion the Sea Cadet officers arranged a ten-day winter training camp at Anglesey in Wales. With permission from my parents I went with about six more lads

from Huddersfield. It was freezing cold there. The food was diabolical and the beds were damp. We had to get up each morning at 5am for a five-mile run. At 9am we had to go swimming in the sea. This particular morning we went down to the beach and there was a small sailing boat about half a mile out to sea. The Petty Officer in charge looked at me and said: 'That's drifted out during the night - go and fetch it Tinsley'. Now even though I could just about manage two lengths at Ramsden Street Baths I didn't wish to look scared in front of the other lads. So I immediately ran down to the sea, sort of dived in and started swimming towards the boat. The water was icy cold and the boat seemed to be about five miles away. The more I swam the further away it seemed to be. My right leg seemed to be seizing up and the coldness of the water was also getting through to me. Then it happened, I got terrible cramp in my right leg. It was dreadful. I couldn't swim any further. I managed to turn around and look to the shore. It seemed to be miles away. I raised my arm and shouted 'Help' then noticed two of the lads raising theirs as if waving to me. I went under and seemed to go down very deep. Eventually though, I surfaced, spluttering and shouting help as I got there. I did get the feeling at the time I was going to die. No doubt in my panic struck mind this was the end. I went under, came up and seemed to go back under again immediately - I was sure of that. Within a few seconds (I can only think it must have been a few seconds although I have no idea what length of time elapsed after going down for the third time) I felt arms around me and someone

grabbed my hair. They were tugging at me and pulling me to the surface. There were three lads who got hold of me and eventually brought me ashore - what a relief. I am sure if they had not arrived when they did I would have died within a couple of minutes. Once they had got me ashore I was encased in all the towels. The petty officer came over and said: 'I thought you were a strong swimmer. You have to be to be a leading seaman.' 'I got cramp sir,' I said. 'The water was so cold it caused me to get cramp.' After that all further bathing in the sea was cancelled.

Saved again! Someone up there was certainly taking good care of me. I only hoped they would continue to do so as I seemed to take a lot of unnecessary chances. I even survived doing more than my share of fire-watch duties for I wanted a bit more extra money so I could go to the pictures with my girlfriend. Margaret was a lovely girl and being out with her was marvellous. She was a year older than me. I met her when I was 16 and we were going very steady. Well - four nights a week to the pictures, back row if possible. I paid twice and she paid twice. Kissing was as far as we ever went. To go any further would have been unchartered territory for either of us and I had a built-in fear that if my penis got within three inches of her she would become immediately pregnant. I am not making a joke of that - my knowledge of sexual relationships could have been written in large type on the back of a postage stamp. I received 1s 6d a night for fire-watching. Mr Green asked me if I would like to do his watch

each week and earn an extra 1s 6d. So I slept at the print shop Wednesday, Thursday and Friday nights. It never occurred to me to ask my mother if it was okay. My parents just accepted I was old enough to do such duties. During the war anyone over 16 could be asked to fire-watch in their factory in case it was bombed. If it was they had to ring the ARP (Air Raid Precautions). Our factory, the print shop, was four storeys high - all wood floors and stuffed with old paper everywhere. It was more like a tinder box. Rats seemed to have a permanent residence in the fire-watching room which also contained a camp-bed and a single cover. Boy, did I hate fire-watch. Duty commenced at 7pm and finished at 7.30am. After the watch I reported for duty and worked through till 5.30pm.

— CHAPTER 3 —

TOO YOUNG FOR A TOT OF RUM

Since leaving school and taking my first real job as a compositor I had never known life as a teenager without the blackout, rationing, war, utility clothes, war and more war. In 1944, when I was 17 and a half years old, I arrived home one day to find a letter from His Majesty saying my call-up for the Royal Navy had finally come around. It told me to report to *HMS Royal Arthur* at Skegness. It contained a one way rail pass from Huddersfield to Skegness, effective from the following Wednesday.

Mother seemed a little upset at losing her eldest son. Dad gave me a few pieces of advice like... 'Keep all your money safe. Don't gamble with other men and make sure you don't sleep next to or with any old sailors.' To be honest I didn't know what he meant by that but certainly understood it when I came out of the Navy. The money was not a problem. I can never remember

having more than 30 bob (30s) in my pocket at any one time in my life. My weekly wage when I left my place of employment to go into the Navy was 29s for a 48-hour week. Although Margaret knew I had volunteered to go into the Navy, nevertheless she was still very upset to hear I had received my call-up papers. We saw each other every evening until the fateful day that I had to go to 'war'. She came to Huddersfield Railway Station to see me off. We had a few rather passionate kisses, a tear or two and I was on my way. There were about a dozen other fresh-faced lads on the train that day and once we got into conversation it was soon apparent they were also Skegness bound. It was a thoroughly miserable winters day, the train was like an ice-box and we all stood together clutching our parcels. Mine contained a pair of clean underpants, one pair of socks, one toothbrush and Gillette razor, brush and soap. Mother said she knew someone whose son had joined up and that was all he requested. So that was all I had - plus 4s 'to keep you going to pay-day'. Mother also asked me if I could send something home so that I would have some money to spend when I returned on leave. She was going to miss the pound or so I had brought in each week. Upon arrival at Skegness other trains were coming in from all over the country. It was snowing and freezing cold. I didn't have an overcoat and my shoes had a hole in the sole and let in the water. The Royal Navy had, however, sent a bus to the station and a very old petty officer was there to meet us. He read out about 70 names - mine was near the last. The Navy did

everything in alphabetical order. I learnt that to my cost over the next three and a half years. Once on the bus the petty officer told us in no uncertain terms from that day we were men, would be treated like men and they didn't have a single mother to go and cry to if we felt like it. (Even so, I understood there were quite a number of single mothers in Skegness after the Navy took up camp there.) *HMS Royal Arthur* was the old Butlins Holiday Camp which had been commandeered by the Navy to act as a training base for young recruits - mainly to provide them with kit. I had become friendly with a lad called George Lumb and they allocated us a chalet with a bunk-bed that was to be home for the next 15 days. We were ordered to report next morning to the large hall called Nelson which would act as a kitting out base. There we were told exactly what we would be getting - and that was that. From that day on every other item of clothing we required in the Navy we had to buy ourselves and with this in mind they paid us an extra 2s 6d a week. It was nice to get two pairs of very strong socks and boots (a big size ten) plus the entire uniform. Every one of us got kitted out completely with only one exception. They didn't have anything above a seven and one eighth size hat. We were told to go back to our chalets, change into our naval uniform and report to the parade ground in one hour. We just about managed it. The Chief Petty Officer arranged us in some sort of ranks, questioned me about the absence of a hat, and then informed us the commanding officer wished to speak to the unit. He said we were

entering the most exciting phase of our life. He was happy we were all perfectly normal as they had managed to kit out every man completely except one lad who had proved a problem with his head. Being the only bare-headed recruit there I had to take quite a lot of good natured ridicule. They did manage to fix me up two days later.

As it was more than likely we would be shipped out to the Far East fairly quickly we had to have a number of very painful innoculations. We just lined up, bared the top of our arms and let the sickbay attendant stick in the needle. He seemed to enjoy it intensely! For the next five days I was in utter agony - as were most of the other lads. It was totally impossible to take off my naval uniform and I had to sleep in it. We also went through a sort of basic training - mainly marching. It was icy cold with snow every day. There was no hot water and we had to do all our own washing. We could use a commercial launderette and we went down there if we had no training as it was the warmest place in the camp. After seven days they allowed us 'shore leave' - in the Navy they called it 'shore leave' even if you were based in camp. We were allowed out at 6pm but had to return at 11pm. Fully kitted out in our uniforms, George and I found a local dance. 'HM Forces Half Price' it said - that meant 9d and we could just about manage that. Once I had got my new naval boots I had thrown my old shoes away. Being very heavy and size tens those naval boots took a bit of trailing about the dance floor - looking back I must have crushed a few female toes that

evening. Upon arrival back at camp we were told to report on the parade-ground at 7am the next morning with full kit, including hammock/bedding etc. We were going to be shipped out.

No one knew where we were going, not even the petty officer who accompanied us to Skegness Station. The train eventually pulled in about three hours late which was about the 'norm' during the war. About six hours later we arrived in Malvern in Worcestershire at a place called *HMS Duke*. There we were to undertake six weeks intensive training. This was like a five star hotel after Royal Arthur. We were put into groups of 24 under a Petty Officer and awarded marks of merit for everything like drill, smartness, sport, general attitude and discipline. The petty officers had a real competitive attitude and this came over greatly to all of us. I loved every minute of Basic Training - it was superb. As a lad a neighbour of ours used to take me shooting rabbits and taught me how to sight a rifle. We had to take target practice and with my previous experience I came out on top. I also played Rugby League before joining up. Once the Petty Officer knew this he put me in the Rugby Union team. After the first game I was made captain and we remained undefeated during our time there. When I joined up at Skegness they had coded me as an 'officer's steward' and that was how I was going to serve my time in the Navy. Our Petty Officer in charge, who was a Stoker Petty Officer, kept me behind after training and pleaded with me not to stay in the Navy as an 'officer's bumboy' as he called it. 'If

you see about a change of rank now I may be able to fix it for you,' he said. 'You will hate the steward's job.' He arranged for me to see a superior officer and explained that I had made a major mistake and would like to change to a stoker - it also meant a change of uniform. Happily with his help and a considerate officer they let me change to a stoker. It was to prove the best thing I ever did in the Navy. The Petty Officer told me that as there were only three coal burning ships left in the Navy it was a very good job now - 'just turning oil taps on and off' he said. As a matter of fact the first three ships I was on abroad were coal burners but to be honest the excessive hard work did me good. My Naval admittance records showed that I weighed ten stone and was five feet seven when I joined. Three and a half years later I weighed 12 and a half stone and was five feet nine and a half inches.

Malvern was a happy camp. I remembered my time at *HMS Duke* as one of the happiest spells I had in the Navy. Plenty of sport, good food, very clean barracks and some very good mates. The town itself was also a very happy place - although when we went on shore leave in the evenings it was totally blacked out. If you called in the pubs the locals were very friendly and you would quite often get bought the odd drink or two. The ironical part about it - I was old enough to be in the Navy and to fight for King and Country but I was not old enough to go into a pub. Not that it worried me at all - I had been going in them since I was 16 and found a couple of halves gave me a

bit more confidence with the girls at the local dances. One particular evening in Malvern, Mac (Ray Magnoni, one of my best mates) and I decided to go on shore leave, have a couple of drinks at the local and go into the cinema where a film called *The Four Feathers* was being shown. We calculated our total worldly possessions amounted to 4s. We had three halves each which accounted for 2s 3d which left us 1s 9d for the pictures. It was usually half price for HM Forces and we expected to pay 10d each. Unfortunately the only seats available for the second performance were 1s each, so we were 3d short. One thing for certain - we were not going back to the barracks so we hatched a plot.

There must have been about 50 people in the queue for the cinema. I suggested Mac stood at the side of them all and I would do a bit of busking - just the odd song and if he went round with my hat we would soon have the necessary funds. Mac thought it was a wonderful idea and he wanted to take the hat round. With three halves of the local brew inside me I felt like taking a chance but was worried I might get nothing. There were two GIs behind us in the queue with a couple of the local girls. It was then that Mac hit on a good idea. 'Bet you guys a shilling my mate dare get out and sing in front of all these people,' he said. It was a beautiful moonlit night and even in the blackout everyone would be able to see me. 'What you gonna sing buddy?' one of the Yanks said. 'What does it bloody matter?' Mac asked. 'The bet is he dare get out and sing.' 'Okay,' the Yank

replied. 'Sing *I belong to Glasgow* and I'll bet you a shilling.' 'We're in,' said Mac. 'We're in.' 'I'm in,' I responded. 'It's me that's actually making a pillock of myself.' It seemed like a good idea, however, so out I went in front of the queue. Mac announced that I was a world famous singer who didn't have enough money to get into the cinema and would like to entertain them. Everyone - and I mean everyone went absolutely silent. I then went out and gave the best rendition of a song I have ever sung. After the first few notes one or two people threw the odd coin. This developed into a torrent - mostly pennies I might add. The GI was absolutely helpless. I never thought he would stop laughing. He gave Mac 2s. Between us we collected about 10s off the road and pavement. We were in the money for the next week or so.

After six weeks training at Malvern we were put on a train again. Not one of us had any idea of the destination. As we were all stokers we eventually finished up in Devonport where we were going to receive further training on a battleship called *HMS Revenge*, which was anchored in the harbour. We were put in various messes and here I teamed up with a couple of mates who were to remain firm friends for the rest of my time in the Navy and much longer than that in the case of Mac. There was fighting in our mess for the first few days. We had a good element but we also had a few very awkward lads who were always on the lookout for trouble. One of the worst fights I ever witnessed turned out to be a good laugh at the end but I still don't know to this

day how neither was not killed or permanently disabled. Both were exceptionally big lads - about six feet tall - and they had quite a lot of verbal battles. One morning while Ken Price was lashing up his hammock, Bill McEwen threw a punch at him. What followed was like World War III. Never have I seen two guys hit each other as often and as hard. All round the mess - over the tables etc. until they came to the top of a hold. In the hold we kept our hammocks after they had been lashed. It had a four feet high wall or bulk head around the top with a 15 feet drop inside. There was a ladder so you could take your hammock down. Eventually Price had McEwen bending over the bulkhead with his hand on his throat. McEwen was shouting: 'Get off you bastard - I'm falling - I'm falling.' Eventually they both went over the top and went down head first onto the metal deck of the hold. There were about 12 of us on the mess while the fight was taking place. When they went over everyone dashed to the top of the hold and expected one or both of them to be either dead or very badly injured. Instead we saw both of them - arms around each other - laughing their heads off. They came back up the ladder - laughing all the way. Then everyone joined in. It was just like a party. Silly as it sounds the whole event seemed to bond a sort of friendship between all the stokers on that mess. I cannot remember another fight or theft for the next eight weeks that I was on board. Training there was pretty good but I had a feeling they were pushing us through as fast as possible. The news on the grapevine was that most of us were going to be shipped to the Far

East as the war against the Germans was almost won. But the Japanese campaign was a different matter. It should have been a 12-week course but it was shortened to eight. We were then promised a ten-day leave which was shortened to seven. Having passed my exams - just - I was now Second-Class Stoker Tinsley. And still only 17.

Going home on leave was one of the most exciting days of my life. Margaret met me at the station. Quite a weepy homecoming that was. We then caught a bus and went to see mother, dad and my two brothers. Although they were pleased to see me, mother seemed more interested in how much money the Navy had given me for 'my keep' while I was at home. In fact I had come home quite rich. I had about £5, but after giving mother £3 for 'my keep' I was struggling financially somewhat for the rest of the leave. Margaret and I had a wonderful time. Still no further than kissing but the night before I went back to Devonport I managed to get my forefinger down her blouse. She cried the night we parted and said 'We may never see each other again'. We promised to write very regularly and parted in much the same way as all the wartime sweethearts did. On arrival at Devonport we returned to *HMS Revenge*. We were told to report with full kit the next morning at 7am and were driven to Portsmouth where we were taken on board *HMS Enterprise* - a cruiser.

Within two hours of getting on board we were informed our destination was the Mediterranean. About two days out to sea the conditions became

very rough. Just about every lad aboard was going to sea for the first time and 99 per cent of us were very, very sick. I felt like throwing myself over the side of the ship because I felt so ill. Yet after about four days I recovered and was never sea-sick again during my entire service in the Royal Navy. Two really old salts in our mess were put in charge of about 40 young ratings. In many ways they were very helpful, giving us many useful tips, and making sure we kept ourselves and the mess clean. They also had a very nice little dice game for the young lads to pass away their time at sea called Crown and Anchor. We had been told by one of the officers that if anyone knew of there being games of Crown and Anchor going on they should report it. Before leaving Portsmouth we had received a month's pay. As I was on 28s a week, this was just over £5. I had bought a few necessities - soap, fags, toothpaste etc. and had just under £4 left. I bumped into my old mate Taxi Wilson about five days out and he had £11. He said he had won it at Crown and Anchor. Even though I had never gambled in my entire life and knew nothing about it, I went with Taxi. Thirty minutes later I had lost my month's pay as had about every other lad in our mess, except Tiny Curtis. This lad seemed to have the Midas Touch and over a three day period amassed about £50 - a great deal of money in those days. We all had money belts as standard issue and he kept his £50 in that. One night I heard a terrible shriek and clank. I shot out of my hammock and found Tiny Curtis with the biggest lump over his eye I had ever seen and, of course, his money belt was

missing. It was no good reporting it - we shouldn't have been playing Crown and Anchor and anyway who would believe that a stoker would have had £50? The two old salts heard about the robbery and gave Tiny £10 out of their tremendous winnings. I don't know to this day if it was one of them who robbed him but Crown and Anchor ceased that night, not just because of the robbery but because everyone was cleaned out.

How the hell was I going to get through the next month without a cent? I needn't have worried for my best mates Mac and Jack Garaway (Gary) came to the rescue. We were inseparable. We shared our soap, razors, toothpaste - everything. Each night the *Enterprise* would stop in the Mediterranean and announce over the Tannoy - 'Hands to bathe'. We used to get on a pair of trunks and dive from the upper deck straight into the sea. It was only three months earlier I had managed to swim those two lengths at the local swimming baths so to be diving 60 feet into the Mediterranean was like tempting suicide. But like many other things in the Navy I came through okay. Eventually we stopped in Port Said and were informed we could go on shore leave. Shore leave in a foreign country - I couldn't believe it. There was an announcement over the Tannoy stating 'Ratings requiring contraceptives should report to the sickbay'. I honestly did not know what a contraceptive was but as all the other lads were going I decided to get one too. I held out my hat as everybody else did and the sickbay attendant simply dropped one into it. We were told we could go in the 10am

liberty boat and would have to be back on board about 11pm. Mac, Gary and myself had about £1 between us plus a few fags. As soon as we got ashore we were surrounded by about 50 beggars, a further 50 people selling everything from a carved elephant to a large carpet and about 20 pimps. I only learned later those guys were called 'pimps'. All had cars and were shouting: 'Want a jump Jack? We have the most beautiful girls in the world.' As we didn't expect very much pleasure out of £1 between the three of us we set out for a bazaar of some sort - or so we were told by a young lad who asked us to follow him. We must have walked about three miles until we came into a square which resembled everything you imagined about the mystic East. There were stalls, fires, donkeys or asses laden up, and many fruiterers. Now I hadn't seen a banana for three years so that proved quite interesting. Walking around eyes open in wonderment the three of us must have got split. One minute I was with them - the next I was on my own surrounded by what seemed to be hundreds of dark skinned unfriendly natives. I was absolutely petrified and must have looked it. Remember I was 17 years old and had never been much further than Huddersfield in my life. Here I was in Port Said on my own with no money - so not worth robbing - and absolutely terrified. All of a sudden I let out a loud shriek, and I yelled: 'Gary, Mac - where are you? Gary - Mac - help!' There was not a white face anywhere, everyone seemed to be staring at me. Was I scared. Then from out of nowhere I heard this London voice: 'Hiya Tins - where you been?' Never in my life

have I been so pleased to see a mate than I was then. 'Oh Mac,' I said. 'Thank God you're here - let's go back.' Gary and Mac had found a little bar and couldn't understand why I wasn't with them. They ordered three beers and then couldn't find me. Gary guarded the beers while Mac came looking for me. After a few minutes I calmed down and began to regain my confidence. But for a while I had felt I was going to be murdered in that bazaar. The next day we went through the Suez Canal. I had heard about this wonderful feat of engineering at school but never thought I would see it or even go through it. What an experience! It left me spellbound - to be on a large cruiser like the Enterprise sailing through that narrow strip of water defied description. The maximum speed allowed us was five knots. To see the desert on both banks and witness all the different facets of life on either side was an experience I would never forget. Once out of the Suez we sailed into the Red Sea. This could be very rough and was particularly so while we sailed through. Having now got my "sea legs" I didn't feel sick again and thoroughly enjoyed it.

Eventually we dropped anchor at Colombo Harbour in what was then known as Ceylon (now Sri Lanka). When we dropped anchor at Colombo there was an announcement on the Tannoy stating, 'All ratings taking passage, report on deck in 30 minutes with all their kit.' This differentiated us from the regular crew of the Enterprise. Once we were on the upper deck the Chief Petty Officer in charge read names in batches of about 30. When

we arrived on shore we were eventually picked up by a large lorry. It was only then that I realised my two best mates had been put in a different batch. I was not to see them for another one and a half years.

My group was taken through the jungle to a shore base called *HMS Mayina*. There we found 500 Royal Naval personnel waiting in transit. Some were going home, some en route to Australia and South Africa, and others to pick up different ships in Colombo. Reporting to the Chief Petty Officer he said: 'Name?' 'Stoker Tinsley sir.' 'You only have to report once - dingbat,' he replied, flicking through a file of papers. 'But sir.....' 'On your way,' he shouted. So there I was, a young 17-year-old in the middle of the jungle, surrounded by all my kit, and with nowhere to go. When I had left Portsmouth I had been given this little slip of paper marked *'HMS Mayina'*. Perhaps I had booked in - I'd arrived. 'Who knows?' I thought. Looking at a large hut plan I went through all the names in alphabetical order and saw 'Stoker Tinsley - Hut 13B'. Finding Hut 13B was fairly easy and inside were many camp beds with mosquito nets around them. An old hand told me to pick any one that didn't have any bedding on it. As there were about 20 spare this proved straight forward. I unwrapped my hammock and spread it on a bed and went for a shower. The shower room was at the end of the hut and there I got talking to another guy who was waiting to go home. He had been out in the Far East for two and a half years. He filled me in about where everything was - the

canteen, parade-ground, transit barracks etc. Everyone reported to the transit hut each morning and looked at a list of names to see where they had to go. For eight days I went there and never saw my name. People were leaving every day but I was stuck in that dump not knowing where the hell I was going. Eventually I decided to go and see the Chief Petty Officer again. Bracing myself up to my full five feet and seven inches I said: 'Sir, sorry Chief', I corrected myself. 'I've been here eight days and I don't know where I'm going or what I'm supposed to do. Can you help me sir - Chief?' 'Name?' 'Tinsley.' He checked through the list and replied: 'You checked out last week.' 'I didn't - I'm here Chief.'

It seemed there had been another Stoker Tinsley (and I never met one the whole time I was in the Navy) in hut 13B who was waiting for transit back to the UK and that cocky, arrogant Chief Petty Officer had told me I could only 'check in once' because he had got me mixed up with him. My request had now started a panic with more people hustling about in the transit room. Eventually the Chief Petty Officer came out with a paper in his hand. 'You should have checked in here eight days ago,' he stated. 'I did check in eight days ago,' I responded. 'Not to me you didn't,' he said. 'I did try Chief.' He ordered me to get all my kit and report back in 15 minutes, which I just about managed. He then gave me a chit which said '*HMS Gombroon*' and a rail pass from Colombo Station for a place called Trincomalee. A jeep was laid on with a driver who took me to Colombo Station and

simply dropped me off there. Carrying my kit bag over one shoulder, my hammock over the other and the rail pass in my mouth, I went over to a platform where there was a train. I sort of moved my mouth up and down and the ticket collector took the pass, clipped it with a pair of pliers and indicated a train. I got on it and put my kit at the side of me. There were just wooden seats and open windows. Within ten minutes the train was packed to capacity, including a couple of mangy looking dogs and two goats. I swear that train stopped at every soap box and crossing from Colombo to Trincomalee. It seemed like an eternity aboard that train. To this day I don't know how long I was on it but it did seem like days.

When we did arrive in Trincomalee it seemed about a thousand other people also got off the train. It was then I noticed two other sailors alighting. They had been on a carriage nearer to the front and I hadn't known they were on the train. We immediately made contact and they said they were expecting to be picked up at the station. Sure enough there was a jeep waiting outside. The leading seaman driving it asked to look at our draft chits, nodded in approval, told us to get in and set off. I dread to think what would have happened to me if I hadn't seen the other two matelots because I didn't expect to be picked up. In fact I didn't know what to expect at all. We went through some fairly dense forest on very bad roads until we eventually saw the sea. He pulled alongside a very long jetty. 'That's as far as I can

go in the jeep,' he said. 'A liberty boat will come and collect you soon from the end of the jetty.' The end of the jetty was about a mile away. The three of us had all our kit - everything including the hammocks. The jetty was one of those floating type about six feet above the water, about a yard wide and no hand-rails at all. At the end of the jetty we collapsed onto our kit. I was absolutely knackered. There were quite a lot of ships in the harbour including a large aircraft carrier. Once we were seated we checked each other's draft chits. All three of us were allocated to different ships. We had no idea whatsoever where we were going, which ship would pick us up and how soon we would be split up. To my amazement I saw two dozen troops get off a lorry and start the long trek along the jetty. Once they arrived we soon figured out they were French. One of them could speak a little English but one of the guys with me started speaking to him in his own language. We were all staggered. The French sergeant was dumbstruck for a while but then let flow into a very long conversation with the sailor who replied just as fluently. All the French soldiers spontaneously applauded - and so did the other British sailor and I. Upon enquiry the linguist explained that his father was a former Mayor of Rangoon. He had been called up two years ago when they moved to Bombay and had now volunteered to go back to Burma. He spoke seven different languages fluently and had told no one in the services of his obvious talent. He was only an AB (Able Seaman) and intended to stay one. It seemed that Europeans in India were still

called up during the war. The French soldiers had a lot of cigarettes - we had none. I had three bars of chocolate so gave them all about one piece each and so became friends immediately. We were given to understand that the French troops were heading for Burma. This may come as a surprise to a lot of people but French troops they were and Burma was their destination - to fight the Japs. We had been at the end of the jetty for about two hours and there were heavy, ominous clouds on the horizon. About half an hour later we could see a liberty boat leaving the aircraft carrier and heading towards us. When it was about 200 yards away the heavens opened. I had never seen rain like that before. It was a monsoon. There was no shelter or cover on the jetty and we just sat there and became completely soaked to the skin. To make matters worse all our kit was completely drenched. The liberty boat came alongside. We were informed that everyone had to get aboard. It took about another half an hour to get to the aircraft carrier and the rain continued to beat down upon us. We eventually pulled up at the side of the ship and went up the gangplank steps. The kitbag and hammock now seemed to weigh a ton each. I had no dry clothes of any sort. When aboard a French officer spoke to his men and a British officer to us.

We were informed we were setting sail for Rangoon within the hour. There were about 1,000 French soldiers on board who were 'taking passage' plus 300 matelots who would join other ships in Burma or would be shore based there. Within five minutes of the announcement the anchor was lifted and we were setting sail. The name of the aircraft

carrier was *HMS Begum* - a former banana boat we heard.

The *Begum* had its own ship's company who had their own messes and their own duties to perform. As we were taking passage we had to bed down anywhere and that was in the hangar. Was I wet and miserable. One of the regular crew members saw this young lad looking absolutely sick and wet through and told me to pick up my kit and follow him. He was a fellow stoker who took me through the hold marked Engine Room. As soon as he clamped the door closed the heat met us. There were literally thousands of pipes. 'Hang all your kit over these,' he said. 'The whole lot will be dry in a couple of hours.' And they were. I just thanked him, went back to the hangar and returned two hours later and collected them. I stowed them all in my kit bag and felt a new man. Upon my return I informed all the other men who had been on the jetty with me and they did likewise. As a matter of fact I had become a very popular lad overnight. Eventually I was allocated a mess number - in case I was qualified for a tot of rum.

During my time in the Navy any man aged 20 years or over received a tot of rum. At 17 I wasn't old enough. Before I qualified for that rum I had served in Burma and could hold the Burma Star and had been aboard the first ship into Singapore after the liberation; been minesweeping; been a sentry in charge of Japanese prisoners of war; been in charge of three lascars (Indian crewmen);

been up the Persian Gulf and through the Suez twice; spent time in Bombay, Calcutta, Karachi and Madras; and been a member of the 27-strong retard party who were the last Naval personnel to leave India following Independence. We were stoned, abused and maltreated before we boarded a liner to finally return to Trincomalee - but I was not old enough to qualify for my tot of rum.

— CHAPTER 4 —

FAR EASTERN PROMISE

I celebrated my 18th birthday on board *HMS Begum* - I didn't tell anyone as I didn't want them to know how young I was. We eventually reached Rangoon, the capital of Burma. There was still heavy gunfire coming from the main town and beyond but we were given to understand the war with the Japanese was being won. As we docked we were told to have all our kit ready and report on deck immediately. After a roll call for all the Navy lads - there were about 20 of us - we went down the ladder to the liberty boat. We were taken by lorry to a building that was formerly a school. The Navy had taken it over as a transit camp. It was a complete dump. There must have been about 100 matelots there, all awaiting further movement to different ships. There was no sickbay, no canteen, no facilities of any sort except one tap between the lot of us. This was out in the yard. There was constant gunfire going on all around and I hoped I wouldn't have to stay there very

long. I managed to find a place to sling my hammock that evening and after a dreadful night woke up the next morning covered in mosquito bites. A leading hand came in to see us and shouted: 'Stoker Second Class Tinsley report here.' I raised my hand and shot over to him saying 'Stoker Tinsley'. 'Get your kit - at the double - and report back here in five minutes,' was his response. I probably did it in four minutes. He then took my hammock and said 'Follow me'. With my kit bag I did exactly that. He led me to a jeep, we threw the hammock and kit bag in the back and we set off - I knew not where. The road was diabolical with huge craters everywhere. He had obviously been down it a few times as he seemed to be aware of the holes before we got to them. We came to the dirtiest, fastest moving, huge river I had ever seen. Later I was told it was the Irrawaddy. There was a small jetty jutting out from the bank and anchored in the river was this horrible old wreck of a ship - it seemed to date back to the last century. The only clean thing about it was the *White Ensign* (the Royal Navy flag) flowing in the strong breeze right at the stern of the ship. I got into a boat manned by two other seamen. The leading hand helped me on with my hammock and shouted 'so long' and I was on my way to the ship - or whatever you could call it. The boat seemed to be having a titanic struggle to beat the strong current. A very strong breeze had also struck up and I was having difficulty staying upright and keeping on my hat. Eventually we got alongside the steps at the side of the ship and just as I was putting my kit bag on

one shoulder and the hammock on the other, my hat blew off and shot down the Irrawaddy like something shooting the rapids. Once on board I was met by Leading Stoker Courcey. He welcomed me, shook my hand and introduced me to a Stoker Sheard. 'This is the man you have come to relieve,' he said. Stoker Sheard added: 'Am I glad to see you, I thought you weren't going to make it!' Within minutes of my arrival Stoker Sheard had got all his kit together and had taken the same boat back to the mainland. I was to learn later that once you had been abroad 21 months you could apply for a relief as 'A Commission' overseas was for a maximum of 30 months. I had been earmarked for this guy's relief when I was in England and had managed to make it with about half an hour to spare. If I had not arrived he would have had to stay aboard HMS Gombroon and set sail for Singapore - which was to be the next exciting phase of my career in the Navy.

Leading Stoker Courcey was great. He showed me to the stokers' mess and introduced me to the other eleven stokers.
'This kid's Sheardie's relief. He's green - don't take the piss out of him and show him the ropes.' He then turned to me and added:
'You'll be on watch tomorrow in the boiler room. Sheardie was on duty with Fucksie. He's up on deck somewhere. Go and let him know who you are.'
'What's his name chief?' I asked.
'Fucksie.'

Green I was but I didn't feel like going on deck and asking for 'Fucksie'. I felt like it was a wind-up but had to follow it through. On deck I spotted a guy and said:

'I'm just on board. Can you tell me who is Fucksie?'

'Sure,' he responded, 'Foxy - yes he's over there.'

It then registered... 'Foxy' was Stoker Fox. He was aged about 25 with blonde hair, slightly built and a nice guy with whom to start your first watch in the Navy. Foxy expected someone like Sheardie who knew what he was doing. I knew nowt. It was a very old ship that had been converted from a coal burner to using oil. All I could do was follow him around the engine room learning as much as I could. We were also in charge of the three lascars on our watch. Foxy was a good friend and taught me well. Slowly I became more and more confident. The lascars looked up to me and I felt good having the responsibility. It was always my job to wake Foxy when we were due on watch. He slept on the upper deck. He would throw his hammock on a camp bed and crash out. He said he had been bitten by a huge rat below deck so vowed he would not sleep down there again. I had heard the odd scurrying at night but had seen no rats.

After about two weeks with Foxy I was feeling more confident so didn't wake him at all for the middle watch (midnight to 4am) and with the three lascars intended carrying it out myself. About 3.30am Foxy stormed down the ladder into

the boiler room and gave me the biggest bollocking I had ever had. It seemed the Stoker Petty Officer had spotted him on his camp bed, checked up, found he should have been on watch and not only woke him up but also reported him to the officer of the watch. Here I was thinking I was doing Foxy a favour as he had been so good to me and instead I had landed him in the biggest mess of his Navy life. Foxy knew I was green and after the initial bollocking had calmed down somewhat. I said it was completely my fault and would he - Foxy - first let me do the talking when we reported back to the officer of the watch. Foxy replied, 'You might as well 'cos I don't know what the f.... h... I'm going to say anyway.' After the watch we duly reported to the officer in charge. He wasn't a bad guy at all. I gave him my best salute and said: 'Can I speak first sir?' 'Alright with you Stoker Fox?' the officer asked. 'Yes sir,' responded Foxy, and so I began... 'Sir, I know I am very green and have not been in the Navy very long. Stoker Fox has been a very good friend to me and has helped me every day. I noticed on our last watch together he looked very ill sir, but he didn't complain. It was up to me to wake him up for the middle watch but when I went to wake him he looked worse than ever. I decided to leave him as I knew I could do the watch myself. It was entirely my decision sir. No one else sir! I have now got both of us into serious trouble sir and no one has really done anything wrong sir. If there is punishment to come I am prepared to take it all sir.' Foxy looked dumbfounded. I felt I could go on for ever but the officer broke in: 'How old are

53

you Tinsley?' '18 sir.' '18?' 'Yes sir, 18'. 'Okay, forget it this time - both of you - but, Stoker Fox, you do the waking up from now on.' 'Yes sir,' replied Foxy. We went back to the mess. It was now 5am. 'Get your head down Tins,' Foxy said. 'See you on the next watch. I'll wake you.'

Unfortunately of all the mosquito bites I had picked up in Rangoon, one must have been the pregnant one - you know, the one that gives you malaria. We had gone back to the mess and I keeled over. They took me to the sickbay which had three beds and a sickbay attendant. I eventually woke up feeling dreadful. I was informed I had malaria. I had no idea how long I was in the sickbay. All I knew was that Foxy came round with another couple of stokers and tried to comfort me somewhat. I felt I was going to die. An eternity seemed to pass before I was eventually released to go back to the mess. I had been excused duties, so my time in the boiler room with Foxy had ended for a while.

We were still on the high seas heading for Singapore and I remember calling at a small island called Port Swettenham. We had no sooner dropped anchor than about a dozen boats pulled alongside full of bananas plus a couple of locals. They were signalling to me they would like a cigarette so I started to do a bit of business giving one cigarette for a bunch of bananas. They kept throwing up a rope. I passed down a fag and they sent up a bunch of bananas. After sending down ten fags I went back to the mess with ten bunches

of bananas. I became very popular with the rest of the stokers' mess and I felt more than a little cocky. There were a couple of stokers in our mess who were constantly having verbal battles. One - an Irishman named Paddy Maguire - was a professional boxer before entering the Royal Navy as a volunteer. The other was a Geordie lad - six feet two inches tall, aged about 30 and built like a brick wall. He would often say (after his tot of rum), 'I am afraid of no man.' Paddy Maguire would then shout, 'There is no man I fear - no man.' It never seemed to go any further though. It was a sort of show of bravado, nothing more. I had just returned after tot of rum time (still being the only man too young to qualify). Having given out most of the bananas I sat in the mess with a sense of satisfaction written all over my face. All of a sudden Paddy Maguire shouted: 'There is no man I fear - no man in the world and no one in this mess,' and glared at Geordie. Geordie immediately responded: 'I will fight anyone in the world - anywhere, anytime.' I simply said: 'Instead of farting about why don't you fight each other.' Within seconds I received a tremendous blow over my left eye. It sent me reeling backwards. It was Paddy Maguire who had delivered the punch. Within seconds pandemonium broke out - verbally anyway. Geordie said something like, 'He's only a green kid - why did you do that you Irish bastard?' 'He's too feckin' cheeky - that's why. He needs teaching a lesson,' stormed Paddy Maguire. Just about everyone turned on Paddy telling him what a diabolical bastard he was, I simply opened up my locker, picked up my towel and fighting the

tears back, shot to the bathroom. The bathroom was empty - thank God. I sat down in the corner and burst into tears. My eyebrow was split open and the eye was closing fast. All of a sudden the bathroom door burst open and Courcey came in. He was one of the most kindly guys I ever met in the Forces. He had helped me a lot and given me sound advice. He was another Irishman, from Dublin. He came over and said: 'Look kid - he was out of order. He should never have hit you and everyone on the mess has told him so.' I just sobbed, 'He's a bastard. He only picked on me 'cos I'm the youngest. Well I'm going back to kick him in the bollocks.' 'Don't be feckin stupid kid - he'll kill you. Leave it - all the sympathy is with you.' He spent about ten minutes with me and calmed me down. He got a plaster from the sickbay, repaired my eye somewhat and accompanied me back to the mess. 'Don't tell 'em I've been crying Courcey will you?' 'No way kid - no way.' It was a bit difficult going back to the mess. There were about 12 guys there altogether and four on watch who hadn't witnessed the incident. 'Are you okay kid?' asked Geordie. 'Yes - I'm okay.' 'I've told him, if he wants to hit anyone else to hit me,' Geordie said. Paddy Maguire was sat by himself at the end of the mess looking very sorry for himself.

I looked straight at him and said: 'Why did you do it? Why? I never did you any harm.' 'Okay, okay,' he said. 'You're such a cheeky bastard - you get on my feckin' nerves. I just lashed out. I don't know why but you feckin' well deserved it.' 'No green kid deserved that,' responded Geordie. It ended right there and there was no more talk

about it until the next day at tot time. Courcey came up with a tot of rum and said: 'Paddy has sent you round sippers - say cheers.' I picked up the tot, took a sip and said 'Cheers'. Now in the Navy if someone gives you 'sippers' of his tot of rum it is either your birthday or you have done someone a good turn. For the next TEN DAYS Paddy sent me round 'sippers' and for the next TEN DAYS I took it and said 'cheers'. It then stopped. We never spoke another word to each other for the next six months until I left the ship. He then came up to me, shook my hand and said 'Good luck kid - sorry about that punch.'

We were now getting near to Singapore. We heard the radio on regular occasions and according to the news the war with Japan was just about over. We understood there were still pockets of resistance in Singapore but a lot of the city had now been occupied by our Forces. The old tramp ship *Gombroon* was about 60 years old and the Royal Navy used it as a repair ship. It was felt that when the other ships came into Singapore it would be advisable to have a repair ship in dock to assist. I was aboard *HMS Gombroon* about a year and cannot remember us repairing anything.

We were the first ship to sail into Singapore after the liberation - a dirty old tramp steamer with most of its crew immaculately dressed in their uniforms on the upper deck with the gleaming White Ensign flying in the breeze. Quite a few other ships followed within days but we were the first. Steaming into Singapore was a very exciting

time for me. Never in my life had I seen any place more devastated. There were a lot of local townspeople to meet us as we tied up at the jetty. They weren't there really to greet us. They wanted to buy soap, medical supplies, cigarettes - anything at all that had been in short supply during the occupation. Courcey gave me a bar of toilet soap and 50 fags and said 'You will have a good run ashore with that.' He was so right. I got about 10 dollars for the soap and 20 dollars for the cigarettes.

There was going to be a concert in the evening at a place called *The New World*. It was an old broken down pleasure park and the captain asked as many as possible to go as Gracie Fields had flown out especially to entertain the first troops in Singapore. Now I've never been a lover of Gracie Fields, nor of the other woman who claimed a lot of fame during World War II, Vera Lynn, who had been dubbed 'The Forces Sweetheart'. She was no sweetheart of mine I can tell you. Another was Ann Shelton who I felt had as much sex appeal as an Alf Garnett sock. However, back to the story. A few of us decided to go down to *The New World* and see 'Our Gracie' as she was called. When we got there we found a guy tinkering with the microphone but he was getting absolutely no sound out of it. There were about a hundred soldiers and maybe forty sailors in the audience. Gracie arrived on stage with her pianist about two hours late. She told us the microphone was broken and being a true star, she was going to sing without one. Now most of the guys were drunk

by then and had been sort of 'force marched' there anyway. The thought of listening to Gracie singing with this wimp of a pianist had about as much appeal as a wet day in Cleethorpes, so we decided to leave by the side entrance. Gracie was giving us a sort of sideways look and said, 'It's a long way to come from Rochdale to sing.' 'It's a long way to come from Dublin to have a jump but I'm having one,' Courcey replied to us.

I was very young and something like 'little boy lost' in the company of Courcey and two other stokers aged about 35 and 40. Courcey said he had been there before about 1938 and knew some very nice brothels and would see if they were still in existence. Believe it or not I had no idea what a brothel was - not a clue - honestly. I thought it was a cafe or something. Perhaps I got that idea from the 'broth'. I tagged along with them, however. We had a couple of rickshaws, two in each and followed Courcey. We didn't seem to go very far when Courcey's rickshaw stopped and we all got out. We had pulled up alongside a broken down house which was open at the front, with some steps leading up to a sort of platform. As soon as we arrived about six very nice looking girls came up to us and one made immediately for me. We all wore our white naval shirts and shorts - and immediately her hands were all over me. I had never masterbated in my life and here I was in a brothel and a lovely Chinese girl had her hand in my shorts. 'Ten dollars for a good time,' she said. 'Five dollars,' Courcey said. 'Seven dollars,' she bargained   'Five dollars,' insisted Courcey   'Six

dollars,' I offered. She removed her hand, took mine and led me upstairs to a tiny bedroom. She immediately took everything off and laid on the bed. I had no idea what to do. Sex to me had been kissing and a wet dream once a week. I did know she wanted me on top of her so I obliged. I was delighted with her and had a delightful first sexual experience. The only English she could speak was numbers and dollars. We eventually went downstairs together. The other three were waiting. 'What the hell have you been up to kid?' Courcey asked. 'Same as you I suppose,' I replied. We left the house and got into a couple of rickshaws and went back to *The New World* and got there as Gracie was winding up the concert. From what I could hear it had been a good choice in leaving when we did.

We eventually got back on board and I had to go down to the boiler room at midnight for the middle watch. I had swapped with someone else. During my time to date on the Gombroon I had never seen the Engineer Officer. I had heard he was permanently under the influence of drink and contributed nothing whatsoever to the running of the ship. Our excellent Stoker Petty Officer (Welbourne) virtually carried the Engineer Officer. Courcey requested we should be granted 'watchman's leave'. This meant that if we came off watch at 8am and had a 24 hour break we could go ashore at 8.30am and come back on board one hour before our next watch. This was a perfectly normal request and was usually granted without any problem. On this occasion the Stoker Petty

Officer said he needed the request to be signed by the Engineer Officer. The latter had refused, however, and demanded that the four stokers requesting 'watchman's leave' should be sent to him. The Stoker Petty Officer took us to the Engineer Officer's cabin. He knocked - no reply. He knocked louder - still no reply. He repeatedly knocked until eventually the door was opened by a greasy looking man wearing shorts and a dirty white shirt. On the shoulders of this shirt were the stripes for his rank - he had two and a half rings which meant he was a Lieutenant Commander. He spoke in a very slurred voice: 'Are you trying to wake the dead you dumb bastards?' I was a bit dumbstruck to say the least. The Stoker Petty Officer replied: 'You requested to speak to the stokers who requested watchman's leave sir. Here they are.' 'What is this feckin' watchman's leave?' the Senior Officer said slurring and staggering. 'The men here are the only ones on watch while we are in harbour sir and wish to go ashore after they complete their 24 hour shift.' 'No the c...s can't have leave - feckin' c...s, can't have leave. Do you hear? Get out.' The Stoker Petty Officer was trying to appear unruffled but he was now beginning to show it: 'With respect sir - you cannot speak to my men like that.' 'Who are you and what feckin' right have you got to be here?' the drunken officer asked and then collapsed back into his chair. He tried in vain to get up and couldn't. 'I came here with my men to request watchman's leave sir,' the Stoker Petty Officer reiterated. 'Well you can't have it an' f... off the lot of you,' and the Engineer Officer closed his

eyes. He was absolutely paralytic and looked as though he had been in that state for some considerable time. Welbourne left the cabin saying: 'Come on lads, let's go below.' As soon as we got out of the cabin I said: 'He can't talk to us like that chief. I want to make a complaint.' 'Okay lad, okay. We all feel the same I'm sure,' said Foxy and the others nodded in agreement. 'Lock the bastard up,' I retorted. The Stoker Petty Officer said he would try to sort things out and would come down as soon as he could. About a couple of hours later I was on watch in the boiler room. Stoker Price came down to relieve me for half an hour and said the Chief wanted to see me in the mess. I found him sitting with the other three. He told us: 'Watchman's leave has been granted and I am here to bring the Lieutenant Commander's profound apologies for his verbal outburst this afternoon. He has been under a lot of pressure lately and he does not know what came over him.' There was a pause for about a minute, I suppose, when no one spoke. Then I ejaculated: 'Bullshit, utter bullshit.' 'Leave it kid,' one of the stokers said. 'We've got leave, that's all we really wanted.' 'You made that up Chief,' I said. 'Why protect somebody like that?' 'No more comments - nothing,' the Stoker Petty Officer stated and he left the mess. I was far from happy. 'There's nothing we can do kid - let it go,' Courcey said. So we did.

Three of us went ashore one day in Singapore and as usual found a bar. We managed to drink something in the region of ten pints each. I could vaguely remember coming out of the bar and

looking for a taxi. After a while we got into one and to be honest I was the least drunk of all. The taxi driver seemed to be driving very erratically and eventually stopped. He was met by two other Chinese who pulled all three of us from the taxi. Then a big fight took place but my two mates were so paralytic they put up only token resistance. I received a couple of very hard punches in the stomach which reduced my contribution to the affray. Finally we were dragged into a ditch, our money belts removed, all our cigarettes taken and one of my mates received a sickening kick to the head. The ditch was about eight feet deep and we were a very sorry sight lying down at the bottom. It did occur to my particularly drunken mind that someone had better make a move and seek some help. I clambered to the top and set off walking down a very dark, unlit road for what seemed to be an eternity. What had happened to us had almost made me sober. Call it luck, call it an act of God, I don't know, but eventually a jeep came up behind me and stopped. Out got two Army sergeants (military policemen) who were patrolling the area. About a hundred Army personnel had arrived in the dockland area of Singapore two days before and there had been reports of servicemen being "mugged" in that district - and that was why they were out on patrol. I explained what had happened to the three of us and they immediately got me in the jeep, turned it around and proceeded back to where I thought my two mates were. When we arrived they were still at the bottom of the ditch in a drunken stupor. The military police loaded them into the jeep and took all three of us

back to the docks and put us right before we went back on board. I will be eternally grateful for their timely intervention.

HMS Gombroon was like a large edition of the *African Queen*, the ship that helped Humphrey Bogart obtain an Oscar. It was old, decrepit, over run with rats and anything seemed to go, if you know what I mean. We had two ship's cats who couldn't cope and two parrots. The ship's cook kept two dozen Rhode Island Red chickens for a fresh supply of eggs. So it was a bit like Noah's Ark. One of the biggest characters we had on board was a stoker called Arthur Corrigan who swore he was a full time burglar in civvy street. One night as he was going ashore with Courcey and another mate we asked him to bring us a dog back. One of the lads used to run a kennel club back home and was always complaining we had no dog.
'A dog?' queried Arthur.
'Yes - a dog,' we replied
'What kind?' asked Arthur.
'It doesn't matter what kind,' said the ex-kennel boy. 'Just bring a dog.' 'What do you think - one with a pedigree?' insisted Arthur.
'Just bring a feckin' dog!'

They went ashore about 12 noon with one thing in mind - to get as drunk as possible before they were due back by midnight. We were tied up alongside the jetty and the last of the guys had already reported back on board. There was no sign of Arthur and Courcey. A few of us were

very concerned especially after what had happened to me and my mates only three days earlier. We had visions of Arthur and Courcey lying in a ditch stripped of their money and watches. Three of us went up on deck and peered down the jetty. It was now about 1.30am. We could hear Courcey's voice "effing and blinding" at Corrigan to hurry up as they would be in all sorts of trouble for being late. Then we spotted Corrigan with the biggest dog I had ever seen. He had a rope under it's collar and he was pulling it like hell while Courcey and the other guy were pushing it as hard as they could. It was snapping at them and not very happy. They were all absolutely paralytic. Eventually they got to the gangplank. It must have taken them about ten minutes to get to the top. They made so much noise that about 20 guys had come on deck and that included the officer of the watch. When they got to the top of the gangplank Corrigan came face to face with the officer. He gave the most drunken salute I have ever witnessed.

'Good evening sir,' he said nearly falling over.

'Stoker Corrigan reporting for duty sir.'

'Corrigan,' shouted the officer. 'What the hell do you think you are doing? You have awakened the whole ship's company. You are inebriated and your dress is a disgrace to His Majesty.'

'Shorry sir,' said Corrigan. 'Very shorry - we have been set upon by bandits and had to fight 'em off.'

'Nonsense.' replied the Officer.

All the time they were talking, the dog had been restrained by Courcey and the other guy.

Where did you get that dog?' asked the officer. It was then I heard one of the best replies I have ever heard in my life. Corrigan retorted:

'It followed us sir.' The officer was flabbergasted.

'Let it go Courcey,' he ordered.

Courcey did. It turned round and shot down the gangplank like a bat out of hell and was never seen again. A few of us went down to help Courcey, Corrigan and his mate back to the mess. 'Thank you sir for being so understanding. It is Corrigan's birthday sir and they have been out to celebrate,' I tried to explain to the officer. 'Button it Tinsley,' he responded. 'I will sort it out in the morning.' They were never asked to report back for coming aboard late. The whole matter was forgotten and I'm sure that Corrigan's brilliant answer of 'It followed us sir,' got them off the hook.

Singapore harbour was now becoming crowded. Ten other ships had arrived since our historic entrance. What made matters worse, an American destroyer had also pulled up alongside and the excellent value for money we were getting for say a couple of fags or a bar of soap suddenly went 'for a burton'. The yanks were giving a tin of fags (50) for the same favours as we were getting for ten. My salary of about £2 a week seemed a pittance compared with what the US sailors got. However, I can't think of any great problems apart from the rate of exchange and I certainly enjoyed my time in Singapore. Most of the guys on board HMS Gombroon had been out in the Far East for a couple of years. A very strong rumour was going

around the ship that we were going to Bombay shortly and from there home. I was writing very regularly to Margaret and receiving a good stream of letters from her. Although I had been away from England about six months by then I missed her very much and felt if things worked out well I could be home again in about three months. Not wishing to raise her hopes too high I decided to wait until we were actually departing on the voyage back to the UK before I let her know. Sure enough about seven days after the rumour began we set sail again. Two days into the voyage it was announced that we were heading for Bombay and further orders would be released then.

We eventually arrived in Bombay after a stop in Colombo. I went ashore with a few lads, got absolutely paralytic and then went on to a barber's shop. My mates had normal haircuts. I fell asleep in the chair and they told the barber to cut the lot off. At that time my hair was my crowning glory. It was jet black, wavy and I did try to keep it looking good. When they woke me out of the barber's chair and looked in the mirror I nearly died. It sobered me up immediately. I know I didn't burst into tears but I nearly did. 'The bastards' I thought. They were not my usual mates and two of them were nearly bald anyway. I swear they did it because they were jealous. Back at the ship I took constant ribbing. It was so non-stop it drove me mad. I bought a sort of dustcap to wear on board. Some of the other stokers used to wear them in the boiler room as they tended to absorb sweat. When it came to meal times,

however, I was told to take it off, saying it was very impolite to wear a 'cap' whilst dining with friends.

Bombay proved a real eye-opener to me. I remember my first run ashore, going up the steps and through the big archway there which is known as the Gateway of India. There must have been 50 beggars waiting for us. 'Buck sheesh, buck sheesh,' they were all shouting. We had a difficult job getting through but eventually made it. Courcey said he knew some bars and eating houses and we followed him. He certainly did know his way around and we had a wonderful time and I seemed to get a feel for the place. I never took my hat off, the pain of my bald dome haunted me. A sort of stubble was beginning to break through although it was a painfully long job.

We had been in Bombay about a week when there was an announcement from the skipper to 'clear lower deck' which meant we all had to appear on the upper deck for a very important announcement. Full of anticipation we assembled and he told us he had received the very good news that within three days we were to sail for home. I couldn't believe it. Everyone was ecstatic. 'You lucky sod Tins,' they said. 'You haven't been out here long enough to get your knees brown and you're on your way home.' I could understand how they felt but even so I was desperate to go home. I sat down that night and wrote to Margaret with the good news - 'Home in eight weeks'. I posted the letter and then started worrying about my

bloody hair. The guys ribbed me saying it would be about four to five months before it would be back to normal. I was sure if Margaret saw me like that she would pack up with me. Call it an act of God, call it what you want, I don't know, but about ten minutes after all the ribbing the Chief Stoker came down to the mess to see me: 'I've got some bad news for you kid,' he said. 'As you have only been out here seven months, they feel you should act as a relief for someone else. He can then take your place on ship and go home.' I was speechless - couldn't believe it. Courcey, who was near, said: 'Don't take the piss Chief - the kid will have a heart attack.' 'The Engineer Officer feels the kid will broaden his experience out here, so he suggested it.' I swore and asked: 'What does he know?' I could not believe this was happening to me but it was. The next day I packed my kit bag and hammock and had quite a tearful farewell with all the lads in the stokers' mess. If I'd had a gun I would have gone looking for the Engineer Officer - but I didn't.

— CHAPTER 5 —

BOMBAY - CITY OF SCHEMES & DREAMS

Again I went through the Gateway of India but not on shore leave this time. Petty Officer Williams was waiting for me with a jeep. 'Stoker Tinsley?' I assented and he continued: 'Come with me. I've been told to pick you up and take you down to *GCB*.' 'What's *GCB*?' '*Gun Carriage Barracks*. It's a naval base. I've got to pick up another stoker there. They say he's going home on the Gombroon.' 'Do you know him?' I asked 'Know of him,' he replied. 'He's been out here two and a half years and has got serious matrimonial problems. He's going on compassionate grounds I think.' Being a decent lad at heart I felt a little better that some poor guy with a lot more problems than me was going home in my place. Only a little better though - not a lot.

GCB was not a bad place. There were about 50 matelots there, all waiting to join various ships. During the day, we were transported out of camp

to a place called Chembur about 15 miles from
Bombay. It was a large ammunition depot and we
were in a working party of 12 moving all sorts of
metal cases and other equipment into large
hangars. We had to help about 20 local coolies
who were really nice blokes and grafted ten hours
a day for about three rupees (4s 6d then and 24p
now). As we had to travel about in a large party I
asked the chief if I could learn to drive. Without a
hair on my head and always a load of stubble
round my face he thought I was about 29. So I
learnt to drive on a three-ton Dodge truck and I
will always be grateful for that.

I spent about three months there and made a few
good friends. George Ray from Bolton was one
and we had some enjoyable nights out together in
Bombay. He was a smashing lad, about 20 years old
and one of the sentries on duty at the gate on
alternate shifts. If there were some good lads in
the camp there were also some crooks and I kept
well away from those. They were always well
dressed and were rolling in money. One day
George came to me in confidence and said he had
been approached by two of the crooks, Mac and
Jock, and asked to turn his head the other way at
2am the next morning whilst on duty. They said
he would receive Rs100 for his trouble. Now Rs100
was a fortune - about a month's wages (£8). He
asked me what he should do. He was in a dilemma
because they hadn't asked him if he would, they
told him he should. Poor George - I wasn't able to
give him much advice really. They were the kind
of guys who would have cut him up if he didn't.

George's bed was next to mine in the hut. I was still awake when he came off watch at 4am. 'What happened George?' I whispered. He told me that at 2am the two guys in question drove out of the front gate in a virtually new jeep - just gave him a wave, nothing else. He was supposed to report any comings and goings at the front gate in a book and sign it after coming off watch. 'How did you sign the book?' I asked. 'Nothing to report,' he replied. About 6am Mac, one of the crooks, came up to the side of George's bed and gave him an envelope and then shot away as fast and as silent as he came. George said it contained the Rs100. He had the next night off and we decided to go for a few jars and perhaps the pictures. I even remember the picture, *"My Foolish Heart"* with Susan Hayward and Dennis Morgan. I enjoyed it but not so George. He was worried sick. We got back to camp about 11pm. Stoker Pickles was on sentry duty. When he saw us he said:
'Hey George, the officer of the watch wants to see you.'
'Now or tomorrow?'
'He said if you came back before midnight to let him know.' George knew what it was about and so did I. Stoker Pickles continued:
'You're okay Tins. It's just George he wants.'
I went back to the hut and waited. Eventually he came in - he looked in a right state. 'Are you awake Tins?' he said and added: 'I don't know what we've eaten tonight but I feel bloody awful. Coming for a walk?' Three or four of the lads were obviously still awake and George wanted to speak to me alone. When we got outside he told

me the officer had questioned him about his duty the night before. George had stuck to his story that there was nothing to report. I asked him if he thought the officer believed him and he said 'No'. I then went and did one of the most stupidest things I ever did in the Navy. I went to see Mac and told him I knew about the theft and George was very scared of what was going to happen to him. 'Know what?' he asked. 'Know what? Feck off kid - I don't know what you are talking about.' How stupid could I get? I had now landed George in further trouble. They came round that night pretending to be drunk, went up to his bed, and laughing and joking dragged him out and said they were taking him for a drink. I lay in bed petrified as George went with them. He came back about half-an-hour later and said: 'Didn't fancy going for a drink with them Tins. Are you coming out?' 'Yes,' I said and was dressed in about ten seconds. Once outside George told me they had given him another Rs100 and said if he split on them it would probably be the last thing he would ever do. He was obviously very scared and so was I. Knowing the two guys very well and that they would carry out their threats we decided to keep quiet. George was interrogated at least six times but stuck to his original report that nothing passed through whilst he was on duty. It transpired Mac and his friend had sold the jeep for Rs5,000 to a Bombay businessman.

About that time George and I were shipped to another camp about 20 miles out of Bombay where we were supposed to be 'in transit' waiting to join

a ship within three to four weeks. It seemed like another act of God, for Mac and his friends were left back at *GCB*. George and I were delighted to leave *GCB* - a more appropriate name would have been GBH. The three to four weeks at the new camp turned out to be about four months. All the guys there were given various duties which amounted to about four hours a day. They delegated me to be in charge of a galley and share duties with a leading cook. He was about 40 and must have been one of the laziest buggars around. In fact he became an embarrassment. He was supposed to be in charge one day and I the next. He told me such a sob story about his bad back and feet and wondered if I would take his shift until he got better. The only thing wrong with his back was he couldn't get it off the bed in the morning. The Indian lads in the cookhouse were a great bunch and we got on fine. We tried to learn from each other English and Hindustani and I became quite proficient in their language. It seemed the Royal Navy had sold the catering rights for the camp to an English guy who had been in India about 50 years. All the Indian staff were paid by him once a month when he came round to inspect the kitchens. He was about six feet tall, with blonde hair and covered in tattoos. He was very arrogant and spoke to the lads in the galley as if they had just crawled out of the local swamp.

I took an instant dislike to him but fortunately didn't come in contact with him very much. It was the monsoon season while we were at that camp. I had seen it rain in Huddersfield but nothing like this. It made the camp resemble a lake.

Two really big uncouth sailors ran the camp as they liked with virtually no interference from anyone else. They organised bullock cart racing, tombola, darts matches, football matches and ran a betting book on every sports event. We had a cinema of sorts which was supposed to be free for all the crew in the camp but they still charged us and nobody argued! The cinema operator, Edwin, was called Edwina by most of the men there. He had a bed in our hut and could be a real nuisance. He slept just four beds away from me. One night about 1am Chief Burns came in shouting at the top of his voice: 'Edwina, Edwina, are you in this hut? Where the feckin' hell are you?' 'Here chief,' he replied. Chief went up to his bed, pulled the mosquito netting to one side and jumped on top of him. No one dared to say a word. For the next ten minutes all we could hear was the chief's heavy groaning, the bed squeaking like a rusty gate and Edwina screaming. I was still 18 and had never seen or heard anything like it. Eventually the climax must have happened and the Chief took his drunken body off Edwina and staggered out of the hut - obviously satisfied and, by the sounds of ecstasy which had come from Edwina's bed, so was he.

The camp was beginning to get me down - we seemed to be heading nowhere. One day while going past the main office a leading seaman was putting up a notice on the board. I must have been the first to see it. It said they were looking for four stokers to join *HMS Bushwood*, a small supply ship that had been converted into a

minesweeper. The ship was then at Bombay harbour and would be going back to the UK in about three months. I immediately went into the office and volunteered. It seemed too easy and too good to be true. I went back to the mess, told some of the lads there what I was going to do and asked George to volunteer as well. One of the guys in the hut retorted: '*Bushwood* - I've just booked off that. It's a coal yaffler you know.' A coal yaffler meant it ran on coal and not oil. 'Well I'm sick of it here,' I said. 'And I've volunteered to go. Come on George, join me. We'll be home in three months.' George was a good mate but he had also heard a strong rumour that all the guys in the camp would be shipped home soon, as the war was now completely over. Try as I might he wouldn't come and I was the only stoker who applied.

Reporting at noon with all my kit I was told to board an old van. One of the local Indian drivers got in and we set off towards Bombay. I was alone again. He dropped me off at the steps to the Gateway of India. I waited for maybe an hour until a liberty boat came up to the steps. About four sailors got out and the seaman in charge of the boat yelled: 'Anyone for *HMS Bushwood*?' 'Yes, me,' I replied and he helped me put all my kit on board. We headed towards the dirtiest, scruffiest ship in the harbour. As we were nearing it I felt this could not be it. Then I noticed the White Ensign flying at the back and realised that, as it was the only Royal Navy ship in the harbour, it definitely was *HMS Bushwood*. The next four

months proved to be my happiest in the Royal Navy. It was an amazing coincidence but two of my old mates from training days were on board - Jack Garaway (Gary) and Ray Magnoni (Mac). We became inseparable. Mac and I were on duty in the boiler room and Gary managed to get himself a really cushy number - he was steward to the Engineer Officer, and this one, too, I never saw sober. There were eight stokers on board and the leading stoker was a fantastic character called Montgomery (Monty). He was never seen without the stokers' mascot - Chico the monkey - on his shoulder. The Captain had sent instructions down to get rid of Chico but we never took any notice of him and when there was a mess inspection we just got one of the lads to take Chico to the bathroom. We heard that we were going to 'coal ship' the next day and all stokers who were not on watch had to report to the upper deck at 6am. I came off the middle watch at 4am and after a shower and an hour's sleep I had to report for duty. There was a very old dilapidated barge alongside the *Bushwood*. Mac said: 'We'll be dead in about three hours Tins. Look at that lot we have to load!' We were each given a large basket that fitted onto our shoulders. We went slowly down the steps on one side of the ship to the barge. The coolies on the barge filled our baskets and we took them up the other steps and along the deck to tip them into the coal bunker. It was worse than donkey work. After about an hour I sat down, absolutely knackered. There was an officer looking on - he was known as the welfare officer but more about him later. 'Tinsley,' he said. 'We

have five hours to coal ship and we are not going to complete it if you lie down on the job.' 'I just came off watch sir. I'm dead beat. I'll be okay in a minute.' 'You've got five minutes Tinsley then back on the job,' he ordered. He was dressed in white shirt, white shorts, white socks and shoes and looked like something out of South Pacific. By this time I was the same colour as the coal I was carrying and like Mac had long white streaks down my face where the sweat had run. After four hours we had emptied the barge. Someone else had been designated to do my morning watch from 8am till midday when I was due on again. Keeping watch in the boiler room was just as hard work as coaling ship. I had three boilers to fire, rake and slice. By the time I had finished the third it was time to move onto the first again. The work was really hard but it certainly broadened me out. I put on about four inches across my chest, three inches on my biceps and increased my weight by two and a half stone. One particular shift I was shovelling coal from the bunker. It came down a narrow passage about two feet wide by two and a half feet high. Unfortunately I could not get any out. It was pretty obvious a couple of very large pieces of coal had jammed at the front and were not allowing any to get through. I was also panicking as No.1 fire was beginning to go down and the steam pressure was falling. I could just about squeeze through on the left of the bunker and wormed my way along till I could reach the three large chunks of coal which were blocking the flow. I could hardly see a thing, there was just a little light coming in through a hole from the

boiler room. I had dragged my shovel with me. I managed to lift out one of the large chunks and there was an almighty crash as it released about ten tons of coal that came tumbling down from the top of the bunker and trapped my right foot. It was pitch black and even if I could have moved I couldn't go back the way I had come for that was now blocked by coal. Was I scared. I started banging on the side of the bulk-head from inside the coal bunker using my shovel. It seemed to be making a hell of a noise but it must have been 15 minutes before anyone heard me. That was my old mate Mac. He lifted the top of the coal bunker, shone a torch down and said: 'God Tins, what's happened? How the hell have you got there?' 'Get me some help quick Mac,' I yelled. 'My foot's stuck'. Mac rounded up a few of the lads and they climbed down into the bunker. One of the stokers was called 'Buck' Jones. He had been in the Boy Scouts and knew something about first aid and tying knots. As Mac dug furiously others managed to release my foot, tie the rope around me and pull me out. No one could recognise me for I was covered from head to toe in coal dust. Mac knew me by my voice. By the time I got out the lights on the ship had faded to about that of a 15 watt bulb. The No.2 boiler had gone out and steam was down way below the red danger mark. Mac and Buck came down to the boiler room with me and we tackled one fire each. After working long and hard for about 40 minutes the steam gauge started to rise and the lights on the ship became a little brighter. What a watch I had had - I nearly died, my foot was up like a balloon and I was absolutely

knackered. But we had all the fires up to scratch again and that was all due to two wonderful mates who had helped enormously. 'We'll go in the shower now Tins,' said Mac. 'Who's relieving you?' I told them and Mac said they would see if he could relieve me half-an-hour sooner so I could go to the sick bay to have my ankle checked. They had just gone up the step ladder when I saw this figure coming down the ladder. There was coal dust everywhere, steam, and hot clinkers on the boiler room steel deck and he was dressed all in white. It was only when he got right to the bottom that I realised it was the Engineer Officer. He was drunk as usual. 'Who are you?' he slurred. 'Stoker First Class Tinsley sir,' I replied. If he had known any of his stokers - and he certainly didn't - he would not have recognised me, I was so covered in coal dust. He slurred again: 'Lights have nearly gone out. My refrigeration has gone off, and so has the one in the Captain's cabin. It is your responsibility to keep steam up on watch - anything amongst the food and drink goes rotten. Due to your negligence I will personally see you get reprimanded and the cost of any food or drink spoilt will be deducted from your pay. Got that Kingsley?' he said and tried to get back up the ladder. It was not an easy climb at the best of times even for a fit young man. He had no chance. He made about five abortive attempts and finally slipped off the bottom step onto his arse. His 'whites' were suddenly becoming 'blacks'.

The engine room was adjacent to the boiler room and that was Monty's domain. It wasn't necessary

for anyone to be on watch in the engine room when we were in harbour but thankfully I found Monty there, with Chico on his shoulder. 'Quick Monty, the Engineer Officer is in the boiler room now and he's pissed.' Monty shot past me into the boiler room with Chico hanging on like a limpet mine. There was the Engineer Officer at the bottom of the ladder trying to lift his hand to the first rung. 'Steady sir,' said Monty. 'Had an accident sir?' 'He hasn't fallen down the ladder if that's what you mean,' I retorted. 'Quiet Tins - we must help our Engineer Officer up on deck. He has obviously sprained his ankle trying to keep a check on all his work. Don't worry sir, we will have you on upper deck in no time. Tins - go and fetch Petty Officer Craig and a very strong rope.' I went up top to the PO's mess, saw Petty Officer Craig and explained as quickly as I could about the situation. He grabbed a rope and shot down to the boiler room. By this time No.3 boiler was going down and needed re-firing. I just started shovelling away at the side of the Engineer Officer and made sure he got plenty of dust all over his face and uniform. It never ceased to amaze me how much some of these officers were protected by the old regulars in the Navy. Monty and Petty Officer Craig were so busy helping that drunken officer to get out of the boiler room - a place he had never visited before. They followed that through by covering up for him. Gary, as the Engineer Officer's batman, was very relieved when they brought him back. He knew the officer was drunk when he left his cabin and thought he might have fallen over the side of the ship. He helped

Monty and Petty Officer Craig to get him into the cabin and then took his blackened clothes off and helped him into the shower. Gary had as much respect for him as I did so he put the shower on at full power and used it like a hosepipe. While the officer was washing Gary took his wallet out of his filthy uniform and removed Rs10. He then put the officer to bed, slipped out of the cabin and came down to the stokers' mess. He came up to Mac and me and said: 'Come on lads, let's have a run ashore - I've just nicked this,' and he showed us the Rs10 note. Neither Mac or I were due back on watch for 24 hours and Gary said the Engineer Officer would probably be asleep through all that. We had a super run ashore. We first went to the Metro cinema in Bombay. They were showing 'The Rookies' starring Abbot and Costello and preceding this there was a sing-a-long. The words of the songs were projected onto the screen with a ball bouncing along on top of each word in time with the music. You could have heard a pin drop. As the audience was 95 per cent Indian you couldn't expect them to sing *Roll out the Barrel* and *There'll be Bluebirds over the White Cliffs of Dover*. My old favourite *April Showers* came up next so, as I had done in Malvern beside the cinema queue, I let forth in full voice. Mac and Gary nearly burst laughing and so did the audience of about 700. It was like a solo performance although I did get quite a few joining in with *April Showers*. By the time we got to *I belong to Glasgow* all those in the cinema were singing their heads off. At the end of the short film everyone started clapping and the management was forced to

put it on again immediately. That set us up well and we were in very high spirits.

CHAPTER 6

SPEED TRIALS
AND
HOME PROSPECTS

Life aboard the *Bushwood* was quite good. We had to cater for ourselves. We were allowed about 3s a day per stoker to get the food ashore in Bombay. We then had a rota for cooking the meals. We had to share the galley with the seamen. Monty, Herbie and Buck Jones were the best cooks. My breakfasts were quite good. Mac and I were together on rota, however, and when it was. our week the stokers didn't get much variety. There were beans on toast for breakfast; egg and chips for lunch; and a mixture of soup or meat with sweet potatoes for tea. There was plenty of tea, coffee, biscuits and fruit. It says a lot for the stokers' cooking that whenever any of us went ashore the first place we aimed for was a little cafe about 200 yards from the *Gateway of India*. We always had the same. We called it SEAC. SEAC actually stood for South East Asia Command of which we were a part. But SEAC to us stood for Steak, Egg and Chips. We could have a really good

plateful for about 16 annas - 1s 6d in old money and 9p in present currency. I was still only 19 and there I was running my own end of the boiler room and cooking meals. I had done my own washing, ironing and sewing since the day I joined the Navy. I was writing home very regularly and writing to Margaret every other day. The last letter I received from home was about two months earlier and it was written by my dad. He said mother had been very ill and was getting worried that she would not see me again. I was very concerned but I didn't know what to do about it. I wrote straight back to them to let them know I was fine and could well be home earlier than they expected. One of the seamen on board was also the wireless operator. That was not a full-time job on an old wreck like the *Bushwood*. His name was Hardy and obviously he was nicknamed 'Ollie'. One day he came down to the stokers' mess and asked to have a word with me privately. He explained that he was surprised I was still there. He had received a radio message from the UK, addressed to the skipper, saying Stoker Tinsley should be released on immediate compassionate leave as his mother was desperately ill. He had received the message four weeks previously! He dared not divulge to the Captain that he had told me. I couldn't do anything about it as I was not supposed to know. The Captain of the *Bushwood* spent virtually all his time at the Bombay Yacht Club. His next in command was the Engineer Officer who was permanently stoned out of his mind. The only other officer was a Sub-Lieutenant who had about as much idea of running a ship as I

did of mountaineering. Monty was livid about it. For once we had an old regular who couldn't find any excuse for the Captain.

He did eventually come up with a brilliant idea. He suggested I should see the welfare officer (every ship was supposed to have one officer delegated as a welfare officer) and ask him if they could cable the UK because I was very worried about my mother as my last letter from my dad had stated she was very ill. The welfare officer was, of course, that young Sub-Lieutenant. He promised to look into the matter for me. About half-an-hour after my meeting with him I heard an announcement on the Tannoy for Stoker Tinsley to report to the bridge. The young Sub-Lieutenant was there looking very embarrassed. He said it seemed like an amazing coincidence but they had just received a wire from the UK saying that I should be considered for compassionate leave. I obviously felt like calling him a lying bastard but that would have got Ollie into trouble. He went on to say that when they received such cables they immediately checked back to the UK to see if things were still the same expediting a return home. He promised to keep me informed. Two days later he sent for me again and showed me a cable they had just received. It said my mother had made a complete recovery and if I had not already been granted compassionate leave it was no longer a request. I decided to question the cable. 'What is this about compassionate leave Sir? It seems to say I should have been granted compassionate leave a while ago sir.'

'Compassionate leave has never been a consideration Tinsley - never. We are a fighting force in His Majesty's Navy and we have a job to do out here. Ratings cannot be released from their duties because of the illness of relatives. Now a wife, that would be a different story.' 'I'm not married sir. All I'm questioning is the second cable about compassionate leave. I never saw the first cable. What did it say sir?' 'I told you what it said Tinsley. That is the end of the matter. It seems you would have been happier going home knowing your mother was ill rather than receiving the news of her complete recovery. Dismiss!' I went back to the stokers' mess and all the lads wanted to know the news. I told them the excellent news of my mother's complete recovery but couldn't push the situation about the four week delay from the first cable without implicating Ollie. It was indeed frustrating that we were members of the Royal Navy, working our nuts off, always smiling, always smart when necessary and yet we were being 'led' by what seemed to be a set of bloody idiots. The *Bushwood* had been anchored out in the harbour in Bombay ever since I was drafted aboard - about five months by then. There had been no mention of us going back to the UK and I was feeling a bit fed up with the whole situation. It was just as hard work being a stoker if your ship was in the harbour. You still had to fire one of the boilers to keep steam up to keep the generator going for all the lights etc. There were something like 20 ships anchored out in Bombay harbour - USA tankers, French tankers, various Indian and East African ships. When I

came off watch I went straight to the shower room, got myself all clean again and then went on the upper deck. Ollie was usually on watch when I got up there. We talked about the cable that never was and the idiots who were running the ship and our present situation. He said he had volunteered for the *Bushwood* because it was going back home.

Every night it was the duty of the rating on watch to turn off all the upper deck lights on the ship. Instructions came from the officer of the watch that this had to be done at 8.30pm. Ollie said: 'You might not believe this Tins but virtually every ship in the harbour waits until we turn out our lights before turning out theirs. They look to us for a lead as they feel that a ship of the Royal Navy must have it right.' 'You're kidding,' I said. 'Wanna bet?' laughed Ollie. 'Yes five rupees.' 'You're on,' he agreed. It was 7.37pm by then. He said: 'You say when Tins'. I waited until 7.51pm. Then right in the middle of our conversation I said to Ollie: 'Right now turn 'em off.' He had a master switch on the upper deck. He pulled it down and all the upper deck lights went out. Within 20 seconds every ship we could see in the harbour had done the same. I couldn't believe it. Ollie refused the Rs5 but we decided to have a little game together every night he was on watch and I could join him. We turned off at a different time every night and once left them on until 8.50pm. The rest of the ships always followed. On the 8.50pm night we heard a clattering along the upper deck and saw the Chief Engineer

approaching. Gary had turned him out very smart - his whites were immaculate. As usual he was very drunk. 'It's nearly nine o'clock, you should have had lights out an hour ago. What do you think you are doing?' he slurred. 'They have put the clock on in the UK sir and we are working to UK time sir. Sorry sir, should we continue with Indian time sir?' I responded. He looked at me absolutely dumbstruck. 'UK time, what the feckin' hell do you think you're talking about?' 'It's a UK ship sir, we are members of His Majesty's Navy and we are proud to serve him and proud to stick to UK time sir.' His face was getting redder and redder. He slurred: 'Report to me first thing in the morning. You are on a charge.' 'Yes sir, certainly sir.' Ollie had stood open mouthed at it all. 'You bloody idiot Tins. He'll throw the book at you tomorrow.' 'He won't remember a thing about it tomorrow,' I said. 'You mean you won't report.' 'No way,' I said. The next day I sat next to Gary in the stokers' mess and asked him what the Chief Engineer had been up to the night before. Gary said he had got him ready to go ashore and waited for him to ask for a liberty boat. It had gone 8.30pm. Gary left and went to the stokers' mess. The Chief Engineer had been drinking all night so he had left him there. He had no idea he had come up on deck. I asked him to chase up to his cabin and see what state he was in, having first explained to Gary what had happened the night before. Gary came back about half an hour later. He had found the Chief Engineer fast asleep in his chair. Gary had undressed him, put him into bed, waited five minutes and then awoke him and told

him it was morning. He mixed a gin and tonic for the officer and said: 'Glad you decided to stay on board last night sir. You have been in need of an early night.' He looked straight at Gary and asked him what time he had returned. Gary had said 7.30pm. He believed him and anyway he was completely drunk again by 11am. That day proved quite eventful. For a start I didn't report to the Chief Engineer and he didn't send for me. A Tannoy announcement requested everyone to meet on the upper deck in ten minutes for a major announcement. Everyone was in the same mind - we were sure we were going home. When all the ships' company - about 30 in all - were assembled, the Captain announced we were going to have speed trials. If everything proved satisfactory and the performance of the ship came up to standard there was a probability we were going home. 'What's speed trials?' I asked when we got back in the stokers' mess. All the time I had been aboard the Bushwood we had never left Bombay harbour. It seemed the Bushwood had been out in the Far East for about 15 years. The Royal Navy had purchased it from the Merchant Navy. Monty said that it used to be on the South African run and had come up to Bombay on the East coast of Africa route. 'But what about speed trials?' I asked again. 'It's got to be the slowest ship in the Navy Monty. You must know that.' Nobody could understand why we were to have speed trials. It didn't matter to me how long it took to get home just so long as we were heading in the right direction. I then hit on a good idea. The Chief Engineer would know why we had to have speed

trials. Gary was his batman. If he could catch him sober Gary might be able to glean that information. About four hours later Gary came into the mess. He didn't say the Engineer Officer was sober but he had told him the reason. To go home we would probably go through the Suez Canal. To pass through the Canal we would have to maintain the accepted speed of five knots. To most ships that was slow but the *Bushwood's* cruising speed was only four knots! Our skipper didn't believe *Bushwood* could maintain the correct speed. It sounded like the most far-fetched story I had ever heard but Gary assured me it was true. We would have to go full steam ahead all the way through the Suez Canal. One big problem seemed to be looming - the skipper did not want to go back home just yet. We had heard he had recently been made President of the Bombay Yacht Club and was living like a Maharajah at that time!

Three days later we held the speed trials. That morning a beautiful small cruiser came alongside - obviously a pleasure ship belonging to some Bombay millionaire. The skipper was at the top of the steps to welcome about ten dignitaries (six men and four women) who came aboard from the cruiser. The skipper was fussing about like a mother hen. He was impeccably dressed in his full whites and my mate Gary was also immaculate as he served them with drinks. Our Captain had brought all his furniture from his cabin and put it on the upper deck. It looked as though they had stepped straight from one pleasure cruiser onto another. The young welfare officer was also in

evidence and fussing about. The skipper said his Engineer Officer couldn't be present as he was in the engine room supervising the trials. In fact he was in his cabin blind drunk and Monty was supervising everything. It was the first time we lifted the anchor since I joined the ship. The really telling watch to be on was the forenoon (8am till 12am) and Mac and I had drawn that. As mentioned before we had to keep a reasonable amount of steam up to keep the engine ticking over for the generator. To move the ship out of the harbour for a speed test was going to be a super-human effort. Monty was on duty in the engine room and we were told we would lift the anchor and commence the trials at 10am. Before Mac and I came on duty Buck Jones and George Bartle had fired and sliced the boilers and prepared everything very well for us. Mac and I had never worked so hard in our lives as we fired and sliced, fired and sliced all six boilers - three each - until they were at their raging best. Monty came through from the engine room and said he had never seen the Bushwood with as much steam up - ever. We could hear the anchor being winched up about 9.50am and knew we had to maintain the amount of steam we had already produced for the next two hours at least. Then we were on the move. The feeling from the boiler room, where we were working our nuts off, was that we were speeding along at about 30 knots. In reality we were doing only four to five. Mac and I managed to sustain the steam required. The heat was unbearable. I was completely exhausted by 12 noon when Buck and George relieved us. They also did very well.

By 4pm when I went back on watch I was somewhat refreshed. The trials went on until about 5pm. We had then returned to Bombay harbour and dropped anchor. What was to be the answer? All the lads on the lower deck - stokers and seamen - felt the old ship had performed magnificently. We were fully prepared to keep up full steam all the way through the Suez Canal if it meant we were going home.

— CHAPTER 7 —

GOODBYE BUSHWOOD
I Belong to Glasgow

Nothing happened for about a week. The skipper
was away at the Yacht Club. The Engineer Officer
was in his drunken stupor. The welfare officer
was here and there and Monty was just about
running the ship with a little help from the lads
around him. I can remember that particular
morning as if it was yesterday. It was announced
on the Tannoy: 'All hands report on upper deck in
ten minutes.' I was convinced the skipper was
going to give us the good news about going home.
On the upper deck Monty put us in some sort of
order and waited for the skipper to come and
address us. He never came. Instead it was the
welfare officer who told us to stand easy and
began: 'Men - it is my unpleasant duty to inform
you that our ship has failed the speed trials and
will "pay off" here in Bombay harbour. The ship
has been sold to a Bombay company whose chief
came aboard during the trials. It is expected that
the ships' company will leave *HMS Bushwood*

within the next few days and will be sent to the local Indian Naval Station where onward arrangements will be made. Dismiss.' 'Hold on sir,' I shouted. Monty then said: 'One of my men wishes to speak sir.' 'What about?' asked the officer. 'With respect sir - what do you think it's about?' I queried. 'Go ahead then,' he said. 'What exactly does onward arrangements mean sir?' I continued. 'It means you will be leaving *HMS Bushwood* and presumably picking up another ship fairly soon.' 'Every man aboard this ship was expecting to go home sir,' I retorted to which he replied: 'Every man aboard this ship would have been going home if our ship had past its speed trials. As it is, it has now been sold on instructions from the Admiralty. There is nothing more to be said. Dismiss.' We got back to the stokers' mess and slumped around the table. All of us were devastated - Monty more than most. We were only kids but he had a wife and three children in Newcastle who were living for his return. All of a sudden it occurred to me that we had been hoodwinked for why had the Indian businessman been allowed on ship during the so-called speed trials. It was my opinion that they had never planned to send the *Bushwood* back to England - we had only been told that so we would volunteer to work on such an old tramp ship. Once they had a crew who could run it well enough they had put it up for sale. That was the theory I put to the rest of the stokers. They felt my assessment was logical but there was absolutely nothing we could do about it - nothing. That night I had a couple of letters to write - one to Margaret

and one to my parents telling them my home-coming had been cancelled for the time being. I said I would write again once I knew what was happening. It was now almost 1947. I had been abroad about 18 months I suppose. India was in the process of attaining Independence and virtually all the Army and Air Force had departed. There were about 30 sailors left in the Royal Navy Barracks and they were going to be joined by the crew of the Bushwood. We were eventually 'paid off' on the Bushwood and the two Petty Officers and all the ratings reported to the Naval Barracks. We arrived early one Sunday morning and found the men already there were pulling out as we arrived. They were obviously very elated for they were being flown home. In fact, it took us by surprise to find we were relieving them! Some of those matelots had only been abroad about 12 months and we were taking their places. If only we had had a skipper who cared for his crew or an Engineer Officer who could keep sober we might well have been the ones flying home. As that Sunday dragged on we waited for any news or further orders. Then Monty told us to report to the parade ground immediately. Once we had assembled the skipper from the *Bushwood* ordered us to stand easy and told us: 'We have been selected to carry out a very important task for His Majesty's Government. We are all seasoned campaigners in the Far East and as you know India has now been granted Independence. Virtually all the Army has moved out. There is only a small band of men attached to the Royal Air Force still in the country and we have been chosen as the

Navy's Retard Party. There are some very important jobs to carry out before we will be allowed to leave the country and it is an honour for us to be chosen for such a responsible job.'   There were about 24 of us including my two best mates, Mac and Gary. As the Captain completed his speech I shouted: 'Sir, permission to ask a question sir.' 'Carry on,' he replied. 'Can you give us an idea of how long this responsible job will take and whether we will be returning to the UK after it's completion?'   The Captain replied: 'Obviously I would have expected someone to ask that question and thought it might well have come from you Stoker Tinsley! We would expect the job to last at least a month.   After that I cannot tell you anything. We must await further orders from the Admiralty. Dismiss.'

That month became two months. Each week we were taken down to the large depot in Bombay docks.   There we had to load case after case of ammunition, ovens, lorries, machine guns and so much more of the sundry articles of war into a landing craft. Once it was full we took it about ten miles out to sea and proceeded to pick everything up by crane and drop each item into the ocean.   By the time this commission was completed we must have thrown a million pounds worth of equipment into the sea.   Upon my enquiries I was told, it was all American lease-lend equipment. With the war over it was not required. The Indian government refused to buy it - they wanted it free. The USA refused to take it back so some big noise at the Admiralty decided we should

throw it into the ocean. It seemed that every time we set out to sea in those landing craft it was rough. They were the flat-bottomed type and we were tossed about like corks. Often it became too rough to use winch equipment and the small crane we had aboard, and the skipper would abandon work for the day. On one occasion it was fairly calm and I was working one winch, Mac the other and Ged Brewer was using the crane, swinging the jib over the side of the craft. The cases were tied on with a special knot which had a long lead. Once they were over the sea the lads would pull the release rope and the goods would plunge into the water. Mac and I lifted the really heavy goods with steam winches and Ged took the smaller stuff. As I looked down from the winch I could see that Ged had quite a big load on and shouted to him. He obviously didn't hear. He swung his crane jib over the side and the weight of the load took the crane and Ged straight over the side. We all rushed over in time to see the load, the crane and Ged plunge straight into the water and disappear within two seconds. It was dreadful. He was a good mate, 20-years-old - and he was lying at the bottom of the Indian Ocean. Work was immediately suspended. The landing craft was stopped - and then moved into 'slow'. We circled the area for about two hours but we all realised there was no hope. The Captain said a few prayers over the spot and work continued as normal again the next day. Once that job was completed we prepared to leave the Naval Barracks - destination unknown.

That night there was a hell of a noise at the front gate of the camp. We heard a few shots fired and then there was an announcement over the Tannoy that all ships' company should report to the main building immediately. We all ran like rabbits out of our hut and into the main building, pulling the large door closed behind us. Within seconds there was the sound of stones and bricks hammering at the door. It seemed a group of young activists wanted the last remnants of the British Forces out of India that very night. It was very scary and it seemed they would break the door down at any second. After about five minutes of bedlam we heard some more shots and then there was peace. The two lads on sentry duty had rifles but they were only loaded with blanks. They had pointed them in the air and fired, warning the mob they would fire at them next time if they didn't disperse. Happily they did just that. It was about four in the morning and the officer suggested it would be as well if we got all our kit together as soon as possible and met on the parade ground within the hour, which we did. Three vehicles picked us up and took us down to Bombay harbour.

We were collected at 6am by a large liberty boat. It took us alongside a very large steamer marked *SS Scythia* and with our kit over our shoulders we boarded that magnificent old pleasure cruiser. We were allocated cabins, three to each (Gary, Mac and I were together) and for the next four days we were treated to luxury such as I had never known before. It was on a cruise from Bombay to South

Africa. There were many wealthy Indian and South African families on board and the ship was to make an unscheduled drop in Trincomalee to drop off the 'war heroes'. The crew treated us magnificently and we dined with all the other passengers enjoying food we had never before tasted.

The trip came to an end far too quickly (I could have travelled around the world in those conditions) and we disembarked at Trincomalee. At the jetty we boarded a coach and were told we were going to *HMS Golden Hind* - a Naval Shore Base which had been carved out of the jungle. The coach driver warned us 'Keep all the windows closed'. As we travelled along a mud road something - maybe a large brick - hit the window beside me. The coach driver retorted, 'Feckin baboons'. 'Baboons' thought I. 'He must be joking!' But as he turned the coach into the main gates of the base there were about five baboons on their hind legs surveying us as though they were the old hands at the camp and we were the new kids on the block. *HMS Golden Hind* was a complete dump. I spent Christmas of 1946 there and it was the most miserable Christmas I can remember. The baboons were a bloody nuisance. They followed us when we went to the camp cinema in the evening and would throw sticks and stones at us. We were told to always go in threes, for about six months previously a rating had gone out alone one night and was killed by the baboons.

Each morning we had to report to HQ for any orders. There was nothing to do. All the other guys in the camp had just arrived from the UK and were on their way to relieve others who had been out for two years or more. We seemed no nearer to going home and all news was conspicuous by the lack of it. The huts we lived and slept in were made from dried leaves and wood with no lights - not even a Tilley lamp. One night Gary, Mac and I were asleep in our hut when we heard a tremendous screeching and bellowing outside. It sounded as if a regiment of soldiers were descending on us at great speed through the bush. It was so loud we all sat up in our beds. Then all of a sudden a sacred cow burst through the side of the hut chased by about five baboons. Looking back it was like a comedy film and we can laugh now. But at the time it was frightening. It was just about the last straw for me. Even though I carried out all the duties assigned to me satisfactorily I felt I was getting nowhere. I had been commanded by some of the most ridiculous officers there could possibly be in the Royal Navy. On the *HMS Gombroon* I had been the only one kept back when all the others sailed home. Now I was stuck in the middle of nowhere on an island with only bad-tempered baboons for company. The only redeeming factor was my friendship with Mac and Gary. The next morning when I reported to HQ I asked the Petty Officer which ships in the harbour needed stoker volunteers. He said he had been instructed to wait until there was a ship going back to the UK and then offer it to the lads from Bombay. I pushed him further and asked if

any were due. He replied he knew of none but, of course, orders could easily be changed. For instance *HMS Glasgow* was looking for ten stokers, one leading stoker and eight seamen but it was unlikely to return to the UK for some considerable time. He went on to explain what a great ship it was and felt I would be very happy aboard it with all its sporting activities. I had a very long chat with Gary and Mac and told them I was going to volunteer to join *HMS Glasgow* and tried to talk them into going with me. I didn't want to be split up from such very good mates but I had had my fill of that God forsaken hole and decided to go whether they did or not. They decided against it. So we wished each other well and the next day I was aboard *HMS Glasgow* along with my old mate Monty (Leading Stoker) and four other lads from *HMS Bushwood*. It was to prove the best move I made in the Royal Navy. The moment I went aboard I felt at home. It was a magnificent ship. After some of the rat infested hulks I had been on, it was superb. In a very short time I made friends with a lad from Bradford called Ben Peacock and with two from London, Ginger Greenwood and Ginger Bloor. They were brilliant characters with whom I had hours of laughter and a few hours of anguish as well. I was a watch keeper in the engine room and I found the job a doddle. No pressure, no problems, good mates - life was good. It was unbelievable but within 24 hours of my joining *HMS Glasgow* it set sail for .... Bombay.

The first stop, however, was Colombo where three cricket matches had been arranged for the first and

second XIs. The names for both teams were on the noticeboard and what I found significant was the first XI comprised of eight officers, two midshipmen (junior officers) and one petty officer. The second XI had a chief petty officer as captain, four midshipman, three petty officers and three leading seamen. Not one of the other ranks were in either team. Cricket was my great love at school and I always felt I could make a good account of myself at the game. I decided to call and see the welfare officer (sports) - a Lieutenant MacDonald - and asked if I could be considered for selection. He was a young officer, pleasant and understanding who said he would mention it to the selection committees. The matches were to be played against RAF, British Army, Indian Army, Indian Air Force, Indian and Ceylonese Navy teams and some local clubs. All of these were of a very good standard. Lieutenant MacDonald scored a 100 runs playing for the first XI in their first match - and helped them to win. The second XI lost. Looking at the noticeboard next day I saw that the teams were unchanged. I went to see Lieutenant MacDonald again and he assured me I would be considered for the third game. Both teams lost their next matches and this time I felt sure I would be in a team. Checking on the noticeboard, there it was - Stoker Tinsley, the last name at the bottom of the second XI. I can remember that game vividly. We batted first and I went in at number ten. I knocked a couple of lusty hits and scored 13 not out. Our total for that innings was 120. Our opponents, however, were soon 60 for no wickets after 12 overs. I decided to have a quiet word with

the skipper when he was about to bring back one of his opening bowlers. The two men who had relieved them earlier were getting nowhere. 'Do you bowl?' he asked. 'Well I'm not a batter if I'm put in at number ten am I?' He promptly gave me a lecture on who was skipper and that he didn't welcome suggestions from someone who had just joined the team. I was feeling and looking a bit upset when the opening bowler said: 'Let him come on skip - I'm not getting anywhere.' The captain gave me the ball and a further lecture about interfering with his captaincy. I bowled a very good maiden and had a catch dropped in the slips. In the next over I clean bowled the opening batsman and had the next man caught at the wicket. My tail was really up by then and I took a further two wickets in my next over. The other bowler took two wickets, one batsman was run out and at 111 for seven our opponents were decidedly shaky. They did manage, however, to get to 121 with no further loss. I had taken four wickets for 13 runs. The skipper congratulated me and did go so far as to admit he should have brought me on sooner.

Over the next three months I continued to represent *HMS Glasgow* as the opening bowler for the second XI, playing in Bombay, Colombo, Calcutta and Madras. We were the flagship of the Royal Navy in the Far East and were constantly on the move making goodwill stops at every port of call. Cricket matches were arranged by radio before we even reached a port. At Trincomalee we were unable to play the proposed matches against

some Royal Air Force teams. It was then decided that there should be a match between our own first and second XIs - to give the first XI some much needed practice. That game for me was a personal triumph and will forever remain in my memory. It was decided that the first XI should bat first - for surely the game wouldn't last long if we opened the batting. That rankled all the second team for a start. The second XI skipper had managed to get a new ball and handed it to me like a cherished possession. 'Put everything into it Tins', he said. 'We can beat them.' I achieved something in that match I have never managed again in my cricketing life (and I'm still playing in my late 60s). Their opening pair came to the wicket their No.1 being Midshipman Ellis. He took guard, surveyed the field and prepared to take my first ball. It was a real fizzer. He played forward - and it went between bat and pad and uprooted the middle stump. A wicket with my first ball! Lieutenant MacDonald then came into bat and I remembered how he had scored a century in his last match. He was determined to knock me off a length but could not get to the ball and was extremely lucky not to get a touch. They proceeded to 46 for one and at that stage I had taken one for 14 off seven overs. Our skipper asked if I wanted a rest but I said I would like to bowl a couple more overs. With the second ball of the next over I clean bowled MacDonald. He had scored 30. Their captain then came in and nibbled at my next two balls which were just pitched outside the off stump. He tried to do the same with the next, got a very thick edge and was taken

by the wicket keeper. He then had the audacity to wait at the wicket hoping not to be given out. I took a further two wickets and finished with match figures of five for 25. I also took a catch. They were all out for 120. We were elated and felt sure we could inflict a humiliating defeat on them. We went out to bat, got 35 without loss and then suffered a mini-collapse to 73 for six. It rose to 95 for six but then we lost two more wickets. That was when I went into bat alongside Petty Officer Patsy Mullins. We struggled through to 121 without losing another wicket. Patsy scored 20 not out and I was 15 not out. We had won by two wickets. That day was the finest I ever experienced in my sporting life. Our captain came over and shook me warmly by the hand. I was applauded off the field as a batsman. The only thing that spoilt it was the reaction of the captain of the first XI who stated: 'The whole idea of the game nauseated me. Nothing can be read into it.' He never came over to shake my hand but MacDonald and Ellis did. The highlight for me was when we got back to *HMS Glasgow*. Just as we got on board it was announced over the Tannoy: 'Cricket result - *HMS Glasgow* first XI 120 all out - Stoker Tinsley five for 25. *HMS Glasgow* second XI 121 for eight. *HMS Glasgow* second XI won by two wickets.' As I got back to the stokers' mess (there were 90 stokers on *HMS Glasgow*) I was applauded all the way to my locker. Ginger Greenwood started shouting 'Speech, speech'. All the stokers knew the first XI was made up entirely of officers and to have Stoker Tinsley beat them was a fantastic tonic for everyone. From that day on I was the opening

bowler for the first XI! We played at some magnificent venues and I enjoyed every minute. I never played in one match where I took less than four wickets. I was the only "other ranks" in the team. Life aboard *HMS Glasgow* was good. I was also playing in the Rugby Union side (if the game didn't clash with cricket) and in the *Stokers' Cutter* Rowing team that won first prize in the *Trincomalee Regatta* of 1947.

I was still writing regularly to Margaret and receiving a good supply back. Letters from mother and father were few and far between but I was in good spirits and hoped I would be sent home soon. After 21 months abroad I, along with 55 others, was entitled to ten days leave. Around India there were several leave camps which had been set up for Forces personnel and I was eventually sent to one about 30 miles inland from Calcutta. I met quite a few Royal Indian Navy personnel there along with men from the Army, Royal Air Force and Royal Navy. It was a very happy camp. There were snooker tables, football and rugby pitches but no cricket pitch. We decided to hold football and snooker tournaments. By then, even though I was desperate to get back to my family and Margaret, I was also enjoying the life of a full-time sportsman. I was developing a strong desire to sign on and make the Royal Navy my career. Sadly my leave was cut short from ten days to seven. *HMS Glasgow* had been summoned to quell some problems in the Persian Gulf. By the time we got there most of the problems had been resolved. The Anglo-American Company operating in Bahrain,

however, requested that *HMS Glasgow* should stay anchored alongside for a few days as a show of strength. This we did and no further problems arose. Then, at long last, the news we were waiting for - *HMS Glasgow* was to return to its home port of Portsmouth.

Was I pleased to be able to write to my mother and father and tell them I was coming home. And I wrote about ten pages to Margaret telling her the great day had finally arrived and within about 28 days we would be re-united. I was elated - God life was good! About three days into the Mediterranean having already chartered the Red Sea and the Suez Canal we received a large batch of letters. There were two from mother and dad. The first asked when I expected to come home. The second stated that they had received my letter with the good news and had decided to take a holiday in Southsea at the same time I was due home so they could be there as our ship docked. Was I delighted! We were used to receiving letters in batches and opened them according to their postmarks so they were in the order they were sent. There were three from Margaret in that particular batch. I read them in date order and the first two were the usual sort of loving letter in which she assured me of her love and how much she was looking forward to my return. Then I opened the third letter. What a shock! Margaret had just received my letter bearing the good news of my home-coming. She usually started her letters with 'My beloved Roy'. This one began 'Dear Roy....' In it she explained how very hard it had

been waiting all that time for me to return home and absence does not always make the heart grow fonder. She had met a young man who had been excused from going into the Forces on medical grounds and played saxophone with a local dance orchestra. When she went to night school to learn Italian he had given her a lift home on his motorbike. Their platonic friendship had materialised into love and although she didn't wish to hurt me, especially as I was now homeward bound, she was sorry to tell me our courtship was over and she was going to become engaged to her new love. I had to read the letter over again. I couldn't believe it. I was absolutely devastated. Ginger Greenwood had seen my face change since reading the letter. 'What's wrong Tins?' he enquired. I just handed him the letter and never said a word. He read it through, put his arm round my shoulder and said: 'You're better off without her Tins - but listen don't do anything drastic. No jumping over the side of the ship or anything like that.' Life was one big joke for Ginger. He could see I was down in the dumps so he was trying to cheer me up. Over the next few days he and Ginger Bloor followed me everywhere. It was now the biggest joke on the ship as far as they were concerned. If I just leant on the rail on the upper deck they would rush up, grab me and say 'Don't do it Tins - don't do it. Nobody's worth killing yourself for.' 'I am not killing myself you stupid bastards. I'm just taking in the evening air,' I retorted. We would eventually go into the stokers' mess and Ginger Bloor would announce in a loud voice: 'When you have all unlashed your

hammocks - all rope to me - immediately. Tins has a suicide wish and we don't want him picking up any ropes.' They teased me constantly - it was brilliantly done and by the time we got to Gibraltar, Margaret was nearly out of my mind. Ginger Bloor, Ginger Greenwood and I went ashore in Gibraltar to search for suitable presents to take home.

Aboard *HMS Glasgow* we had one of the most miserable stoker Petty Officers I had ever met. I never saw him smile once. We were walking down a narrow street in Gibraltar when I saw this particular Petty Officer coming towards us with two of his mates. When they were about a yard away, Ginger Greenwood stopped right in front of them and said, in his loudest voice: 'Look Tins - chief is here now. Tell him to his face... I don't like this talking behind peoples' backs. If you feel he is a miserable bastard - tell him. He's here now - tell him! I nearly died. 'Tell him what? I said nowt chief - honest.' Ginger was going to keep it going at all costs. 'Tins has been through a lot recently chief an' you know me - I cannot stand all this talking behind peoples' backs. So I thought he should tell you to your face.' The chief looked at Greenwood, looked at me and then burst out laughing. He then said: 'Piss off Greenwood, you two faced pillock.'

a

b

c

d

e

f

g

h

i

j

Photograph Captions

A) Roy and Don on front step with Cousin Audrey (1936).

B) Gary, Steven and Carol (1963).

C) The three brothers Roy, Don and Dave.

D) Tommy and Roy near Lake Lucerne.

E) Cricketing Days.

F) Rugby League days.

G) Roy and Shirley on Steven's Wedding Day.

H) Shirley and Chris.

I) Home on Leave (1947).

J) Roy and Shirley at a friends Wedding (1989).

K) Eldest son - Gary and wife Sandra.

L) Son No.2 and wife - Steven and Debbie.

M) Daughter Carol and husband Steven.

N) Roy and Shirley - overweight - but happy!

O) The Tinsley Clan - females.

P) Roy the happy Compositor (Huddersfield Examiner 1957).

Q) Greenhead Park during Printers strike - 1959/60.

R) With 'best man' Gordon, on our Wedding Day.

S) Family party.

T) This is how I used to dress to go on the beach!

U) Carol, Chris, Shirley and mother.

V) Honeymoon photograph 1953.

W) Roy on Tinsley-Robor golf day (1986).

X) The day before I joined the Royal Navy (1944).

k

1

n

o

p

q

r

s

t

u

v

w

x

— CHAPTER 8 —

HOME AT LAST

It was a tumultuous welcome. Thousands lined the jetty to welcome us home and British Movietone News was there to record the historic event of our heroes returning from the Far East. And I had only five minutes to enjoy it! We docked at 3.55pm and I was due on watch in the boiler room at 4pm. I went down to relieve Stoker Hoton who shot up on deck to see that splendid sight. I only had the 'dog-watch' of two hours to do though and hopefully by the time I finished at 6pm, mother, father and young brother David would be on board and down in the stokers' mess waiting to greet me.

Sure enough as soon as I came off watch I went straight to the stokers' mess - covered in sweat. I immediately saw my dad - rushed up to him and threw my arms around him and then did the same to my mother and David. I did apologise for being soaked in sweat and went to the bathroom saying I

would rejoin them in about 15 minutes. The Navy was marvellous for every relative and friend of the ships' company were invited aboard. Food and drinks were plentiful - it was a magnificent day. Dad obviously felt for me when he explained how he had gone to see Margaret about my homecoming and she had told him we were finished. Thankfully, with the help of Ginger Greenwood, I was over it by then. We were allowed shore leave with no restrictions. Mother and dad took me to their boarding house and we were very close for the next three days. They then returned home and I assured them I would be with them again in four days time. We had drawn lots aboard ship. The starboard watch would go home immediately with their loved ones for four days leave and the port watch would stay back. Then the port watch would have their full 15 days leave and when we returned the starboard watch would take their remaining 11 days. Everyone seemed happy with that arrangement. I went home laden with presents for mother, father, Donald and David - some collected over the last two and a half years. Mother received most of those originally earmarked for Margaret. When I arrived at Huddersfield station Donald was there to meet me. I couldn't believe it - the 14-year-old who had bid me farewell was now a 17-year-old man.

After I had been home about five days I felt I should contact Margaret. There were no telephones in the houses those days so I had to take three buses to reach her home. Her father invited me in and both her parents welcomed me warmly. When

she shook my hand, Margaret's mother commented: 'Hello Roy - you look very well.' Her dad then said: 'She did very well for the first two years Roy but for a young lass it's a long time to wait.' 'Where is she?' I asked. 'Oh sorry - she's in the bath lad. She'll be down in a minute.' About ten minutes later she came into the room, looked straight at me and said, 'Hello'. She went first to her father and asked him for a cigarette. She lit it and then asked, 'How are you?' 'Not bad,' I replied. 'Can I see you Margaret - privately - now?' She said something about having just had a bath and not wanting to go outside. I replied I had been waiting for two and a half years to.see her and so asked her to put on her coat. Outside I took her by the hand and led her to a passage we had once used regularly as a "snogging centre". Her home was in a row of terraced houses which had passages between them at regular intervals. My first words were 'Is it all over then?' She said 'Yes'. I then put my arms around her, kissed her and said: 'I don't see why I can't kiss my girlfriend of three and a half years standing.' It was a friendly kiss. She didn't draw away and over the next half hour I kissed her a few more times and we talked and talked and talked. 'If only you had come home three months earlier,' she said. 'Things would be so different.' In my usual cocky way I replied that the timing was out of my hands for it was the Admiralty who decided when I should come home. We seemed to be getting a little warmer towards each other and I asked if there was any chance of us trying again. She said she would like a little more time to think it through.

'Meet me the day after tomorrow outside Heywoods and give me your decision then,' I said. Surprisingly she said 'Yes'.

When we met again she said, 'Give me just a little more time, Roy, please. You are definitely winning at the moment but please give me a couple more days.' What an arrogant, cocky bugger I was, for I replied: 'No Margaret, no more time. I want a decision now - me or him.' She was not prepared to make up her mind there and then and we parted. About a month later I was on leave again and received a letter from her saying she had a lot of photographs I had sent her over the last two and a half years. If everything was finished between us she wanted to give them back to me - and I could return to her all those she had sent me. She suggested we could meet and exchange photographs outside Heywoods. I will never know if Margaret wanted to make a fresh start or just exchange photographs. I did meet her, exchanged photographs and never met or spoke to her again.

— CHAPTER 9 —

DEMOB TIME

I met up with my old mate Gordon Brahney when I was on leave. He was a printer and had been called up during the war to serve down the mines. They were officially known as 'Bevin Boys'. We had corresponded regularly. His girlfriend at that time, Maria, was a close friend of Margaret's and during my first year away they had all gone out in a threesome. Gordon and I teamed up with some other old pals, Alec, Arthur and Syd - all ex Navy. We had some great boozy times together and we seemed to share a similar attitude - enjoy yourself and don't become too seriously involved with anyone. Marriage was definitely taboo.

Back at *HMS Glasgow* we were told the ship was paying off and only a skeleton crew was staying aboard. She was to be based in Pompey, (Portsmouth) for the forseeable future. We were sent to Pompey Barracks to await

demob. When I reported to Pompey Barracks I immediately bumped into Mac and Gary, my old mates from *HMS Bushwood* days. They had been shipped back home about a month before me. I certainly had no regrets about volunteering for *HMS Glasgow* and leaving them back in Ceylon. We had a marvellous reunion and were virtually inseparable until our eventual demob. Come demob day we promised to correspond and keep in touch for the rest of our lives - we were such close friends. Mac and I did so until his death in 1988. Gary went back to Manchester and wrote one letter to which I replied. About three months later I decided to write again but it was sent back marked 'unknown at this address'. I never did learn where Gary eventually finished up - I guessed he may have gone to Australia. He was a very talented lad.

Another memory of demob has stayed with me for the rest of my life. I had just heard I would be demobbed within four weeks and was talking to another mate, Stoker Swann. I was flat broke and asked if I could borrow half-a-crown (2s.6d). He said he was being demobbed that day and we wouldn't see each other again. I promised to post it back and he gave me his address. I genuinely lost that address and all I know was he came from the West Country somewhere. If I could only trace him and settle the debt (it must be worth £20 now with interest) - it would relieve my conscience after all these years. When I was demobbed a wide boy (a spiv) agreed to purchase all my kit - hammock, kit bag and uniform - for £4. I agreed he

could have it all except one uniform. I decided to keep that just in case I re-enlisted. I've still got it at home to this day! The Navy paid me a month's pay, 14 days victualling allowance and gave me a free train pass from Portsmouth to Huddersfield.

When I arrived home I had a demob suit, a change of underwear, a pair of shoes, a mac and a few quid (pounds) in my pocket. The family were there to meet me at the station and I had quite a good homecoming. The house did look nice when I stepped inside. Before there had been just linoleum and a few rugs but now they had a new suite and carpet. Everyone in the Forces was paid a gratuity based on their time served. My total was about £40 - a lot of money then! In addition, when I got home I expected I would have £80 in the bank for the Navy had been paying 10s a week into my account for the past two and a half years. I felt like a rich man. Then my mother broke the news to me. They had been through some hard times financially while I was away and they so wanted the house to look good on my return. So they had decided to withdraw the money I had in the bank and bought that new carpet and suite! What could I say? After being away so long and after such a wonderful homecoming there was little left to say than, 'It's okay mother'. I was sure that if I offered her my victualling allowance of about £6 she would refuse it. But no - she took it! In hindsight I could see the reasons. Dad never did have a large wage and mother now had three big sons as well as dad to feed and probably never had a 'meg' (penny) over each week. I may sound

bitter, but I was not really. Although we were very poor, there was love in the house and mother was not as bad as she may have sounded.

After a couple of weeks at home I felt it was time to visit Mr Green at Swindlehurst and Nicholson to see if I could get my job back. In the 1940s a compositor had to do a seven year apprenticeship and couldn't obtain a full union card until that was complete. I had done three and a half years prior to my call-up and my years in the Navy only counted for one year. I therefore had to do a further two and a half years before gaining my union card. Mr Green, however, received a substantial reimbursement under an agreement that, if an apprenticeship had been interrupted by service in the Forces, the government would pay half until the apprenticeship was completed. It seemed like a very good deal - for Mr Green. Yet he said the best wage he could offer would be £3 10s a week, the union rate at the time being £5 a week. So he was still paying me the apprentice rate and drawing half from the Government. There was nothing I could do. My father was particularly keen for me to finish the apprenticeship and although I was offered a shoe salesman's job at Stead and Simpson for £5 a week he talked me into staying. I might have been receiving only a pittance in wages but I was good at my job and within six months I was helping the foreman (Alf Woolley) to run the company. Mother was finding things hard financially and out of my £3 10s I gave her £2 a week. I never had a meg! I soon used up

my war gratuity and what with going out with my mates and dating a girl occasionally, money was something I definitely did not have. A school pal of mine managed to get me a job in an iron foundry on Saturdays for 10s a shift. That was a very big help. On three occasions I asked Mr Green for a rise but he said he couldn't manage it. My wage did eventually creep up first to £4 10s and, during my last year, it even hit a magical figure of £6. At last the day came when, after nine and a half years in the trade, I finally made it as a fully apprentice-trained compositor. I was over 23-years-old by then. Mr Green called me into his office during the last week of my apprenticeship and told me I would begin receiving the full printer's wage of £7 a week. I told him I was worth considerably more than that and expected him to reward me accordingly, especially for my loyalty. Again he said he could not afford any more.

One of my best mates, Syd Gronow, worked for The *"Huddersfield Examiner"* as a compositor (linotype operator). His wage was £9 a week but he had to work every other Saturday. He told me someone was about to retire and asked me if I would be interested. I agreed and he put my name down. Within a couple of months I received a letter inviting me for an interview. I met with the foreman, Tom Cockin, at 5.30pm one evening. We got on very well and he offered me the job at £9. I was elated. The following day I went to see Mr Green and handed in my notice. He went raving mad! He started pounding me in the chest with

the flat of his hand saying: 'We have great plans for you here. You cannot leave. You could have a job here for life. Don't be stupid. That is the end of the matter - you cannot leave.' When I eventually could speak I said I had given my word to the foreman at the *Huddersfield Examiner* and was going. 'How much are they paying you?' he demanded. 'Nine pounds a week.' 'Right, I'll pay £9 a week. Now go and give back-word.' Mr Green went down in my estimation a lot that day. If he had offered me a little more a month earlier I would have stayed. Now he was offering me a £2 a week rise! I liked my job there but I had given my word, so told Mr Green I was leaving. He never spoke to me for the next two weeks - never even glanced at me. If he wanted me to do a particular job he would give details to Alfred Woolley or Stanley Swift (another good lifetime friend). When it came to within one hour of me leaving I decided to go to Mr Green's office. I knocked on the door and he said 'Come in'. I went over to his desk and said, 'Are we really going to part like this Mr Green? You gave me my chance in printing and we are now at loggerheads. I don't really like leaving like this' and held out my hand. He looked up, smiled and took my hand. 'You're right Roy - the very best of luck. Sorry for accepting it like I have but I did have big plans for you.' We parted friends and he sent me an excellent reference in case it was ever required.

When I returned home from the Navy I tried to relaunch my cricketing career. Unfortunately the clubs I approached had strong cliques and, with my

lack of funds, I was one of the worst turned-out players on practice night. With one club I often bowled out those in the first team but was never selected. One evening I was bowling in the nets when two members of the club committee came over to watch. One remarked: 'This lad can bowl a bit - just look.' I distinctly heard the other man reply, 'He bowls off the wrong foot - he'll never get any wickets.'

The move to The *"Huddersfield Examiner"* proved to be a happy one not just for the work but because they also had a cricket team! I played for them for 20 years, continuing to do so even when I was no longer employed by them. I enjoyed life to the full during my first years there. Alec, Gordon, Arthur, Syd and I did the rounds of pubs, dance halls, and dating girls (so long as they weren't very serious).

— CHAPTER 10—

BRAHNEY & TINSLEY - PRINTERS

I was enjoying work at The *Huddersfield Examiner* and I had some excellent mates there. Gordon Brahney, an old school friend, had joined me in the composing room. One day Gordon was setting an advertisement for a printing business that was up for sale in Golcar, Huddersfield - price £700. He immediately brought it over to me. 'Look at this,' he said. 'Fancy going in with me?' Now I had only just got back on my feet financially and for me £350 for a half share was impossible. Gordon said he could raise £500 and we could ask the bank for a £200 loan. I agreed to go and see the firm with him and we called that very evening after work. It was situated in a lovely old building. Inside we found three hand-fed machines and a hand-rotary guillotine. Originally it had been known as Johnny Moorhouse Printers but was now called Arthur Cook's. It seemed to have quite a good order book. There was only one

problem. Arthur Cook didn't have a clue that the firm was up for sale. It seemed Johnny Moorhouse, the founder, was very ill and had asked Arthur Cook to look after it for him until he got better. Mr Cook had run it for 19 months and had never passed a penny over to Mr Moorhouse, so Mr Moorhouse had asked his son-in-law to sell the business. It was a bit embarrassing. Gordon left the negotiating to me and we bought the actual business for £600 plus 15s a week for use of the building. It would have cost us £300 to buy the property in 1951. In 1990 it changed hands for £115,000! Gordon also left me to do all the talking at the bank and I was able to negotiate a £275 loan.

Then we had to hand in our notices at *"The Examiner"*. That was not easy to do for the company had a policy that anyone who resigned would never be considered for a position with them again. I had made quite an impression there. My main job on Saturday afternoon was to compile the football results by hand into a classified results service and also a league table. I managed the entire job on my own. On the other shift it took three men! And we were always the fastest to bed the forme to press. I gave my notice to the foreman, George Chadwick, and he was staggered. However he took it a lot better than Mr Green had done and added a rider that if it didn't work out he would do his very best to secure my job back for me.

The step into the great unknown as a master printer was a bit of a disaster. It was great being

my own boss but the business just could not support the two of us compared with the salary we had received at *"The Examiner"*. We grafted and worked very hard but we were only drawing about £4 a week and I gave my mother half of that. It seemed I was getting into as much of a financial mess as I was before I joined the *"The Examiner"*.

Arthur, Alec, Syd and I played a lot of rugby. Syd's dad had been a legend with Huddersfield Rugby League Club and his two brothers also played. I joined a local club called Crosland Moor. We were all quite good at the game and Syd was already playing regularly for the great Huddersfield Team Second XIII. He had also played for the England Amateur Team. I remember turning out in a match against Rastrick and scoring a couple of tries and kicking four goals and having quite a good game. Our coach said "A Scout" had asked for my address after the game and he passed it on. Within a week I received a card from Huddersfield Rugby League Club inviting me for trials. I played against Keighley, Hull and Halifax and had reasonable games. The problem in those days was that there was no substitutes and I must have been "stand-by" player for about 10 games. Everyone turned up so I didn't play. It was causing a problem as well. At this time I thought I had a chance of getting my job back at the *"Examiner"* and I would have to work every other Saturday. Taking stock of the whole situation I don't feel I could have ever been good enough to get in the first team. My mate Syd thought the same and we

gave up our chances of becoming Rugby League stars and continued playing amateur with Crosland Moor.

One day we were playing in a cup match at Crosland Moor. The landlord at *"The Sands House"* allowed us to use their best room for changing as he also had a sink and hot water in there. We patronised the pub on all match days and twice a week on training nights so his return from us was quite good. On rugby nights anyone else calling at the pub had to use the tap room until we had finished in the best room. After one match we went into the tap room and saw four girls playing dominoes. I immediately fancied one and asked a mate of mine (Harry Cutler) who had come to watch the game to join me. We sidled over and I immediately moved up to the one I fancied. She had fabulous red hair. If Shirley thought I was a cheeky, cocky sod, she still seemed interested in me. So Harry and I moved in on the domino game. I partnered her and Harry joined up with her mate, Sylvia. For the first time in several years I had met someone who really appealed to me. Harry and I stayed quite late as we were celebrating a victory but the girls had to leave earlier. Sylvia and Shirley said farewell, caught the bus and were gone. I hadn't taken her address and didn't know where she worked. I had no way of finding her again and decided I was a silly sod as I had really liked her. The following weekend we all went to the Town Hall for the local Saturday night dance and the first person I saw when we entered was Shirley. She was dancing with Sylvia, spotted

me and smiled. As they finished the dance I moved over and started talking. We got on so well I saw her home and arranged to take her to the pictures the following evening. We met twice a week for a while and believed we had started a good relationship. She introduced me to her parents and her father gave me quite a lot of printing. He was Secretary of a local Liberal Club.

I suppose Shirley thought I was quite a catch in those days. I was 24-years-old, smart and presentable and joint managing director of my own business. Truth be known I was struggling to make ends meet.

Gordon and I discussed the whole business at great length and decided that, within a month, it would be best to sell up and find employment again in the printing trade. It was a rather traumatic time. Gordon's mother, however, was dead against him pulling out. She said she would back him for 12 months by using her savings. I said it was okay by me. He changed the name to B.T. Printing which rolled off the tongue far better than Brahney and Tinsley! He still has the business to this day.

At that time I was so pre-occupied with leaving the business and my money worries (I left without a penny) that I had not seen Shirley for about three weeks. As Christmas approached I had to find work. I first went to see George Chadwick. He informed me there were no vacancies on *"The Huddersfield Examiner"* at that time but he would

let me know when one became available. I had hit a slack period in the trade and the only place I could get a job was with Lund Humphries in Bradford. I worked from 7.30am until 5.30pm each day with one hour for lunch. The pay wasn't too bad but I had to take three buses to get there and so left home at 6am and didn't get back until 7pm. By then we had moved as a family to a much nicer district in Lower Houses and I enjoyed living there.

Even so it proved to be about the worst Christmas I ever spent at home. The last time I remembered receiving any Christmas gifts was 1937 and never received anything since.

Gordon was seeing Betty who he later married. Alec and Arthur booked into a hotel in Blackpool. My brother Don and I had never really been mates to go out together and anyway he was going steady with Edith who was to become his wife.

Some close family friends, Eve and Frank Coops, had two daughters, Marjorie and Audrey. On their frequent visits my mother and Auntie Eve became set on matchmaking between Audrey and me. Audrey was a nice looking girl and I rather liked her. So when the Coops came to our house one day I asked her out. She accepted and in no time at all we were seeing quite a lot of each other. So much so that Auntie Eve and mother were setting up a wedding date - no kidding! I felt trapped. I liked Audrey but knew I didn't love her and no way could I see us getting married. It called for drastic action. I had to face up to the situation and admit to her I had been blindly allowing us to get

deeper and deeper into this problem.

On the evening when I decided to tell her I felt an absolute cad. Audrey made it very easy for me. She said she thought I hadn't been my usual self the past couple of weeks and understood that might have been on my mind. We parted friends and I felt as though the world had been lifted from my shoulders.

My parents were none too pleased as they thought she would have made me a good wife - and I'm sure they were right - but unfortunately I didn't care enough for Audrey to walk down the aisle with her. I wanted to see Shirley again but without a telephone at home that was difficult to arrange. I did have her works number but wasn't altogether sure whether her employers would let her take a call. It was December 31st and everyone was back at work, we didn't have extended holidays in the 1950s. I plucked up courage and decided to ring. I used a phone in the pub at lunchtime and asked if I could speak to Shirley Brunton. The man who answered muttered about them not being allowed to take personal calls but about five minutes later she came on the phone. 'Hello Shirley - this is Roy. You know - Roy Tinsley. I wondered if you were going anywhere tonight. I know it's short notice but how about it?' She immediately said 'Yes' and we arranged to meet outside Manners Shop in Huddersfield. We had a lovely night with plenty of laughs. I felt so much more at ease with Shirley. She had a similar sense of humour to me. We were to be together for the

next 40 years. We kept up a courtship for about 18 months although when I was at Lund Humphries we saw each other only once a week as I worked such long hours. I told her that if I ever got my job back at *"The Examiner"* I would like to marry her. It was a funny sort of proposal in a way but she accepted. I had to ask her father and mother, of course, and then we became engaged. Just after that I was offered my job back at *"The Examiner"* and readily accepted.

Life was very good! We set September 26th 1953 as the date for the wedding and it was to prove the best day of my life. After our marriage Shirley's parents said we could live with them. That was an especially nice gesture seeing as they had no bathroom and only one tap in the house. We had quite a nice bedroom though. Shirley continued working and with two wages coming in we saved hard for a house of our own. Working at *"The Examiner"* gave me quite an advantage over other people. I used to see the classified advertisements before anyone else. One particular day I spotted: 'Two bedroomed cottage for sale. Inside Toilet, Needs Modernising. £1 a week, (No deposit) or £300 cash.' It gave a telephone number in Golcar. I did a very naughty thing. I put the advert in my drawer so it wouldn't be in the paper for a couple of days and I immediately asked if I could use the phone. They let me and my call was answered by a Mrs Barker, who was somewhat surprised to have someone calling about an advert that hadn't yet appeared in the paper. Shirley and I went to see this empty cottage. It was absolutely dreadful. It

was the second in a row of six of the type known as 'through cottage by light'. In other words it had no back door but did have a window at the back and so wasn't a 'back-to-back'. It had a badly cracked flagged stone floor; an old, old fireplace; a very tiny kitchen; two bedrooms and an inside toilet. We looked around, looked at each other and immediately said 'Yes'. We told Mrs Barker that we would like to spend quite a lot of time modernising it so she agreed to hold up the rent payment for a month.

We went to that house every night after work and received a terrific amount of help from my dad. He was great. He got a pal from work who helped him lay a complete new floor. We decorated from top to bottom. It had very old beams in the ceiling of the living room and we hard-boarded them over! Can you imagine that? They were the best feature in the house and we covered them up. After about nine weeks it was finished. We went to a furnisher in Huddersfield called Roebucks and purchased a three-piece suite, a carpet and a few other necessities. Shirley's mother and father had bought us a bedroom suite and we were ready to move in. It was our intention for Shirley to continue working for another two or three years so we could get some money in the bank. That just didn't work out but neither of us had any regrets. Shirley became pregnant and Gary came upon the scene in August 1955. Shirley's pregnancy went quite well apart from her blood pressure being slightly higher than normal. We went to see our doctor very late in

her pregnancy and he thought it would be a good idea for her to go into the maternity home as the birth was fairly imminent. He believed they might have to induce the birth. She went in the following morning and I visited her that same evening. When I arrived the sister said I couldn't go in just yet. When I asked why she said the doctor was still with Shirley. Eventually I was allowed in and Shirley gave me the good news that we were the parents of a beautiful baby boy. It was difficult to explain how I felt. It was a marvellous feeling. For some reason the baby had been taken away from Shirley without any explanation so our joy was tinged by a sort of regret - even anxiety. I went and asked the sister where my baby was and if there was a problem. She took me to a ward and showed me my son. He seemed fine so I went back to Shirley to let her know everything was okay.

It was great breaking the news to Shirley's mum and dad and to my parents. I walked around with a permanent smile on my face for the next few weeks. We had settled down well in our new house with our new baby and it was nice struggling to get a few things together. I was really enjoying working at *"The Examiner"* but cash wise we never had anything to spare. Shirley took some mending in to do at home and I occasionally helped my mate Gordon at the print shop for the odd 10 bob (10s). I was also very ambitious but there was no way I would ever get any promotion at work as it was only given on 'years of service' and there were quite a lot of

people in front of me in that department. I started looking through the papers to see if there were any jobs going that would give me a little extra money.

After a year in our small cottage I saw a position that might suffice. David Brown's (the Gear People) wanted a man in their printing department. My wage at The Examiner was £10 a week and they were offering £48 a month. I applied for the job and was interviewed by one of the most curt people I could ever imagine - a right miserable bugger and he was the man in charge! He must have been suitably impressed and offered me the job. I said I would give my decision the next day. I discussed it at great length with Shirley, because she was always so supportive, and we decided I should take the job. When I saw George Chadwick and handed in my notice he told me very clearly that I was making a great mistake. He then took me to see the manager, Mr Lindley, who also gave me quite a ticking off. He told me he had made a very big gesture in allowing me to come back and now I was doing this - he wasn't at all pleased. We did, however, separate on good terms and I still have many friends there and, of course, continued to play cricket for The Examiner.

My new job was fine, but the first weeks were hell for I had to wait to the month end to get the wage. I think by the time I got it most of it was owed. We managed okay however. The job was quite comfortable and I had no problem with it at all. But oh that miserable manager - he was

something else. We all had to call him Mr Hirst and not use his first name, Doug. Besides Mr Hirst and I there was another compositor (Donald), and eight women who had various duties like collating, feeding the machines etc. They were quite a happy bunch of lasses and we had our fair share of laughs, usually at the expense of Mr Hirst but without his knowledge of course. By then I was active in *The Typographical Association* print union and was on the branch committee. The old *Branch Secretary*, Herbert Killingbeck, was about to retire and he asked me if I would like to take his place at the week-long Union Conference to be held in Belfast (there were no problems in Northern Ireland in 1956). Another pal of mine, William White who worked at *The Examiner* was also chosen to go.

I was appointed Branch Secretary (Designate) and went off for a very interesting conference leaving Shirley at home with Gary. William and I teamed up with four delegates from the Leeds Branch with whom we got on very well. On the second night in Belfast, William said with bravado to the waitress serving our table, 'What time do you finish?' She immediately responded '7.30 - see you in the bar.' We laughed loudly and to be honest William was pushed into keeping that 7.30 rendezvous even if just to see if she would be there. At 7.25 he made his way to the bar. Ten minutes later he was back, doubled up with laughter, for she was there and had asked if he could supply two more mates! He implored me to go and to be honest I did consider it for a minute

or two but I refused. Two of the other lads from Leeds made up the six-some. William and I were sharing a twin-bedded room and I don't think he got back before 4am all that week. It turned out to be one of the wisest decisions I ever made. The day we left Belfast I don't think I had seen three girls so broken up, they cried uncontrollably. They told Walter they were all single and looked forward to the men returning for a prolonged holiday. He did say they had made sure not to give their addresses to the girls and they hadn't seemed worried about that. I had written to Shirley a few times and was pleased to get on the plane (which was my first ever flight) and go home. Three weeks later William White turned up at work three hours late and ash white. He came up to me and explained that he and his wife had had an almighty row. The day before a letter arrived from Belfast and she had opened it. To put it mildly it had been very explicit about his affair during the Conference. He rang the two lads in Leeds - they had received similar letters and one had been that bad his wife had temporarily left him! The girls had simply copied their addresses from the Hotel Guest register and wrote thinking the men were single. - Am I glad I declined the offer.

— CHAPTER 11—

MOVING ABOVE THE BREADLINE...

Step by step we moved above the breadline. The work at David Brown's was quite interesting. I also had the Union Secretary's job which gave me a little more money. As the Union Secretary I met a lot of the master printers and I developed quite a good relationship with many of them. So much so that when the foreman at Alfred Jubb and Son (Colour Printers) retired the Managing Director offered me the job. He offered me £12 a week compared with about £11.15s at David Brown's. It was a step up the ladder but it wasn't worth taking on all the extra responsibility for just 5s extra a week. My job at David Brown's was very secure and it was a staff appointment which meant I received my wage even when off sick.

There was no secret that I wanted the job at Alfred Jubb's but they had to come up with some more money. After very lengthy

negotiations the Managing Director agreed to pay me £12 15s. I gave my notice to Doug Hirst who threw a bit of a 'wobbly'. He went home within ten minutes of my announcement. I had to work a month's notice and he never came in again until after I left. On the last day there I decided to ring him at home to say goodbye and ask how he was. He said my leaving had come as a great shock and he added, 'I know I am losing a good man and I don't like to see you go.' That amazed me. I had never known him give a compliment to anyone. We did part friends but only because I had called him.

About ten months or so before that, there were strong rumours that the local council were going to condemn our row of cottages as it was believed they were not fit for human habitation. Our next door neighbours, Maurice and Janet Brook, had spent all their money modernising their house and were horrified at the news. Between us we followed the whole matter through with the council who stated they could only guarantee the houses had about five years before being demolished. We were devastated. Maurice and Janet immediately put their house up for sale and managed to get £425 for it. It really was a lovely cottage and beautifully restored. They acquired a very nice house about a mile away so didn't fare too badly. We had paid about 15 months' rent at £4 a month so had only knocked £60 off the original price. But we had spent all our money on it and felt it was worth at least £450. I raised hell with the council, wrote to the local newspaper and

got a lot of support - but it mattered not.

Just about this time Shirley found she was pregnant again. She had little security in knowing she might lose her home within five years. I went to one of our local councillors and explained the situation. He was very sympathetic and the following day called to see us. He explained that the council were building some new three-bedroomed corporation houses in Leymoor - about a mile away - and he had got permission to say we had been allocated one. Shirley and I went down to see them and were delighted with their location, the good gardens and the standard of construction. It certainly eased the problem of the condemned house. We advertised our cottage at £450 and several people were interested but I was unable to deceive anyone and told prospective buyers about the expected five years life. It scared everyone off. We tried for about six months but with no luck and the new house was about ready. Eventually someone came and made an offer of £300 at £2 a week. We took it. He missed giving us the rent many times but finally repaid us.

Those cottages are still standing! More than 30 years later the one we left exchanged hands at £29,500. We moved into our new house - 94 Sycamore Avenue - in November and we decided that Shirley would have the baby at home. It was a very cold house and in those days there was no central heating. We had no carpets and it was very sparsely furnished. We were given a telephone number to call for the midwife when

Shirley thought the baby was about due. It was in the very early hours of January 2, 1958 that Shirley felt the labour pains and so I got out and walked about a mile to the nearest telephone box - it was bitterly cold and snowing. The midwife arrived about an hour later. I let her in and took her upstairs to see Shirley but I was not allowed in the bedroom. After examining Shirley the midwife announced that it would be quite a long time before the baby would be born and she said she would come back in a few hours - and then left! About two or three hours later Shirley was sure the baby was going to be born any minute! I dashed to the telephone, told the midwife and said I didn't know what to do. She told me to get back home as soon as possible and she would leave immediately. I ran as fast as I could and dashed upstairs. Gary was crying in the other bedroom and Shirley was virtually ready to give birth. Within five minutes the midwife arrived, ran upstairs and ordered me out of the room. She told me to get a big fire going and to take care of Gary. I did just that and within a very short time I heard the cries of son number two - Steven. I hurried upstairs and knocked at the door but the midwife told me to stay where I was and handed me the afterbirth. 'Get rid of that - burn it,' she said quite curtly. 'Can I see my wife and baby?' I asked. 'Burn that first,' she replied. I carried out her instructions to the letter and then shot upstairs and knocked on the door again. This time she let me in. I rushed over to Shirley but there was no baby! 'Where is it?' I asked. 'Where's our baby?' The midwife then opened the airing cupboard - she

had wrapped Steven in a towel and put him on the top shelf above the hot-water cistern. For all the dashing about and traumas it ended as a very happy day and we were now the proud parents of two boys.

About a week later I joined Alfred Jubb's as foreman. When I left David Brown's they paid me my month's wages and a week's holiday pay. Shirley and I were able to pay off everything we owed and even had £24 left. We felt rich. The week after Steven was born I talked Shirley into letting me buy a car. I had seen one at the local garage - a 1934 Austin 10. The garage wanted £30 for it. I offered £25 and they settled for £28. I bought it, called at a local insurance company and insured it for three months for £3. It was already taxed for a couple of months so I was on the road. It will always stay in my memory the day I took it home. It ran like a Swiss watch. It was magnificent. It was the finest and most enjoyable car I had ever known. I parked it outside the house and dashed inside. Shirley was in the back room feeding Steven. Gary was in his playpen. I asked her to go into the front room and look out of the window. She was pleasantly surprised for it looked good. As soon as she had finished feeding Steven we took it for its first long run. We went to Dewsbury which was about 12 miles away. It went so well that on the Sunday we decided to drive the 65 miles to St. Annes. It ran beautifully. I felt there was no holding me now! I was bringing in a decent wage as a foreman plus my earnings as a Union Secretary. I had a new council house, two

fine sons and a car.

There was one problem - the job at Alfred Jubb's was too easy. I could have done it standing on my head and I was getting bored. It took me just four hours to get through a day's work. The company was making good profits but I had the comp room so well organised that none of us there were busy. The job was getting me down - no motivation at all.

One day I found a magazine there called Printing World. Its 'Situations Vacant' column advertised jobs throughout the country. I studied it at great length and decided I would have nothing to lose if I inserted a small advert myself. It included a box number and read something like this:
EXPERIENCED COMPOSING ROOM FOREMAN - AGED 31 seeks rewarding position where his knowledge of the trade will be acknowledged financially and with prospects.

It cost about five bob and I waited expectantly for that edition to appear. Four days after it came out I received about 20 letters all offering me jobs as Comp-Room Overseer or Works Manager. I sifted through them and replied to a couple which seemed quite interesting. The nearest reply came from Burton-on-Trent from a firm called Tresises. They responded quickly to my letter and invited me to visit them. This was arranged for a Saturday. Shirley's mum agreed to care for Gary and Steven so Shirley and I travelled together in *"Jenny"* as we had named our car, after the film

"Genevieve". At the factory we were met by Ken Tresise who was a rather dapper little man with a very nice infectious laugh. There was no one in the works as he showed us around. It was larger than Alfred Jubb's and seemed to be a very busy jobbing printers. He told us the comp-room foreman had just left and he had appointed a new one from his present staff. Now he needed someone rather urgently to 'sort things out'. He offered me £14 a week and a rent-free semi-detached house. Shirley and I looked at each other and agreed that we would go to see it. It was a very old, large house with a lounge, kitchen, dining room, four bedrooms and a bathroom. It was running with damp in every room. It needed a fortune spending on it. The interview went well and Mr Tresise offered me the job. I said it would require a lot of consideration to move all that way for such a small increase in salary. We promised we would discuss it and let him know as soon as possible. When we got back in the car we immediately decided against the house and went off to look around the town. It was very pleasant with some very nice outlying districts.

Back home we discussed it with Shirley's parents. They seemed dead against it at first but eventually her mum said if it was what we wanted we would have her blessing. During the next week I received three more letters imploring me to take the job. Mr Tresise upped the salary to £15 a week, plus the house. If we didn't want the house he would give us an interest free loan of £100 towards a deposit on the house of our choice and

we would pay it back at £1 a week. Shirley and I had another look around the town, a further meeting with Mr Tresise and finally I agreed to take the job. We felt it would be a good idea for me to take lodgings there for a while and return home at the weekends. I could look for a property during the week and Shirley would stay in the corporation house until we found something suitable. My boss at Alfred Jubb's, Mr May, did not take too kindly to me leaving and immediately offered to match the wage I had been offered. In many ways I wished I had taken it. Burton-on-Trent proved a bit of a disaster.

TRESISES PRINTERS - BURTON-ON-TRENT.

My first day there was quite strange. It was only then that I learnt that the office I had been told was mine belonged to the Works Director - Aubrey Ritchins. Until I arrived he did not know that a new comp-room overseer had been appointed! Aubrey Ritchins was an absolute tyrant who didn't want a comp-room foreman for he wanted to run everything. At lunchtime the bindery overseer could see I looked a little non-plussed and introduced himself. He explained that there had been five comp-room foremen in the last two and a half years. Each one had come to the point where he could take no more of Aubrey Ritchins and had left. Ken Tresise had a very difficult problem. He needed a comp-room foreman badly but dared not say too much to Ritchins because he brought in 25 per cent of the Company's turnover from one client. The buyer there was an old school chum of Ritchins and he would deal only with him. Ken

Tresise had tried to get in himself but could never get an order. I decided I would try and work with Aubrey. If not, I would fight him but one thing for certain - he would not make me resign. We did have some terrible arguments, yet I managed to command the respect of all the compositors. With good organisation I kept a constant flow of work going through the comp-room and machine room. Friday afternoons were an absolute God-send. After all the problems at work it was bliss to get into "Jenny" and motor back to Huddersfield to see my wife and kids.

My lodgings were good but I only spent four nights a week there for I never returned to Burton-on-Trent on a Sunday. I preferred to leave Huddersfield at 4.30am on Monday mornings for the long drive back to work. I didn't complain to Shirley about the problems at Tresises and she never complained once about how much we were separated. Each week we wrote at least two letters to each other and we so enjoyed our weekends together, and our £28 car never let me down once!

Every evening, after work, I went searching for a house but for months could find nothing suitable. Then one evening I went to a local pub in Burton-on-Trent with a fellow who stayed in the same lodgings as myself. We often went out together for a drink for we had much in common - he had been a Petty Officer in the Royal Navy and was an excellent guy. That evening we were discussing houses. He too was searching for a home so that he could bring his wife and two kids to be with

him. A chap at the bar said: 'Are you looking for a house?' When I said 'Yes', he told me he was building some three-bedroomed detached houses in Branston, two miles from Burton. These, however, were £2,150 whereas I had been unwilling to consider anything above £900. When I said I couldn't possibly think of paying that much he replied that he would arrange a 95 per cent mortgage. He took me down to the site which I thought was marvellous. I was even more taken, by the plans he showed me - besides the bedrooms, each house was to have a lounge/dining area, kitchen, boxroom and bathroom plus a large garden. He said they would be ready in three months. I mentioned it to Ken Tresise the next day. He said he would lend me the five per cent deposit and pay the solicitor's fee. I couldn't wait to get home that weekend to tell Shirley. I drove all the way back to Branston the next day so that Shirley could see the site. As I was proudly showing her around the plot a goods train appeared about 200 yards away! All 40 trucks marked ESSO clanked past so very slowly. 'Oh Roy - what have you done?' Shirley cried. 'We're right beside a railway line. Think of the kids!' All my enthusiasm drained away for a while. But as we looked around the area we were particularly impressed by the village - and we were fed-up with being apart. So we decided to go ahead. I went down to the site every day and badgered the builders into improving on that three months. They did eventually complete it within 12 weeks. Before we moved in, I took Shirley to see the house again. Complete with even the walls colour-

washed it looked magnificent. Shirley was over the moon. It was past all our expectations. Just a few more small jobs to do and we could move in about 3-4 weeks.

Unfortunately, my job at Tresises was proving to be a pain. I was constantly battling with Aubrey Ritchins and he seemed determined to get me out. Having just got the house and owing the company £120 there was no way I was going to give in to him and I carried on as best I could. Then it happened - at the worst time. The Printers' Union called a strike. We had a 100 per cent union shop at Tresises and everyone had to come out - and that included me. Most people expected it to go on for a week or two at the most. It continued for seven weeks! I left my lodgings and moved back to the corporation house in Huddersfield to stay with Shirley and the kids and took whatever part-time work I could get. We received just £5 in strike pay each week - we had nothing.

After two weeks I received a letter from Ken Tresise. He explained that they were using the idle period to design a new comp-room and needed my advice. I would even get paid for it - without, it seemed, breaking the strike. So I went. At the factory the dozen or so men on the picket line implored me not to go in. I explained to them that Ken Tresise only wanted my advice - and I needed the money. Eventually I did go in after promising them I would not work on the production side. I felt confident that Ken Tresise had no one running the machines, but when I got inside I realised he

had. One print machine was being operated by a Company Representative and the other by 'scab' labour. They had brought me in by pretence for they had no compositor to keep the machines running all the time. Aubrey Ritchins was working the guillotine and they were managing to complete a few jobs. I was now in an invidious position. Both the management and the fellows in the Trade Union were testing my loyalty. I certainly did not want to lose my union card for, if things didn't work out at Tresises, I would need it when searching for a new job. I was also very annoyed with the management for bringing me in under false pretences. They offered me £2 a week over my basic rate if I would start comping. The money would have been most welcome but I never gave it a thought. After checking with Mr. Tresise that my job would still be there when the strike ended, I then explained that I couldn't do it. He assured me he understood my predicament and my reluctance to go through the picket line every day. I would never have done that anyway! As I left the factory the pickets asked me what I was going to do. I explained that the Company had expected me to do all the comping and so keep the firm going. When I said I had refused and that I was going back to Huddersfield they let out a cheer. Most of them shook hands with me before I returned home. The problem was - Shirley and I didn't know where the next penny would come from. I found a job as a dye-house labourer. I hated it - but they did give me two weeks work at £7 a week. A friend of mine then heard of my plight and found me a job as a 'teazer' in a

weaving mill. That was also dreadful. For two weeks I came home every night covered in flea bites - all for £6 a week.

The Printing Union - *The National Graphical Association* - eventually called in Lord Birkett as an arbiter and after a week's hard negotiations the strike was over. We had demanded a seven per cent increase compared with the bosses' offer of three per cent. We went back for four and a half per cent. We had been on strike for seven weeks and got about 15s extra a week (75p). What a waste of time! I had, however, kept my integrity and I'm sure that at the end of the day, Mr Tresise respected me.

— CHAPTER 12—

MOVING IN

The day finally arrived when we could move into our new house at Branston. It was gorgeous. We loved it. The kids soon settled in and were very happy. Within months Shirley and I were delighted to find we were expecting another child. This time we hoped it might be a girl. To bring in a little extra money we did some outwork for Tresises. We simply had to fold serviettes and stack them in 50s. We got 25p for a box of 5,000. Whenever possible I would take home a box and Shirley and I would sit watching our 14 inch black and white television folding pub serviettes. Then all of a sudden that little bit of revenue dried up. Aubrey took on the job of giving out that work and actually did ten boxes a week himself! At work he was beginning to get through to me and my days there were becoming a nightmare. I began to hate the job and when Tresises advertised for a salesman I applied. Ken Tresise, however, said he was looking for someone with experience and ruled me out. (Years later he told me he had made

a big mistake not giving me that job!) When Shirley was about five months pregnant I had had enough. I turned to my old friend *"The Printing World"* and noticed an advert placed by a company called Partridge Printers in Leeds who wanted a comp-foreman. I knew how to write a good application and my credentials were impressive so I applied for the job. Within a week I was invited to go for an interview with Mr Haydon Scott and Mr Tommy Lambert. We went as a family to Leeds in "Jenny" on a Saturday morning. I had intended to leave Shirley and the kids with her mother but we got lost and I had to go straight to the interview, arriving with just five minutes to spare. I was first met by Haydon Scott who elaborated on the success of the firm and how they were looking for a good man to ensure the efficient running of the comp-room. He then invited Tommy Lambert to join us and I was immediately impressed - especially by his 'Persil white' overall. Tommy helped me to relax and it was a good interview and so began my friendship with him which was to last for the next 30 years. After the interview he came out with me and was astonished to find Shirley and the kids waiting there. He introduced himself to Shirley and immediately impressed her as a very nice, friendly person. He explained to us that they had had a very big response to the advert and had to interview several more candidates. Even so they would let me know their decision within a week. I had a feel for the place immediately and hoped I would be successful and, of course, there was the wage - £18 a week! They also assisted with travelling expenses.

Come the following Saturday morning I received a letter saying I had been selected for the job and would I telephone them and let them know if I wanted to accept it. I desperately wanted to take it, but could I really move my family once more? There we were in such a beautiful detached house in a lovely area and if I accepted the job we wouldn't have a home to move to in Leeds and hardly any money. Shirley understood that I was finding the situation at Tresises intolerable and after a weekend talking it over we decided to take the new job. Shirley's mum and dad were again so helpful and said we could live with them until we found a home of our own. That would give us time to go house-hunting and I still had to give a month's notice at Tresises so had four weekends to look for something. The day I gave my notice to leave Tresises was particularly pleasing to me. Although it was not my intention to start casting aspersions at Aubrey Ritchins I did say to Ken Tresise that 'he had won' and there was no way I could continue working in such an atmosphere. He was amazed and stated: 'You can't leave - you owe me £120. How are you going to pay it back?' 'At the moment I don't know - but I will,' I assured him. He was very kind after that and even offered to forget the loan if I agreed to stay. My mind was made up, however, and I just wanted to get away as soon as possible.

Every weekend, Shirley and I went house-hunting but it was difficult to find something when we had no deposit and already lived in a very nice house. Eventually an estate agent in Leeds told us about a

house in Farsley which had been on the market for a long time and the owners were desperate to sell it. We visited the village of Farsley for the first time in April 1960 and liked it immediately, what with its excellent schools, nice shopping centre and lots of open countryside. As we were searching for 55, Newlands we spotted a building site on Springbank where a Mr Scott was constructing some bungalows and three-bedroomed semi-detached houses. We chatted and even looked around one of the houses but his asking price was £1,950 and even with a 95 per cent mortgage we couldn't consider it, with the outstanding loan from Mr Tresise. By a strange coincidence my Daughter Carol and her husband Steven bought the very house we inspected 33 years later and it is now worth £80,000. We did find 55 Newlands. It overlooked a cricket ground and park and there was a school at the end of the road. The house had a flat-roof, three bedrooms, kitchen, a toilet and bathroom combined on the ground floor and a living room. There was a small garden at the front and an even smaller one at the back. After seeing so many poor properties that one seemed okay. The asking price was £1,250 and the owner, Mr Rawlinson, wouldn't take less. I explained I had a good job but no savings although I was sure the bank would help me. We agreed to take the house if he said I had paid him £50 deposit, when in fact I had given him nothing. We both felt quite good about finally deciding on a place and to make matters better the Rawlinsons wanted to move out very quickly.

Soon after we got back to Burton-on-Trent, a young man knocked at the door and asked if he could look around our house. He was considering buying a house on the estate and ours was still the only one that had been completed. We told him we were leaving and would be willing to sell for the price we had paid. He immediately accepted our offer. Even though the Building Society wanted three months interest to close the deal and the solicitor charged about £16 the sale went through without any trouble. When the deal was concluded the young man told us he had been willing to pay an extra £150!

I was so relieved to leave Tresises. We had to move in with Shirley's parents for a while and Tommy Lambert let us store some of our furniture at Partridge Printers. I had just three days to get everything finalised on the house in Farsley before I started my new job. I had no idea how I was going to raise the money for the remainder of the deposit. Immediately on returning to Yorkshire I went to the first bank I saw in Pudsey. It was the National Westminster in Lidget Hill. On asking to see the manager, Mr Donnington promptly came out to see me and gave me a warm welcome. We talked for at least half an hour - he was a lovely man and a good listener. I walked into that bank with no account and no money although I could show I had good prospects. I came out with a bank account, a facility for a £100 overdraft along with a cheque book and paying-in book. Mr Rawlinson did confirm I had paid him a £50 deposit. The Rock Building Society then gave us a

90 per cent mortgage which meant I had a £120 deposit to pay. They counted the £50 and so that left £70 plus the solicitor's fees. That about finished the £100 overdraft facility but we did have a house. We moved in during June 1960 and were blessed with a beautiful baby girl on August 24th. Carol was born in the front bedroom of the house, we had recently bought and yet again I was not allowed at the birth. I sat outside the bedroom door (which the midwife kept locked). Shirley would have loved me to be there and I would so much have liked to see at least one of my children born. I could hear Shirley struggling with the birth a matter of inches away - but I was not allowed to comfort her. Then the midwife said 'Oh my God the cord is round her neck' - Honestly, I didn't know what that meant. It was obviously something quite alarming by the midwifes voice. Then I heard her say 'Its alright now don't worry'. My God what a relief! It was a wonderfully happy time and both of us felt we had the perfect family with our two boys and one daughter. With a good job too everything looked very healthy.

PARTRIDGE PRINTERS

The job at Partridge was excellent. The standard of workmanship surpassed anything I had seen in the trade and Tommy Lambert was a great boss. We got on exceptionally well and with my past experience I could hold the job down very well. My only problem was the money I still owed Tresises. I sent them £30 and said I would try and pay the rest as soon as possible. Their Accounts Director, Percy Richardson, gave me a couple of

months and then wrote a rather nasty letter demanding the balance by return. I know it seems this life story of mine is all about money - or lack of it. I'm sure that people who never had anything to start with are constantly striving to keep their heads above water. I needed some extra income, not only to pay off the loan but to keep my car on the road. With three children to raise I was finding it difficult to run a car. We had sold *"Jenny"* and had a 1939 Morris 8 - a lovely little car.

About a year after taking the Partridge job I saw an advert in the *'Yorkshire Post'* for a 'Youth Leader at Rawdon Youth Club' and applied. I made it to the short-list of three and was called to what proved to be an interesting interview. Afterwards I was told in front of the other interviewees that I had got the job. I was informed I would be required to work two evenings a week and for that would be paid £3 with 5s travelling expenses. I was overjoyed - and overawed within five minutes. One of the selection committee was a 20-year-old called John Rigg who immediately said: 'Come with me. I would like to introduce you to the members.' He took me to a large hall where there were about 120 members - boys and girls aged between 14 and 20. They all watched me with deep reservation. John told them to turn off the record player and announced: 'This is Roy. He's just been made the leader of Rawdon Youth Club.' They gave me a big round of applause and then looked straight at me, awaiting a response. I froze! I am never usually short of confidence but I was

then. I just stood there for what seemed an eternity and finally blurted out, 'I'm happy to be associated with such a fine youth club and will try to meet you individually as soon as possible.' John clapped and so did a few others. I was over the first hurdle. The next morning I told Tommy I had got the job at the youth club but was worried about the demand from Tresises. He was marvellous as usual. He arranged for Partridges to pay off the debt and that I could repay them at £2 a week. Was I glad to get that problem out of the way. But it was still tight money-wise. Each week £2 of the money from the youth club went to Partridges to repay the loan and the rest we used to put petrol in the car.

Shirley, as usual, was very supportive. I often did extra nights at the youth club and she took on a part-time job at a local nursing home. She went in a couple of nights a week to look after the elderly patients and do some washing, ironing and other household chores. For that she got about £2 a week. In addition she had our three children to care for plus Sally, our dog, who we had for 16 years. I progressed well at Partridges and after a year or so my wages increased to £20 a week. We then bought a four-year-old 1958 Ford Popular. It was a really good car and we managed to go away to St. Annes most Sundays. Although I was happy at Partridges I was still very interested in becoming a salesman. Even when Partridges had vacancies for two salesmen they

turned me down because I had no experience. But how was I to gain that? I certainly felt I could have done better than the two men they employed. The nearest I got to being a salesman then, was when I was shortlisted by Sun Street Printers in Keighley but the other man got the job!

I was still playing cricket and was involved in a lot of sport at the youth club. The club had a decent cricket team, a good football team and even a girls' football team. We had our own monthly newspaper called 'Youth Times' in which we printed many leading articles that provoked a lot of attention from major dailies. We even advocated honours for the Beatles before they were awarded their MBEs. It was a very responsible position for me and during my first four years there it developed into a thriving centre. Then came the directive from our Area Youth Officer that we should try and arrange overseas holidays for youth club members. I decided to try and get a group together. Twenty lads between 16 and 19 signed up and we booked a youth hostel in Bredene near Ostende. From Bredene we were able to visit Paris and Brussels and it proved a wonderful experience for the boys as none of them had been out of England before. We were sharing the hostel with some other British youth groups and some of their leaders weren't that enlightened. Unfortunately on a couple of evenings two or three of our party decided they would like to see how much alcohol they could drink. Some of their language became pretty intemperate but they didn't physically harm anyone. Even so I could in no way excuse their

behaviour especially when one of my lads abused a youth leader when the latter remonstrated with him. That leader reported the boy to me and I duly took him to task over it and we had no further trouble. This was in fact an isolated incident during a holiday which proved to be a complete success.

On our return to England, however, the youth leader made a complaint to the Airedale and Wharfedale leadership. About two weeks later the entire Youth Club committee (who I very rarely saw) came to the club on the Monday and requested a meeting with me. I was actually in the club playing table tennis with three of the members. I went into the meeting and the Chairman spoke first, saying after five good, successful years there, maybe now it was getting in a rut. He had spoken to the Area Youth Officer and the two of them along with the Committee felt it would be a good idea if they advertised for a new youth club leader. Maybe it was time to have a new face, they said, but I would be free to apply! I was dumbfounded. I felt we had one of the best youth clubs in the area. Of the 165 members about 110 attended every night it was open. We were running a successful newspaper and a good drama group which had just won first prize in a competition. I decided not to tell the members about the meeting and just let things proceed. About a couple of weeks later an advertisement appeared in the local paper inviting applications for the position of 'Leader of Rawdon Youth Club'. When I got to the youth club that evening a

contingent of about 20 members told me, 'We didn't know you were leaving Roy!' I decided not to cover up for the committee and so explained to them I didn't want to leave. It was the committee's decision that it was time for a new leader. The kids were great. They got out a petition asking me to stay. They approached the committee and said they didn't want a change but it all made no difference. I refused to apply for a job I already had and a new leader was duly appointed. It was one of the most emotional days of my life when I left in January 1966. The kids organised a surprise party for me and 125 members came along. They even made a presentation to me. I'm afraid the occasion was too much for me and I broke down and cried.

— CHAPTER 13—

MOVING UP THE
LADDER

My next job move proved to be a major stepping stone, but it got off to an inauspicious start. After nearly five years at Partridges I felt it was time to move on to a better position somewhere. I saw a job advertised at Byles and Sons Printers in Bradford for a Comp-Foreman at £22 a week. I chatted it over with Shirley and sent off my application. Within a couple of days I was invited to an interview at 6pm the following evening. I arrived at the factory at 5.55pm, was told that Mr Rothwell was expecting me and was ushered into the waiting room. At 6.30pm no one had been to see me. There were one or two brochures advertising William Byles and Sons there and the back page was blank. So on one of them I wrote:

Dear Mr Rothwell, I had an interview booked at 6pm. At 5.55pm your secretary informed me I was expected and asked me to go to the waiting room. It has never been my habit to be late for appointments and I do expect other people to be

punctual (unless of course there is an excuse and I have been notified). As there was no apology received I felt you had either forgotten the appointment or wished not to see me. Please ignore my application for the position. Yours, Roy Tinsley.

We had no telephone at home in those days. That evening I told Shirley what had happened and went off to Partridges as normal next morning. About 9.05am I received a telephone call there from John Rothwell. He said he had gone to the waiting room to see me and I must have just left. He was very apologetic and asked if I would come again, and he would not keep me waiting. We booked another appointment and that time we had a good meeting and he offered me the job. I said I would give him my decision within two days. Shirley and I talked it over and decided it seemed a good move and I should take it. It was not easy telling Tommy Lambert for we were such good mates. He did understand, however, and we remained life-long friends.

At Byles I became very friendly with a compositor called Jimmy Slack. He and his wife were devout Catholics. They had four sons and we often went on holiday with them. All seven kids were under nine years old but they (and our dog) got on famously. The job was reasonable, there were parts which I enjoyed and others I didn't. There were 52 in the comp-room and most of them were quite good craftsmen. I was able to run the department very efficiently and (happily for John Rothwell) profitably. To be perfectly honest I did

not enjoy it as much as I had at Partridges but the extra money was very useful.

We were still very happy in our flat-topped house especially as it backed onto open fields at the front and back. One morning, however, I was awoken about 6.30am by an almighty noise from outside my front gate. Looking out I saw the largest crane I had ever seen trundling through the field to about six inches of my garden wall. I went downstairs, put on a coat and went outside to see what damage it had done. It had certainly left some big craters. When the driver eventually turned off the engine I asked him what he was doing. He explained it was difficult taking those large cranes out of their front gate onto the road, so their company, George Cohen Ltd, had asked the local builder if they could use his land to leave from the back of their factory. Now our house was the middle one of five. The two on either side of us were rented from the builder whereas we were buying ours. I told him I hadn't been asked and I would have said 'No'. The guy smiled and said he would be coming up each day and going back each night - those were his orders. After about a week I could stand it no longer. The noise was deafening and, what with the rain, the field was turning into a swamp. I wrote to George Cohen Ltd (which is of course a huge International Company) to complain. They totally ignored my letter.

As I was in the Printers' Union I could get free legal advice. I wrote to the Union's solicitors and explained the whole story. To my delight the

solicitor informed me that George Cohen's had no right to use the land outside my front gate without my permission. He advised me to write to the giants at "Cohen's" and inform them that if the practice did not immediately stop I would take further legal action. Again "Cohen's" totally ignored my letter. So one morning I got up about 6am and, with the help of a neighbour, erected a small fence to bar entrance to my land. At about 7am the huge tractor came face to face with me in front of my small fence. 'Get out the bloody way,' the tractor driver yelled. 'You are trespassing,' I told him. 'Go back.' To which his co-driver retorted: 'Drive over the feckin thing.' 'Please do,' I replied. 'The police have been informed of my action and will be here within minutes.' I hadn't told anyone but it sounded good. They eventually turned off the engine and one of them stayed with the crane while the other went back to the factory.

I had to go to work by then and so asked Shirley to let me know if they knocked the fence down. When I arrived home that evening I learnt they had pulled back about 100 yards and then gone through another field to bypass my house - but they had got stuck. As they had been renting the cranes at very high rates it must have been costing them a fortune! The Company obviously took legal advice as well and found they couldn't do a thing. They did eventually come back and said they would make up the road in front of my house if I would give them permission to pass. If they had replied to my letters I might have looked on it sympathetically, but at that point I stood my ground. A lovely case of the little man taking on

the big guys - and winning!

As Christmas approached I thought I had found a way of completely fooling my sons. Byles had one of the finest Father Christmas' outfits I had ever seen and that year they asked me if I would play the part. It was total disguise! I took Gary (7) and Steven (5) to the party and left them with Jimmy Slack and his three boys, telling them I had to go home and would pick them up later. Off I went to the office and put on that marvellous outfit. I walked proudly into the canteen carrying a large bag of presents. As they took their gifts, each with their own name on it, they said 'Thank you Santa'. When I eventually called out 'Steven Tinsley' and gave him his present he said 'Thanks Dad'. So much for my disguise!

Just after Christmas I was looking through the papers and noticed how much house prices had risen. We were a bit better off by then and had often discussed how much we would like a house with a nice garden and a garage. To see what our house was worth we put it on the market and to our amazement were told we could sell it for £1,600, £400 more than we had paid. I couldn't take it in. The agent said he would also look for something suitable for us. Within a couple of weeks ours was sold and we hadn't found anything for ourselves. Then we received a circular about a semi-detached with a large garden and garage in Farsley at £2,200. At 7.30am I drove straight round and so liked the look of it I immediately collected Shirley and showed her. I rang the factory to tell

them I would be a little late that morning. At 8.30am I returned to the house and the owner let me see inside. Again I went back for Shirley and we were so sure it was the right house for us, I went straight to the estate agent and agreed to buy it. We were so pleased with our acquisition that we would walk past it every weekend and most evenings just to look at it. We were absolutely delighted the day we moved in. It had three bedrooms, a kitchen, living room, dining room, hall and a bathroom. The rear garden was lovely and the big thing was that it had a telephone. We decided to keep that!

Even though I was doing very well at Byles and they had given me a bonus as well as a pay rise, I still had this burning desire to be a salesman. On joining Byles I had become a member of the Printers Manager and Overseers Association and so received their monthly magazine. One day I saw the following:

Compositor. Preferably married with a family. Age 35-40 Clean driving licence, required as salesman in the North of England selling a product to the Printing Industry that has a distinct price advantage... Basic salary + car.

I felt it had been written especially for me and sat down that evening to write out an application. It was a bit special to be able to put down on the letterheading a telephone number - Pudsey 4930. Three days later about 8pm I received a telephone call in response. It was a wonderful old man called Percy Austin. He became a dear friend and the man I will always credit for getting me into the

selling game. He explained he had been selling printers' metal for many, many years for a London company and they had asked him to find a salesman to start a completely new round in the North of England. He thought my application was very suitable and suggested we should try to set up a meeting in the near future.

Shirley and I had just booked a one-week holiday at a little place called Penmaenwawr in North Wales and would be travelling there the following Saturday. He asked for the name of the hotel as he planned to be in Llandudno the same week and would like the opportunity to meet me and my family. Shirley wasn't so keen on the idea of meeting someone such as Mr Austin during her holiday. In fact, she seemed quite reluctant. So, after a long discussion, it was agreed I should go alone if he did actually make contact with us. We loved the little resort of Penmaenwawr. It had one of the safest beaches in Britain and we had a beach chalet there where we could change and eat our sandwiches. We really liked it. We had been there about three days when, just as I had left the breakfast table, the landlady told Shirley there was a telephone call from Mr Austin. As I was unavailable Shirley took it. He sounded such a delightful man and was so persuasive that she accepted his invitation for all of the family to join him for lunch. I'm sure if I had answered the phone I would have gone alone.

By then we had progressed to a Ford Consul - a nice looking car and by far the most prestigious we

had ever owned. At 11 o'clock we started to make the kids look presentable and then drove to Llandudno. Mr Austin was staying in a beautiful hotel with a lovely view over the promenade and sea from the dining room. Percy Austin met us at the door and I was pleasantly surprised to find him so friendly and welcoming. He took us into the bar, walked over to a lady who was about 40 and introduced her as his daughter. With her was a five-year-old boy called Thomas who she said was her son. She had no wedding ring and no husband - quite a shock 30 years ago! She was a single parent. Percy was aged 77 and had a wealth of experience in the printing trade. We hit it off immediately and discussed the industry from A to Z. Shirley had quite a talk with both Percy and his daughter. We always looked back on that day as one when our three kids behaved impeccably. They were absolutely brilliant and Carol was a little charmer. He virtually offered me the job but said it would have to be confirmed by a Mr Tilley at the head office in London and he would be in touch with me after the holidays to book an appointment. At that stage we did not discuss salary. For me all that was important was that I would soon be a salesman - the job I had always wanted.

The week after our return from holiday, Percy Austin telephoned and said he had made arrangements for an interview in London. If I came through the interview successfully, I would be offered the job and could possibly pick up a company car while down there and drive home in

it. Shirley's mother and father agreed to take care of the kids and we went down by train. Percy was waiting to meet us when we arrived at the head office of Press Printing Alloys. He took me along to see Mr Tilley who, during the interview, spoke more about their expansion plans in the North. He said if I could get out on the road and bring in about £75,000 worth of orders for Monotype and Linotype metal in the first year I would be able to have a very successful career with their Company. We still had not discussed the wage. The problem was I wanted that job more than any other. When Mr Tilley asked me if I could achieve such figures I assured him I was certain I could. He then pulled a pad from his desk and wrote out £1,000. He pointed at it and said: 'That's the wage we are prepared to pay, plus a car, plus reasonable expenses. What do you think?' I immediately replied, 'That's fine.' Before I had gone to the interview, Shirley and I had worked out our car was costing us £6 a week, with tax, insurance, petrol and servicing plus the hire purchase repayments of £12 a month with 30 months to go. With a company car and £1,000 a year I would actually be £3 a week better off and would have my toe in the selling door for the first time. So I accepted and told them I had to give a month's notice. Mr Tilley still let us take the car. It was a Cortina - the latest style with 12,000 miles on the clock. It was by far the best car I had ever had and I was quite proud to have it parked on our drive at the front of the house.

Our old friends Jimmy and Joyce Slack came to the rescue regarding my car. Joyce's brother Joe had been looking for one and paid me enough for the Consul for me to settle the hire purchase account. When it came to handing in my notice at Byles I didn't find it too difficult. I explained to Mr Rothwell I had always wanted to get into the selling field and this opportunity had arisen and I felt I had to take it. We parted very good friends and he ordered two tons of type metal from me which gave me a great start with my selling career.

— CHAPTER 14 —

A NEW SALESMAN
ON THE ROAD

My first day on the road will always stick in my memory. My first call was at Sunfield Printers in Stanningley where I met Ernest Horne, who I knew slightly. He made me welcome, took my card and said he would consider me when he next ordered. They had about five linotypes and used quite a bit of metal. I continued on my round and called at many printers in Leeds, Bradford and Huddersfield and had a pretty reasonable reception at most companies. I was expected to make a daily report and found I had made 12 calls on my first day. The first week went quite well. I didn't take any orders but I felt confident something would come of my efforts. Then on the Friday afternoon, Shirley answered the telephone at home. It was Ernest Horne. He wanted five hundredweight. I was on my way! Percy Austin was so helpful in those early days. He sent out letters to many of his existing customers introducing me and gave me several lists of printers and who to contact by

name. His help was invaluable. He told me that the two big accounts to crack in the North of England were Horsfalls (Startype) and The Yorkshire Post. It took about ten visits to each plus a few lunches before I finally got in - but get in I did and orders were beginning to roll in from all quarters. I hit my annual budget of £70,000 in the first five months. The *"Yorkshire Post"* and Horsfalls ordered 20 tons each. Business became so good that our company had to open a foundry in the North to service all the orders I was taking. At last I felt I had achieved my life ambition - to be a successful salesman. After about 18 months of successful selling with Press Printing Alloys they gave me a £250 a year increase. What with the car as well, we as a family were feeling the benefit of that job. I certainly didn't have to work at the weekends anymore. However I didn't win them all! I remember one day calling at a large printers (Netherwoods) whose factory overlooked the Huddersfield Town football ground. I knew them through a man called Frank Sykes who was on one of the Printing Trade Committees I was associated with as Trade Union Secretary. He said they had quite a lot of metal (type and blocks) to dispose of and would I buy it from them. I had been advised to 'buy as well as sell' so I said 'Yes'. We managed to have it all collected and I was astonished by how much there was. They had old blocks going back to the last century. Now I wish we had kept some of them. About ten days later our London office informed me the metal had been weighed and they would send the cash by registered letter. When it arrived and I had duly signed for it, I had

quite a shock for when I opened it I found £700. It was a real test of my character because Netherwoods had no idea of the value of the metal. I wondered if those in my head office thought I was making a few quid myself. But I resisted that temptation and took it all to Netherwoods the next day. I had the feeling they were surprised when I handed it over, but the man took it without a word of thanks. A few days later I called there on the chance they might give me an order for some monotype or linotype ingots. They sent a message that they were too busy to see me. I made calls there for the next few years and was never seen, never.

About October 1964 I was asked by our head office to make arrangements to exhibit at a small printing exhibition to be held in Leeds to commemorate the opening of a new factory by Thomas E. Knight & Co. Now Thomas E. Knight was a very reputable Printing Engineering company which not only sold secondhand machines but also new Mercedes letterpress cylinders, Michael-Master guillotines and Fohlmer paper drills. Laurie Baxter was the company manager and was organising the exhibition. We got to know each other quite well and he explained that the salesman they had didn't know much about the printing trade and his sales record was abysmal. So, the following week, they would be interviewing eight prospective salesmen. He wondered if I would be interested. I was so happy with Press Printing Alloys that it never occurred to me to look for another job. Laurie pointed out that

I could earn big money as their company paid a good basic salary and one and a quarter per cent commission on turnover. I discussed this with Shirley when I got home and we decided we should inform Laurie that I was interested in the new job. It wasn't as though I didn't enjoy my work with Press Printing Alloys - I did and it was great. But there was a certain appeal in doing a similar job for more money when we had three young children and a mortgage. In the following weeks Laurie passed on to me several inquiries and I turned them into sales for him. This proved I was as good at selling machines as I was metal and Laurie was so keen to employ me he didn't bother to interview anyone else.

So Mr Knight did offer me the job (by coincidence he played golf every weekend with my boss from Press Printing Alloys). Then I had the difficult job of telling Noel Harding (the Managing Director) and my old friend Percy Austin that I would like to take the new position. They were both very understanding, accepted my resignation and wished me every success. Little did I know what that side of the industry was like. In the Royal Navy I had met a few criminals and con-men but they were choir boys compared with certain characters I was to come across within the secondhand printing machinery trade.

— CHAPTER 15 —

NEW AND SECONDHAND - THE MARKET

Within the first couple of months I picked up more orders for Thomas Knight and Company than they had processed in the previous 15 months. And I loved it. I had found my true vocation amongst all those guillotines, letterpress cylinders, offsets - new and secondhand. On top of all that I had a brand-new Cortina estate car, expenses and, of course, one and a quarter per cent commission. A year after I joined them, Mr Knight said he was coming to Leeds as he had some very good news for me. On arrival he called in Laurie and me and announced that he had great pleasure in making me a director of Thomas E. Knight and Company. He wanted me to sign a contract, one of the clauses of which stated that I would not, for a period of two years, set up a company in competition with him. Now I never had the slightest intention of setting up my own company - that job was fine by me for life (or so I thought at the time). I told Mr Knight I would be proud to be a director and would always conduct myself in

the appropriate manner but I wouldn't sign a contract with that clause inserted as I had no plans to go into competition with him. He agreed to delete it. He then informed the various printing magazines that I had been made a director. In 1966 Mr Knight suggested I should go to Ireland for a week. He believed the company could reap good dividends from the secondhand market in Eire and that I would do well there.

Ireland was to prove the happiest hunting ground of my entire career. I sold machines from Dublin to Galway, from Athlone to Cork and in many other beautiful cities the length and breadth of Ireland. It also gave me the opportunity to meet some of the finest characters that inhabited this earth. After one particularly successful week there, I decided to stay over the weekend and continue again on the Monday. On the Saturday I drove into the country and called in at a beautiful little pub in Bundoran. By a most amazing coincidence inside I met three former colleagues from The *Huddersfield Examiner* who were on a fact-finding tour concerning the latest newspaper presses, one of which had been installed in Cork. Other than the four of us there were about six locals in the pub. Meeting in such a way out place obviously called for quite a booze-up. We started at 7.30pm and by ten past midnight we were still at it. One of my friends said: 'What time do they close? Bloody hell - if she doesn't close before long I'll die.' Sharing the same sentiment I staggered over to the bar for another four pints and enquired: 'When do you close?' 'October' she said without a

glimmer of a smile - one of the finest one word answers I have ever heard seeing it was May. I nearly fell on the floor - partly due to the answer and partly from the excessive booze I had drunk. I found being away from Shirley and the kids for two weeks was far too long and I vowed not to do that again. Even so for the next seven years I did spend one week out of every four in Ireland. As the years went by Shirley and I felt quite affluent and I was enjoying the job immensely.

The Japanese firm Komori is now a big name amongst printers in Europe and the World, but was virtually unknown in 1966. Laurie Baxter came across a book printed in 1965 in Japan which gave the names of Japanese printing machine manufacturers and the machines they were producing. One company seemed to be well in advance of all the others and I decided to write to see if there was a possibility of representing them in the UK. It was none other than Komori. I wrote many letters to them and finally they decided to send a representative to meet me and look at Thomas E. Knight as a company. It wasn't hard to recognise him at Leeds-Bradford airport - he was the only Japanese getting off the plane from London. I approached him and pronounced his name in the best way I could and he nodded his head. It was then I found out he didn't speak a word of English and I didn't speak a word of Japanese. I invited him to stay with Shirley and me. It was the longest three days of our lives. The kids were great. They seemed to get on just fine with him and all we seemed to do was laugh!

We never did find a translator but we got by somehow. Mr Knight came from London to meet him and we managed to find a client who was very interested in a two colour Unikon. I'm sure this was the first time a Komori representative, along with their prospective agents - Thomas E. Knight & Co. had sat down to discuss a sale together, and so I was the first to introduce Komori to Europe! Although I introduced them I believe Michael Knight sold the first Komori machine over here.

From little acorns, big oak trees grow! Knights did Komori proud - and Komori did Knights proud. It seemed like the perfect marriage. It was a most exciting period in the development of Thomas E. Knight. Yet, due to the number of orders coming in from Ireland, I was being persuaded to start up business on my own.

In Ireland I had become firm friends with a master printer called Don McFergus. We spent a lot of time together discussing both my work and his business which was one of the most quality-conscious companies in Ireland. The bulk of their business came from Aer-Lingus. He had bought quite a lot of equipment from me and became my best client in Ireland. Don virtually sold me on the idea of forming a 50-50 partnership with him and he would put the money up to start the company.

It was coming up to DRUPA (the International Printing Machinery Exhibition held in Germany

every five years) and Mr Knight asked me to go along with his two other representatives, John Childs and Ray Lancaster. They were two superb characters who had worked for Mr Knight for many years and had been very successful. While at DRUPA they did their best to talk me out of the idea of going into business with Don McFergus. They told me I could have a wonderful career with Mr Knight's company. I had to admit life was good for after being made up to Sales Director I had been given a fairly free hand to run the Northern office with Laurie Baxter and (with Mr Knight's overall direction) we had been very successful. It was just that as I approached 40 I felt that with all the contacts I had in Ireland and with the help of Don McFergus the venture would prove very successful. Immediately after DRUPA I returned to Ireland and picked up orders for four more machines. Don felt the time was right for us to set up on our own and he was ready to raise £2,000 and transfer it to my bank. I would then need to see the bank manager and obtain an overdraft facility and put things in motion. My main problem was telling Mr Knight I was leaving. He had been such a good employer and I enjoyed such a pleasant relationship with him that it was going to be as bad as the time I had to tell Tommy Lambert I was resigning from Byles.

I discussed everything with Shirley. She felt the job I had was exceptionally good and we were more solvent than we had ever been. She did, however, leave the decision to me - and I decided to go ahead with the new company. Laurie took it

very badly. He said he would close up shop if I left. He asked if he could go with me! I told him he had a very good job and business was going well. If they managed to get another salesman he would be okay. Then I had to tell Mr Knight. I put a call through to his private office in London. 'Good morning Mr Knight. Roy here - I just wanted a private..' 'Hello Roy - had a nice weekend? Been playing cricket? How many did you get?' He went on and on in his inimitable way which demoralised me. 'Sorry Mr Knight - I have a very difficult job to do this morning. I want to give my notice.' 'Roy - don't be silly. Stay where you are. Don't leave the office. I'm coming up to see you.' The London office was 200 miles away but four hours later he walked into the Leeds office. He made out such a good case for me to stay on I was in a terrible dilemma. In the end he saw that my mind was made up and he made the decision easier for me by holding out his hand. He wished me every success and said: 'Okay Roy - try it. Get it out of your system. I hope it works out for you. But if it doesn't you can have your job back any time you like!' I thought, 'What a wonderful man'. After enjoying three wonderful years with Knights, I left on very amicable terms. Mr Knight and I remained excellent friends until his death in February 1994.

— CHAPTER 16 —

ROY W. TINSLEY LIMITED

Within a day of telling him I had handed in my resignation, Don McFergus flew in from Ireland. He was very helpful in those early days and together we searched for suitable premises for our new business. We found a wonderful little factory, half a mile from my home and virtually in the country. It was a pleasure to go there each morning for it was literally surrounded by wildlife. Don gave me a cheque for £1,000. I went to my bank manager, explained that my partner would soon send a further £1,000 and asked for an overdraft facility of £3,000. He said he would authorise that so long as I put up our house as security. Shirley and I agreed and we signed the necessary documents.

Don placed an order for a Heidelberg cylinder worth £2,000. I used the overdraft facility to buy one, rebuilt it and sent it over to Ireland. Although Don sent £2,000 for the machine two months later,

he never did give me the further £1,000 towards setting up the business. So I had to get things moving with hardly any financial support although Don was instrumental in obtaining some good contacts in the 1960s. Business began to pick up well and I was visiting Dublin every other week. I bought a second hand Morris Oxford for £325 and gave myself a salary of £40 a week.

It was at that early stage that I asked my younger brother Dave to consider leaving ICI and to come and work with me. After a lot of soul searching he decided to do that and became a very important member of the company. He worked long and hard hours and thoroughly enjoyed all his visits to Ireland installing the machines I had sold. My trips to Ireland were producing a large amount of business. I was selling in virtually every town out there. I even found myself doing business with the IRA and was glad to get out of that!

The original enquiry came from Linotype in Dublin who said they had a man in their office called Seamus White. He wanted to start a new company in Cavan. The only other printer in that town was called Black. Not a great deal of significance in that but it must have been the only town in Ireland with two printers - one called Black and the other White! Through Linotype I arranged for Seamus White to visit me in Pudsey so we could discuss a package deal for a complete printing company. His business sleeping partner was quite a character called Paddy Smith who toured throughout Ireland doing gigs with his own

showband. We agreed it should all be letterpress - Heidelberg cylinder, platen and linotype. In fact we supplied everything, 'lock, stock and barrel'. Seamus White was in a tremendous hurry to get started but the Irish Bank was in the fourth month of a strike and there was no sign of it ending. There was no way I would accept a cheque as they had no bank account for their new company. They were so determined that Paddy Smith came up with £13,000 in cash within two days! We made the installation and I asked Seamus where the majority of the work was coming from. He seemed very secretive about it and didn't want to tell me. After the company had been going for three months I paid them a surprise visit to see how it was progressing.

When I left the Navy I had bought a Royal Navy badge and I had only recently had it sewn on a blazer. It looked quite nice and it was a good talking point. When we shook hands in the factory, Seamus looked decidedly fidgety and said, 'You're a brave man wearing that badge in this town - especially today.' I didn't attach a lot of significance to his statement until later. It seemed every job Seamus had in his works was for the IRA. He was even printing the official IRA newspaper, *"Pro Blacht"*. Its contents were highly slanderous regarding all that the UK stood for - the Government, Armed Forces, everything. He apologised for the work he was doing and said that he and Paddy wanted to get out of the contract with the IRA and were to meet with them shortly. Before I left he emphatically warned me not to

stay in the town very long as there was a big funeral taking place that afternoon of a senior officer in the IRA who had been killed 'on active service'.

It still didn't register with me how vulnerable I was in Cavan that day wearing that blazer. I bade him farewell and drove off in my hired car only to stop at a pub on the outskirts of the town. I went in and ordered a pint of Guiness and a beef sandwich. The barman looked at me as though I had just crawled out of the local sewer. He did not reply - he just went into a room behind the bar. He came back with a man in a black suit and tie. He took one look at me and then at the badge and asked: 'Are you in the British Forces?' 'No, not now,' I replied. 'I was in the Navy during the war. Why?' 'You are a very foolish man dressed like that in Cavan today.' I still didn't understand what all the fuss was about and said: 'Can I have my order then?' 'Feck off - now!' He was so emphatic and so emphasised the 'now' that I went out, threw my blazer in the back of the car, got in and put my foot down. I never stopped until I got to Dublin. A car followed me fairly closely for about ten miles and then turned back to Cavan. I went straight to some good friends in Dublin (Stewart and Curry) and explained what had happened. They made me a cup of tea. Once I had calmed down I went back to the car only to find that the back window had been smashed and the blazer had gone. Perhaps that was a good thing - I never did replace that badge.

Four weeks later I received a telephone call from Seamus. He said he was giving up the IRA contract within a month and they now wanted to set up their own printing company. Seamus told me that if I could supply them with identical equipment to that I had found for him they would pay half immediately in cash and the balance after installation. It seemed the IRA had obtained the services of a printer, for the list they gave Seamus was very specific and professional. I gave the deal a lot of thought and decided that as I was in the business to sell printing machines, Seamus could set up the meeting for me. The meeting was arranged in a pub one evening in Dublin. Seamus met me at the bar and ushered me over to a dark corner where two very smart, well spoken and friendly men were waiting. I had prepared a quotation - the total cost came to £19,000. They agreed the deal, said they would like everything installed into a factory in Tullamare and proceeded to count out £9,500 in cash. They didn't require a receipt so we shook hands and parted - with a promise that everything would be installed with 21 days. I had arranged to see Don McFergus that evening and I related to him the whole event and produced the £9,500. He was rather taken aback. 'Roy,' he said. 'Get that money back to them as soon as possible. I don't care how - but get it back.'

He went on to explain that if I did install the machines I would never get the balance of the money. I decided to take his advice and contacted Seamus immediately. When I told him I wanted to pull out of the deal he told me the IRA would not be very pleased. He did, however, arrange another

meeting at which I was able to explain I was uncomfortable with the transaction. They accepted this amicably and I returned the £9,500. That thankfully, was the end of the matter.

— CHAPTER 17 —

TOM AND ROY LINK UP AGAIN

Some months earlier (during my first year of trading) Tommy Lambert's wife, Ivy, had rung me to say he was convalescing in bed after a heart attack. I went straight over to visit him and he was certainly pleased to see me. Ivy said he had been overdoing things of late and now had to take it easy. He asked about my new business so I told him how good things were and if he fancied a change when he recovered (as I was sure he would) then I would be delighted to have him working for me.

About two months after my IRA meeting Tommy came to see me, by then fully recovered, and asked if my offer was still open. 'Of course it's still open,' I said and Tommy and I teamed up again the next day. Now everyone is wise with hindsight. What I should have done that very day was to buy Don McFergus out and make Tommy equal partners in the business. We were responsible for all the work and sales and yet we were paying Don a

wage plus expenses to bring family and friends over on regular occasions. Unfortunately I did not go down that road and Tommy just continued to graft and work alongside David and myself to make the company successful. By this time my other brother Donald had joined the company as our lorry driver and installer of machines. He worked long hours and very concientiously for the company. Our first year's figures were excellent. It was then that I fancied building a British guillotine. Tommy and I came up with a basic design, Dave put the electrics together and we contacted a local company called Rhodes-Gill to manufacture it. I had visions of it sweeping the market and producing a guillotine years ahead of its time. We decided on the name Gill-Roy - from Roy and Rhodes-Gill. It seemed like a good name. The first one we produced was sold in 1968 and is still performing satisfactorily to this day. Unfortunately I did not foresee the enormous production costs involved. It began to take most of my time and was absorbing virtually all the profits we were making on the secondhand machines. Rhodes-Gill were a first-class company and the product completed was excellent. We had produced a leaflet in six languages but they wanted to double the price on all future machines. We had already exhibited the first machine at Northprint in Harrogate and it created a lot of interest. We had many enquiries - but not at double the price!

We then decided to take the drawings to another company in Huddersfield called Broomfield

Engineering. They agreed to supply six at the original price. Within two weeks I had sold the first six machines. They were not a patch, however, on the original one built by Rhodes-Gill. We put the first into Dennis Welborne in Pudsey but took it out again as it wouldn't work correctly. The next we installed at Leeds University but again out it came. It was proving to be an absolute disaster.

At enormous cost we decided to exhibit at the international DRUPA show in Dusseldorf (we had the excellent leaflets in many languages). We also worked on another invention - 'The Tinsley Permanent Blanket' for letterpress cylinders and this proved an absolute winner - we decided to take a stock of these to DRUPA as well.

The German Organisers decided in their wisdom to put our booth about 50 yards from the POLAR Guillotine stand. That proved a disaster. The POLAR was and still is acknowledged as the finest guillotine in the world. It was like taking a 1939 car to the 1960 Motor Show - we were so far behind the Polar. After two or three days at the show we realised what a disaster it was. Tommy and I got a couple of engineers to remove it from the stand and put it in the warehouse attached to the exhibition hall. We then proceeded to exhibit our Tinsley Permanent Blanket and sold the lot in four days. We asked David to come over to DRUPA in his car and bring our entire stock over. He arrived the next day and we sold everyone by the end of the show and took orders for many more

this helped to finance the catastrophe of the guillotine.

With great reluctance I pulled out of the guillotine market in 1969/70. It had just about brought my company to its knees financially and I had to accept we could not continue to pour good money after bad. During the first two years of trading I had managed to purchase the factory and another nearby. Sales were still good on the secondhand market so even after the guillotine debacle I was able to gain the assistance of the bank when Don McFergus asked to be bought out. After two pretty bad years I could understand his reluctance to be involved but it wasn't a great moment to deal with that. After putting in £1,000 at the start he had then drawn £20 a week and brought his family and friends to England for several holidays all expenses paid. So he was quite happy to accept £5,000 from me to end his relationship with the company. We did remain on friendly terms. I then had to get the business back on its feet.

We employed 12 people at that time and that included my brother Don who made frequent trips to Ireland during his three or four years with us and always kept a very clean account of all his hours. We had two engineers (one good and one indifferent) plus labourers and an apprentice. For 12 months we all worked like hell but were badly hit by the Irish Bank strike. Everyone said it would be over in three or four weeks - it went on for seven months. I was still securing good

business in Ireland and people were paying me. My bank would not, however, accept their cheques. All they would do was give me an overdraft against those cheques. Banks - they are all the same. They never seem to take any chances whatsoever, but will let you do so. By the time the Irish Bank strike was over I had about £35,000 in Irish cheques. When they were presented and sorted, £8,500 were returned and couldn't be processed through my bank. One particular client had died and his cheque for £2,500 was no longer valid!

It was at this time that a man from Yorkshire Electricity Board came to see me. He said he had some bad news for me - he had been incorrectly reading the meter at the factory for the past six years. He produced a huge sheet of paper with handwritten figures all over it and tried to explain the different ratios from 1967 through to 1971. He did kindly say he would make no charge for 1966 as I hadn't moved in until 1967. I honestly thought it was some sort of practical joke and told him to 'Piss-off'. He got quite "uppity" at that and it was then I realised he wasn't joking. He said the amount I owed was £2,921.12 and he would like to take a cheque with him. I rang my solicitor who thought I had a case for not paying. After two weeks the solicitor sent me a bill for £450 for his services and told me I would have to pay.

I informed the local newspaper who reported on the injustice of it all. This was picked up by *"News at Ten"* and Martyn Lewis came to

interview me and that was broadcast nationally the following evening. Although I received letters of support from all over the country I still had to pay!

With all these financial problems my accountant suggested I would have to close the business and go into bankruptcy. I was devastated. This deeply hurt me even though it was a Limited Company. After six hard years when I had raised my own salary to only £50 a week it was hard to accept I would lose everything. I decided to wind up the business as cleanly as I could. I contacted all those who had outstanding accounts with us and said I would pay half the amount immediately and give them a further good payment against the balance once the company had gone into liquidation. Everyone agreed. Shirley and I had a beautiful five-bedroomed detached bungalow. We sold that and retained just enough money to put a five per cent deposit on a smaller, cheaper house in Farsley. Shirley was as wonderful as ever. She had received a small inheritance and she even gave me that to help pay off my business debts as well as letting me use all our savings. After that I put the company into voluntary liquidation. The only mistake I made was to sell the premises to one of our creditors for a paltry £13,000. He did not receive the initial 50 per cent of his account but still has the premises to this day which are now valued at about £300,000.

When my solicitor had drawn up the agreement to buy out Don McFergus the deeds for the small secondary premises had been overlooked. Now we needed Don's signature to sell them. When he

learnt this Don said he would only sign if we paid him another £1,000 in cash. Again I was devastated. It seemed I couldn't win. He was paid his £1,000 in cash. I voluntarily liquidated and we paid a dividend of around 30 per cent. This meant all those we were in debt to received 80 per cent of their outstanding accounts - except the Electricity Board. I never paid them the initial 50 per cent and they only got 30 per cent of the disputed bill.

So that was the end of Roy W. Tinsley Ltd. I came out without a job, without a penny - but with my head held high. Tommy - God bless him - was very supportive and a big help at that time. He managed to get a job with a firm of printers engineers and stayed with them for quite a while, although they never appreciated his talents. I found a very good job for my brother Don as an ink representative and Tommy and I gave him a lot of our contacts. He was very successful and stayed with them about ten years. I persuaded my other brother to go into business on his own and gave him a lot of help in the early days. He became very successful. All the other members of the staff quickly got fixed up with jobs and I had the satisfaction of succeeding in coming out of the whole affair pretty clean.

Then I had to face the dilemma of what to do myself. I had many good contacts in the business. Among them was John Rose, Chairman of the Tinsley-Robor Group. I had bought some of his old machines. He intimated he would be interested

should I wish to join his group in the printing machinery trade. I was also receiving a few visits from Harry West who suggested I should team up with him and his partner Bill Myers as they were in the secondhand printing machinery business and needed a good salesman. I gave details of their company to my accountant and asked him to check them out. He said he would try and get copies of the balance sheets for their last two years of trading and see if they were as sound as West and Myers had stated. 'You must ask for £3,000 a year and a car Roy,' Tommy Lambert advised me. 'Otherwise look around for something else.' 'Do you really think they will pay me that Tommy?' I asked. 'Of course they will - just see.' I met Harry and Bill at the Stansfield Arms, a rather nice restaurant where I had taken many of my clients during the previous six years. So the owner and the head waiter were fussing around me with Mr Tinsley this and Mr Tinsley that and even a brandy on the house. At the same time Harry and Bill were trying to impress me with the details of how prosperous their company was. The only missing cog was a good salesman they said. I told them my terms and Harry agreed immediately. Bill was flabbergasted for he was only paid £40 a week. Even so I wasn't sure it was the right move and asked for time to think it over.

In the meantime I contacted Ron Roadknight at Dornier and asked if they were considering opening a branch in the North. He had a splendid reputation and I felt it would be a good combination. Ron was very sympathetic on hearing

that my company had closed, but thought the timing was wrong, regarding a move into the North and so declined the offer of my services. I was at least still mobile, for I had managed to raise the deposit for another car and I decided to contact Harry West and offer to work for them for a couple of months. I would use my own car and he would pay me £50 a week plus six pence a mile. I needed to start supporting my family again and that included paying off the big mortgage on the house.

On my first day at Westmyer, Harry took me round his works and showed me the stock. I could hardly believe they had so few valuable machines. The jewel in the crown was a Heidelberg cylinder. In my opinion the total value (including the Heidelberg) was about £1,500. Within four hours I had sold the Heidelberg cylinder to an old customer of mine in Ireland.

When I got home I heard that my accountant, John Milne, had been trying to contact me. He had managed to obtain the accounts for Westmyer. His strict instructions were not to join them warning: 'You have just put your company into voluntary liquidation and it was like ICI compared with Westmyer.' He went on to say they could not possibly last another six months. That evening my old friend John Rose also phoned me. He had just purchased a printing company in Birmingham called James Upton and wondered if I would be interested in buying a two-colour Roland Rekord. Now why I didn't say to John that I was available

there and then I do not know. It would have been the right decision at the right time - but I didn't. Instead Harry West and I went to Birmingham the next day and met John Rose. He was very pleased to see me again, shook my hand warmly and asked how things were. It was then I mentioned my intended team up with Harry West and introduced them. Harry went off to inspect the machine and soon John Rose and I began bargaining. 'I would like ten,' John told me. 'I think it's only worth five,' I responded and John laughed and shook his head. 'How about £8,000 then?' And he agreed, adding that we had to leave a deposit. I went down to the machine room and told Harry I had done a deal at £8,000. He asked me if I could sell it and I said 'Yes'. He seemed a happy man until I mentioned the deposit. He then gave the impression he would have difficulty raising that. There was no way I was going back to John Rose without a deposit. He agreed 5% would be alright, so we managed to give him £400.

Back in the car I asked Harry: 'How bad are things then? Have you difficulty raising £400?' He said it was just a little cash flow problem. He did say he had a very good enquiry for the machine from Bill Mould of Leyland Printing Company. As I also knew Bill Mould it was possible, once Harry had made the initial contact, to go ahead with negotiations. I arranged to meet Bill Mould at James Upton's to show him the machine. He asked me how much and I said: '£15,000 - 'as is' lying there.' 'Come on Roy - you can do better than that,' he replied. I told him it was the best we

could do and we must have his cheque the following day if he wanted to go ahead. He held out his hand, said he would arrange to take it out himself and we would have the cheque within 24 hours.

I had been with Harry West two days and made him £7,000 net profit on one deal! Harry was ecstatic. 'Roy,' he said. 'We can really make big business together. I'll make sure you have a big share in it too.' About two months later Harry offered to buy Bill Myers out and he accepted even though he did not receive a particularly large amount for his share in the company.

After I had been with Harry a few weeks I got a feel for the place and business was booming. All my contacts were coming good, especially from Ireland and we were really beginning to take off. One day I bought six KSBA Heidelberg cylinders from The Three Candles Press in Dublin and sold them all the next day at £10,000 profit. Over the next four months I bought and sold more equipment for Westmyer than they had turned over in the previous 12 months. We also concluded quite a few export orders which resulted in some good 'cash' transactions. Whenever we did such 'cash' deals, Harry was always very fair and split the takings straight down the middle. I didn't tell him then about the balance sheets of his Company that I had received from my accountant. We seemed to get on well and, without telling me, he even put my name on the letterheadings as a Director. He said he looked on me as a 50/50

partner (except for shares) and proceeded to arrange a company car for me - a Jaguar.

However the most important thing was my family. They meant everything to me and we were enjoying a good family life. Gary was 17 by then, Steven 15 and Carol 13. Then came the big surprise! Shirley informed me one evening when we were alone that she was pregnant again. She had it confirmed by our local doctor. I was 47 and Shirley 42. Whilst it was obviously quite a shock we were still very pleased and proceeded to make plans.

I was amazed at how Shirley coped. She had to care for me, the three kids and be a full-time nurse to her father. He was 78 at that time and after some years of bad health had moved in with us. He'd been a wonderful grandad to our kids, playing golf with them and watching them at cricket. He'd always dressed immaculately before he became ill for he was a well educated man who had gained many promotions in his own trade. He had worked for a couple of the really top-quality worsted manufacturers in Yorkshire and had made something of his life. His health problems in later years stemmed from the First World War when he had suffered badly from his nerves in the trenches. The situation grew increasingly difficult as he became very demanding and also incontinent. Our local doctor felt he would be better off being cared for in a hospital for such patients and arranged for him to be admitted to the one at High Royds, Menston.

When we visited him he looked so vulnerable. Many patients had been in that hospital for over 20 years. They had just been left and forgotten by their families. We visited every evening for about two weeks and sometimes we were the only visitors there. He would ask us to take him home and would relate stories of how he had been badly treated. Finally we could take it no more and after discussing the whole matter with the hospital doctor we said we would like to take grandad home again. The doctor seemed quite moved. I don't think anyone had asked to take a patient home before but I can't be sure. We took grandad that evening but decided not to tell him about Shirley's pregnancy. We were eternally grateful for the decision we had taken. In his own way we could see how pleased he was to be back with us and he eventually passed away without ever knowing that another baby was expected.

One life goes and another comes. That is life I suppose. We were bereaved to see dad go but he had enjoyed his life and his grandchildren were very dear to him. We now had to face up to another Tinsley coming on the scene. When we told the kids mum was expecting again they were ecstatic. Gary held out his hand and said: 'Well done Dad.' 'What about Mum?' I asked. 'Oh - well done Mum,' he said and gave her a kiss. On January 19, 1973 we were blessed with the birth of our third son, Christopher. He was a lovely looking baby - he would be wouldn't he? Unfortunately it had been a very taxing birth for Shirley and there had been one or two

complications. He had come out with a very bad skin rash and was not at all well. The doctor said Shirley could come home, but Christopher would have to stay in Hospital a few days more. We went down every day and eventually we were allowed to take him home.

We noticed Chris was taking longer to walk than the other children. He was also way behind in talking and to be honest we did feel Christopher was slower than we would have expected. He had a gorgeous smile and was such a loving baby, and we felt so happy in having such a wonderful addition to our family.

— CHAPTER 18 —

MOVING ON

At work Harry and I found a bright young man called Max Dawson who was very quick to learn. He had an eye for an opening and became very influential in promoting the export side of the business. He proved a very useful addition to the sales force of the company. During the six years I spent at Westmyer I never received one increase in salary without asking. When I joined them they rented their premises. Within three years we had purchased them outright and bought the land in front of the factory, plus the fish and chip shop on that land. We rented it to a tenant who also made a very good profit. Harry's way of life wasn't mine. We seldom socialised and after about five years I noted a certain amount of tension. He was getting a bit of a reputation for hiring and firing people and a few of his business dealings did not receive my blessing.

We were still doing good business and Max was bringing in some excellent export orders. Working

for Westmyer wasn't as trying as some jobs could be, even though I was still doing a lot of good deals. The works staff seemed to prefer me running things while Max travelled to all the corners of the globe. This also enabled me to spend more time with my family.

Gary and Steven were proving to be quite good cricketers. We all played for Kirkstall Educational Cricket Club and so could go as a family and stay on after a match and socialise. Both completed their apprenticeships in the printing business and in 1978 I helped them acquire their own company - John Breare's in Bradford. They retained the original name, for the company dates back to 1912.

When it came to Carol's turn to take driving lessons I would sometimes teach her in the evening. When the morning of her test arrived I decided not to go to work. I informed the lady on the switchboard that I would be late and took Carol out for a warming up session, so by the time she went for her 11 o'clock test she was feeling relaxed and confident. She did in fact pass. I went back to work after lunch and had a visit from one of my Irish clients. He purchased a Heidelberg cylinder and I took him out to dinner that evening. The next day at the office I noticed Harry seemed a little edgy but dismissed it. I went home for lunch and got a telephone call there asking me to meet him at the Peacock Hotel at 1.30pm on my way back to the office. I thought nothing of it as I assumed we were probably going to see a client together. I found him there sitting at the bar. He

asked me what I would like, bought me a drink and then said he had a few things on his mind recently and wanted to have them out with me. He said he had a feeling I was not giving the job my best shot and was disappointed in my attitude in taking the morning off to go with my daughter to a driving lesson. He said it was not the right action of a Director. He also felt that my current buyings were not up to scratch and mentioned a recent deal. I could not believe what I was hearing. 'Are you serious?' I queried him.

'Very serious. Don't think I want you to leave - I don't. But you could put more effort into it.'

I looked him straight in the eye and replied: 'Who the bloody hell are you talking to? This is Roy - Roy Tinsley - the man who turned the company around - remember?'

'That is a matter of conjecture,' he said. 'You joined a very good company and helped me to develop it. You have been well paid for your efforts.'

The discussion went on for about another couple of hours and we also had quite a few drinks. When we returned to the office he told Max Dawson and the company accountant, Freddie Swallow, that he had been concerned something might have been worrying me and we had just had a long discussion. He emphatically told them that I was not leaving the company. Once he had finished reporting to them, I asked him to accompany me to my office. There I brought out my personal files and showed him the balance sheets for Westmyer prior to my appointment. 'Everyone told me I was a mug to join Westmyer,

particularly after I had seen these balance sheets,' I said. 'Yet I felt confident we could make it together. That's why I ignored these - here - have you seen them before?' He took them and started to read through and immediately tore them into shreds saying, 'How did you get these? Don't let anybody see these - nobody!' He went out of my office and I went home. I sat down with Shirley and explained exactly what had happened. One possibility was that he wanted me out because his own son, Graham was now in the wings. If that was so, then Max was doing very well and maybe he thought he could do okay without me.

After pondering the situation very carefully, I felt we had both acted hastily, so I decided to telephone him at home. The phone rang for quite a while and was answered by someone I knew - Jeff Miller, who was the Northern Manager for Heidelberg. He immediately recognised my voice and said, 'Hello Roy, do you want Harry?' 'Yes Jeff, please put him on.' There was a pause for about two minutes, then Jeff came back and said Harry was too busy to speak to me at that moment. I had never felt so humiliated. I drove to the factory and left all my keys and credit cards on Harry's desk with a note stating: 'If you cannot even take the time to speak to me on the telephone then it would be better if I resigned. Herewith are my keys and credit cards. Please send me whatever my one share in the company is worth along with my holiday pay.' I went outside, locked the door of the works with the remaining key I had and pushed that back through the letterbox. Shirley

had followed me there in her car and took me back home. Six wasted years - that's what I call my Westmyer experience. And here I was again - no job, no car. What should I do?

About two weeks later, a friend of mine in the trade rang me and said he was sorry to hear about my ill-health and hoped I would soon get better. When I questioned him he said he had telephoned Westmyer and asked for me. Harry West, he said, had told him I had a bit of a scare with my heart and had decided to help my two sons on a part-time basis as they built up their own business in the printing industry. I hit the roof. I rang Harry demanding to know why he had circulated such a rumour and told him to refute it immediately or I would contact my solicitor. He said little or nothing but the very next day he did a blanket mailing shot to all printers stating I had resigned my directorship of Westmyer, left of my own accord and as far as they were concerned remained in good health. About three days after that mailing I received a letter from Freddie Swallow. He told me that, as a Director, I was not entitled to holiday pay as I was paid in advance. There was no pay due and he enclosed £1 being the amount my share was worth in Westmyer. By return of post I sent Harry West my personal cheque for £1 to cover what they had sent me. I never saw or spoke to Harry West again for something like five years. We then bumped into each other at an exhibition and he asked me to have a drink with him. I didn't particularly have any feelings for him either way by then so accepted his invitation. He

said a few things about my leaving which didn't really count for much as far as I was concerned and we parted. I occasionally come across him but more by luck than judgment.

"DOWN -BUT NOT OUT" - Lets have a laugh!
We decided to take a weeks holiday and booked one of those "Square Deal" ones and went to Spain with our good friends Cora and Dennis Pease and Iris and Ken Favell. It helped enormously and seemed to be one long laugh. We hired three cars and went around in a convoy. We went right into the middle of Spain, meeting some of the local villagers who spoke no English. Dennis always bragged he could speak Spanish so we left the talking to him.

We went to a small newsagents who also sold ice cream - but he couldn't really understand what we were asking for. Dennis said to leave it to him and came out with the classic line *"Ice-a-de-creamo for De Bambino Monsieur"*, what was more amazing the guy understood him! On the way back to the Hotel, Dennis said he would lead our convoy back as he had a good idea for a very scenic route. We left matters to him, but when we got near Palma he seemed to take a wrong turn and we finished up in a field. Dennis, not liking to be beat, kept plodding on - and we like lost sheep followed him. We turned another couple of times and finished up on a very, very wide road. We then slowed down, just to see where we were, when a jet plane soared above us. We were on the runway at Palma Airport!!!

We immediately spotted a jeep loaded with four policemen - all armed with machine guns chasing after us. We turned around and drove like the clappers towards a side road which seemed like an exit. The police got within 100 yards of us, but when we got to the exit road and headed in the direction of Palma, they turned around and went back. Frightening at the time, but funny to look back on.

— CHAPTER 19 —

THE TINSLEY-ROBOR EXPERIENCE

After two weeks out of work I needed to find a job and quick. I had kept in touch with John Rose throughout my time at Westmyer and had recently purchased a two-colour Solna from one of John's companies called Howards of Slough. We had even discussed the idea of sometime setting up something together. So I contacted John and told him I had decided to leave Westmyer and asked if he was still interested in starting a printing machinery company with me. He certainly was! He immediately asked me to go and see him at his home in Sussex. When I explained I no longer had a car he said, 'Come down by train and we will arrange something.' Within a couple of hours he called back: 'Take a train to Slough and call at St. Michael's Garage in Windsor. There you will find a new car ordered on your behalf. Pick it up and then motor down here to see me.' I did just that and collected a brand new Ford Granada GLE and went to see John. He later apologised for only

supplying me with a Granada after I had been used to a Jaguar but I assured him that was the least of my worries. At his home he introduced me to his wife, Eileen. I found her charming and easy to get along with but she soon left us so that John and I could discuss business.

For years within the Tinsley-Robor Group there had been a dormant company called S.Tinsley Ltd. We decided to re-activate it for, as John pointed out, 'Your name fits the group perfectly'. He then offered me a salary which made me realise how underpaid I had been at Westmyer and helped me to appreciate how fair my new boss was going to be. We decided to try and keep the company small to start with and budgeted for a turnover of about £1 million in the first year. We did need premises and John arranged for a director in the group, Barry Walford, to come to Bradford and assist with obtaining a suitable place. Barry and I hit it off immediately and I had a lot of respect for him. We were to remain friends for the next eight years or so. Barry was most helpful in obtaining some good premises for our start-up operation. We managed to negotiate a deal with Bradford Council for a 3,500 sq.ft. factory in Hockney Road. I approached a printing engineer friend called Billy Clubb to join me and found a girl to work in the office, plus a couple of labourers and an apprentice. We were ready to put the show on the road except for one important person. I needed someone to work with me on sales, administrative work and be my deputy when I was away from the office. Who better than my old friend Tommy Lambert. Tommy

was by then semi-retired but I managed to talk him into joining up again. We soon developed into a good team once more.

The first machine we purchased was a Heidelberg KORD for £5,000 and we sold it for £12,000. We then bought a few small Heidelbergs and we were on our way. We weren't setting the world on fire but all my old friends in the trade were responding positively. In the first few years we progressed well, managed to build up a good customer base and made a small profit. We gained a good name in the industry, particularly for the quality of the secondhand presses that we had reconditioned. The girl in the office was a devout Jehovah's Witness and wanted more time off to go out converting people to her faith. I felt, therefore, it was time to part company and appointed my daughter as secretary. Carol was the sort of daughter all parents would like their girls to be. She had a formal education, progressed to Grammar School and did reasonably well there. She started her working life as a secretary at a printing business and then found a better job in the office of a shipping company. She was extremely competent, a good typist and very confident. She was like a breath of fresh air in my office and organised the whole place very well. One day I received a call from the Forward Trust Group in Glasgow. They said they now owned a six-colour Heidelberg Speedmaster. It was located at a local company that had recently gone bust. They wondered if we would like to purchase it from them. I immediately went off to inspect it, taking

Shirley with me. She couldn't always travel with me, but there were many occasions when we did manage to go away together. At the factory in Glasgow I was led into a huge, morgue-like building, not a soul anywhere, with plastic covers over all the machines. The caretaker took me to see this beautiful Speedmaster and to say I was impressed was an understatement. After giving it a full inspection I went to the Forward Trust offices and told the man there I was very interested in buying the machine. After some very hard bargaining we hit on a price of £196,000. Then I had to convince John Rose it was a good buy and we could make money out of it. That would be the hard part of the deal! I decided to stick my neck out and right there in the Glasgow office I said we would take it and asked for an invoice. We shook hands on the deal and I left. I did phone Tommy and told him what I had done.

Back at our hotel Shirley and I celebrated with wine and a good meal. Before I got back to our Bradford office the next day Tommy had sold the Speedmaster! Another company, Dornier, had heard about the Speedmaster and for the past ten days had been involved in negotiations concerning it. They had actually offered it to a company in the States but when they went back to Forward Trust to purchase it they found I had already nipped in and completed the deal. Dornier then offered us £210,000. Tommy and John Rose decided to accept this so long as Dornier paid in full the following day. And they did. We had not parted with a penny. We had the money to pay

for the press without touching our own capital and Dornier moved the press out themselves. My own cost sheet was: petrol £16 and a meal £5. Profit for the day was £13,979! About three weeks after this nice deal a very large printing company in London asked me to make an offer for one of their Heidelbergs. The trip there and back was completed in a day. I offered £14,000 which they accepted and we arranged to take it out within seven days. Three days later their accountant - who didn't speak good English and seemed to have difficulty understanding my Yorkshire accent - called me to say they had decided to sell a second Heidelberg and would I pay £14,000 for that also. I agreed. The next day I received an invoice for one machine at £14,000. Two days later we went to London and took out both machines. We paid the first invoice but never received the second. Perhaps the accountant was happy to sell both for £14,000. Maybe that is what he thought he had negotiated. I will never know. To us £14,000 was a very attractive price for one machine. If Jimmy Greaves could say of football "It's a funny old game" - then so is the printing machinery business.

In another deal one of the largest companies in the UK asked me to remove two Heidelbergs within 24 hours. They had new machinery arriving and had been let down by another printers' engineer who had promised to take out the Heidelbergs. I negotiated a ridiculously low figure for the two, took them both out the same day - and never even received an invoice. With those sort of deals going through, the business looked good. Our staff had now built up to ten

and we were increasing turnover astronomically. Unfortunately our profits were not growing at the same rate although we were certainly holding our own. Perhaps we were too quality conscious! I refused, however, to cut down on the quality because we were beginning to get repeat orders on the strength of our previously supplied machines. I found working with John Rose was marvellous - he was so straight and there was no deceit. I knew exactly where I stood and had already received two increases in salary without asking!

Life was good. Earning a good salary. Working with a good company who appreciated my efforts and rewarded me accordingly.

As a family we were engrossed in the Cricket scene and Shirley and I went to many matches, including those I played. We watched Gary and Steven who were developing into very good players. A very proud moment for all the family was the day they represented the league side playing on the 'hallowed' turf of Headingley Cricket Ground.

Just previous to this I was talked into entering the local election as a Conservative candidate. Being a member of the local Conservative Club, I enjoyed all their facilities and felt it was time I put a bit back into our local town. Having been a Trade Union secretary, I had always voted Labour, but recently had taken on the conservative badge. A young man called Andrew Carter asked if he could be my agent and did a magnificent job. We

won by about 300 votes. Andrew is still in local politics and was Deputy Lord Mayor of Leeds in recent years.

Ireland was still proving a good ground for second-hand printing machines and I enjoyed visiting such a wonderful country. Shirley managed to make the occasional trip with me and we never failed to enjoy ourselves.

I remember vividly one particular visit. A premier printing house over there is 'Alpha-Print' and I helped them get started in their early days. Cecil Wheatley and "P.J." were lovely people and they were the founders of the company. P.J. had been courting 'Kitty' about eight years and had been engaged about six years. One day after we had a couple of drinks I said to P.J. "don't you think it's time you both got married." "Yes" said P.J., "But who would have us?" I said we would love to come to the wedding if it ever happened.

A few months later we got an invitation and Shirley and I went over, we had a super time and it seemed to go on for days. Being in that wonderful Catholic Church in Athlone, listening to the beautiful solo tenor voice and the magnificent choir, and the lovely wedding ceremony re-activated my religious belief again and I will always be grateful for that.

On a later trip to Ireland, I went to see a Printer in Mullingar who placed a nice order with me. He asked me to go to the pub with him and his

partners to celebrate the deal. I know we all bought a round of Harp Lagers, so after about an hour I had drank about four pints. Having arranged to meet someone in Dublin that evening I felt it was time to go. In Ireland there is no problem getting into a pub, the problem is getting out, especially when you are in good company and the pints are flowing. However I did eventually make it.

There are some very quiet roads out of Mullingar, and it was very dark. After about twenty miles I was bursting to 'spend a penny'. I'd gone through a couple of small hamlets but had not been able to find a toilet. I was now at bursting point and pulled up at the side of the road. It was very dark but I could make out a small wall about three feet high, twenty yards away. It seemed the perfect place, so I decided to jump over it. putting my left hand on the wall I leapt over. To my horror there was a twenty to thirty foot drop on the other side. It wasn't a straight drop, more of a steep slope. I rolled over and over down the hill until I reached the bottom. My left ankle was killing me and the new mohair suit I was wearing was ripped to shreds. I had gone through blackberry bushes and some barbed wire. After collecting my thoughts I managed to clamber up the bank and crawl over the wall. I was in agony, such agony that I'd forgotten to have a leak. Eventually I managed that and stumbled back to the car. My ankle was coming up like a balloon. Sitting in the driving seat I couldn't put any pressure on the clutch to engage gear. I felt I had broken my ankle in about

twelve places. Switching feet I got into second and then third gear. Keeping that gear I got back to Dublin and went immediately to hospital. After various X-rays they confirmed it was a very bad sprain and I would be incapacitated for some considerable time. I must have taken about a year to get completely right. For part of the time I had to wear a shoe with a leg-iron. Needless to say, I have never jumped over a wall since that day!

It had got around to the time of my re-election for Pudsey Council. It was another part of my life I enjoyed. It's surprising how much sway councillors carry and I used to get many requests from constituents asking me if I could get their street lights attended to, their drains cleared out, dustbins emptied and such like on a regular basis. In just about every case I was successful in attending to their requests. One man came to see me one day and asked me if I could get his wife a Council Flat as he was "sick of the sight of her" and she was a "bad influence on their dog and four children". I didn't manage to help that constituent. He took it badly and said he would not vote for me in the following week's local election. My ankle was a real burden and I couldn't get out canvassing as much as I would have liked to have done. Come the election I lost to the Labour Candidate (Stanley Pearson) a very good friend, by seven votes after two recounts.

— CHAPTER 20 —

THE HANSON INTERVENTION

After six years of trading, John Rose felt the time was right to obtain the services of a proven salesman and we advertised nationally. There was a fair response with at least a couple worth interviewing. It was then I received a telephone call from an old friend of mine - Phil Padmore, a former Sales Director of T.C. Thompson. He mentioned a young man called Ken Hanson who had been quite successful for their company selling Thompson Crown Offsets. He went on to say that Hanson was now working with Graphic Arts Equipment selling Fuji presses. Phil spoke highly of him and asked if we were interested. I said with a personal recommendation like that I certainly was. So Ken Hanson made contact and was called for an interview. I was impressed. He came through as a go-ahead, confident salesman and although he had no knowledge of the Heidelberg and Roland range of equipment he assured me he was quite quick to learn. After

sifting through all the applications we decided to shortlist two - Ken Hanson and Keith Billings. Keith Billings subsequently worked for many years with Bradley Graphics and I was to rue the day we chose Ken Hanson instead of him. John Rose came along for the final interviews and we both agreed that Hanson just shaded it so we offered him the job. It was the biggest mistake I have ever made in over 50 years in the printing industry. At the time, however, I checked carefully with his two previous employers. Phil Padmore, of course, gave him an excellent report and Graphic Arts didn't say anything wrong. If I had gone to a previous employer, a printer in Accrington, he would never have been appointed. It was only after I fired him that I checked with them and found out what I had come to suspect.

He had come into the job with all the confidence of an experienced salesman. All his thoughts seemed to be for my concern. He couldn't do enough for me. I was making frequent trips to Germany and apart from being time-consuming, I was suffering badly from my back again. "Why don't you let me do these trips for you" he would say, "I know enough about Heidelbergs now".

Before Ken went to view machines in Germany, I had already agreed a 'ball-park' figure for the presses. Invariably he would call me from Germany and say 'It's a very good machine Roy, but there are more extras on it than we realised so we will have to pay more for it. But don't worry, I'm sure I can sell it' and invariably he did!

Nevertheless I still felt uncomfortable about a lot of the transactions Hanson concluded.

It was about that time that Ken came into my office and locked the door after him. He told me that on a recent visit to Meissner in Germany he had seen a lot of rebuilt Heidelberg platens. He had, therefore, asked Mr Meissner to 'throw one in' on the next order as he felt it would be a good asset to my two sons. We negotiated with Mr Meissner for a couple of Heidelberg GTOs and while I thought they were a bit expensive we agreed to go ahead. When they arrived at our factory we found there was an extra Heidelberg platen. I asked Hanson for the invoice and he showed me a copy invoice with no mention of the Heidelberg platen. My sons could certainly use another platen and Ken said, 'Put it in - who's to know?' I still felt uncomfortable so, without telling him, I spoke to John Rose and explained the situation. John asked how much it was worth and I told him at least £1,000. John agreed they could have it for £750. The lads paid us and we put it in. The significance of that little story comes later.

Some months later, after much deliberation, I had given in to Hanson's persuasions to be allowed to take on our business in the States. We had been doing a huge amount of work there and our profits were so good I had introduced John Rose to my nephew in California - Jim Magouhey. This successful meeting led to us appointing Jim to our staff and opening a factory over there. Jim pulled in a lot of business and we even sold a

Speedmaster to the University of California. I went to shows in San Francisco and Chicago where I obtained some big orders. However all that travelling was making my back trouble far worse and I was suffering badly. So I relented and let Ken Hanson go to an exhibition in Long Beach, California, where we had decided to exhibit a four-colour Heidelberg. He teamed up with my nephew there. On his return he told us the exhibition had been a complete flop so far as S. Tinsley and Co. were concerned. There hadn't been a single order. Yet within days there were telephone calls from clients in the USA asking for Ken Hanson and demanding to know when their machines would be delivered! He was later to set up his own company in the States using many of the contacts he had gained while with us. With all my investigations I found many discrepancies but didn't have 100 per cent proof of my suspicions.

I had booked to go to our caravan at Ulrome near Bridlington for a ten day holiday. I left specific instructions that Ken was not to buy anything or to attempt to sell any of the large stock we had accumulated. Nor did I want him to go abroad on our behalf. Shirley and I had been away for about six days when my daughter drove over to see us. She told me that a big lorry had arrived at our factory with two large machines consigned to 'Hanson'. Hanson had stored them in Jim McElroy's factory next door and told one of our engineers that he had just bought them for £36,000. They were his property, he said, not Tinsley's. Even though it was a Sunday morning I

went straight to the factory. I telephoned him at home and told him to come there immediately and to bring his keys. When he arrived I told him that was the end of our association. It was fortunate I did not uncover much of what he had done till after he had left. Otherwise I would probably have done something drastic or said things I might have regretted. As it was I forced myself to remain calm - or I might have had a heart attack. I asked him for his keys to the car (a very nice white Opel Manta) and saw him to the front door. It was all over in three minutes. The very next day he arrived at Jim McElroy's factory in a brand new brown Opel Manta!

While investigating all the Hanson deals that seemed suspicious, I went to Germany and interviewed the management of one of the German companies that we purchased machines from. They would or could not produce any evidence about commissions paid to Ken Hanson. I went onto the second firm called Wolfgang Alves. We had purchased many machines from them and the boss could not understand my investigations. That wasn't surprising since most deals Ken Hanson negotiated with them had included an additional cash payment which, Wolfgang Alves had been told, I urgently required for my new house. After the first such payments he had become a little worried because I hadn't discussed this arrangement with him. So for all subsequent payments he asked Hanson to sign for them. He then went to his safe and brought out proper authenticated documents containing Hanson's

signature. This was the evidence I required. He gave them to me and I brought them back to England. When I informed John Rose about what I had obtained he agreed we should call in the police. The tie-up I couldn't understand was Hanson and Jim McElroy. Jim was an engineer who I had personally helped. I had given him a lot of work and made many deals with him. As I considered him a personal friend and with the police becoming involved, I decided to tell him how matters were progressing concerning Hanson. I phoned him and we had a private meeting during which I told him about the signed documents at Wolfgang Alves, the false invoices and fictitious cost sheets. I argued I had enough to make a strong case against Hanson and, as a friend, felt that Jim should think carefully about doing any business with him. That proved to be a big mistake on my part. By forewarning Jim I had forewarned Hanson so he knew exactly what I had against him. As the saying goes 'forewarned is forearmed'. It did not surprise me about Hanson but I was staggered about Jim McElroy. Sgt John Hesketh was in charge of the case and he made a very thorough investigation. Wolfgang Alves was invited to the opening of our new factory in Saltaire and Sgt Hesketh spent many hours with him. He also checked on the altered invoices, cash payments and everything else. It all seemed to be taking a very long time but I felt the police were making headway.

Three months after Ken had been dismissed he wrote to John Rose stating I had stolen a platen.

He gave the machine number, said the platen could be found at my sons' factory and that he had lodged the original invoice with his solicitors! This was the same Heidelberg platen which had come from Meissner's. My whole career could have been ruined if I hadn't been straight with John Rose at the time!

At long last Sgt. Hesketh was able to announce that Hanson had admitted to taking the cash he had signed for in Germany.
'That proves it then', 'We've finally got him', I said, 'I'm afraid not,' he replied. 'Hanson's defence is "Yes, I took the money but on Roy Tinsley's instructions and I passed it all back to him." And with that the Director of Public Prosecutions has decided not to go ahead!' I couldn't believe he was going to get away with it. I was devastated. A few days later Hanson wrote to me. In a spiteful letter he said his solicitor would be writing to me about certain malicious and slanderous statements I had made about him to a German company and Jim McElroy! His solicitor did contact me and informed me that those comments were damning as to Hanson's professional integrity and character and demanded I should write a letter of apology within seven days retracting them. If I did not, civil proceedings would be taken against me to claim substantial damages for defamation of character. I was absolutely delighted as that would give me the opportunity to state my full case in court. I instructed my solicitors to reply that I would in no way retract and would be pleased to see them in court. I never received any more

correspondence from that solicitor. Need I say more!

I have never spoken to Hanson since the day he left. During a trip to Holland in 1995 I met Jim McElroy on the plane. We had a drink together and exchanged a few words. He went on to say how his association with Hanson had worked out badly for him and I consider we have renewed our friendship.

My family and other interests kept me sane after the Hanson Incident. The three cricket clubs that gave me most pleasure were, Kirkstall Educational in the Leeds League, Lockwood in the Huddersfield League and Farsley in the Bradford League. Gary, Steven and myself played for all three clubs and we enjoyed endless happy hours with all of them. My association with Farsley goes back many years, and the present President is Ray Illingworth of England fame. In the seventies we had a very useful junior in the same side as Gary and Steven called Phil Carrick. He was approached by the Yorkshire County Cricket Club to play with the Colts, but he needed a kind hearted employer to give him a job and release him when he was required by Yorkshire, Who else? He was such a nice respectful lad I had no hesitation in giving him a job. He progressed into being a regular with the first team and later as captain was successful winning the Benson & Hedges Trophy in 1987. We are still good friends along with all the other characters associated with those very happy years.

Now in my seventieth year, I still manage to play cricket in the Bradford Evening League. My career having spanned from 1939 (Rastrick 2nd XI) to 1996. No fool like an old fool they say!

— CHAPTER 21 —

PICKING UP THE PIECES

The year Hanson left was a disaster so far as profits were concerned. We made a trading loss of £150,000 after we had taken into consideration all those fictitious cost sheets and altered invoices. John Rose was tremendous and gave me wonderful support at a time when it was most needed. In the following months I worked a 60 to 70 hour week to try and turn things around. Shirley never complained. She made sure there was always a nice meal awaiting me when I did get home and occasionally would phone me at the office and suggest we went out for a meal instead. We continued to make time for any events at the special school that Chris attended. Chris had an amazing memory for routes and was very good at map reading. We often asked him to plan a Sunday tour for us and he would be our guide as we drove through various parts of the Yorkshire Dales. We especially liked Grassington or dropping off for a meal at the Three Sisters in Haworth.

At work the new factory in Saltaire had been sorely needed, for we had been bursting at the seams for extra space. We were also receiving many calls from the States and so became aware of how many deals Hanson had made with my nephew - at our expense. With the dollar so strong it was still a very good market and I decided to put a lot more time into developing our contacts there. It was tough though for there were many rogues in the business and it was a difficult and painstaking job to sort out the "goodies from the baddies". Among those we came into contact with was a company called Bob Shwermer Graphics. They asked for our complete stock list. They selected about five machines and asked us to send pro-forma invoices and photographs of the presses. They presented themselves very well and the enquiry seemed genuine. About a week after we sent the photographs we received a telephone call from Mr Wood of Wood Printing Company in Washington asking if we had a specific Heidelberg in stock and he gave the serial number. We confirmed we had it and asked how he knew all the details. He said they had been shown the pro-forma invoice and a photograph of the press by a Mr Dale Silver of Shwermer Graphics. We pointed out that we had not as yet sold the machine. Mr Wood, however, said they would prefer to obtain it through a US company like Shwermer Graphics as Mr Silver had guaranteed they would service the machine. Four weeks later we received another call from Mr Wood asking how long it would be before his machine was delivered. We informed him we had not received any order for it. He said

Mr Silver had visited him three weeks before, informed him that Tinsley's were ready to despatch the machine and had requested him to pay 90 per cent of the purchase price. So he had handed Mr Silver US $86,500. Mr Silver had then told him to contact us about a delivery date! Poor Mr Wood. He never got his press and he never got a penny back from Shwermer Graphics. It seemed they had 'sold' all the machines we had sent photographs of - not just once in some cases but up to three times! Some friends of mine - Tomkins Printing Company in Chicago - telephoned me and warned me to beware of Shwermer Graphics and they sent me a newspaper cutting. Later Shwermer Graphics went into liquidation.

For ourselves our efforts on the export side began to pay off and even in the States we were often selling machines direct to printers rather than going through dealers. We continued to do business through Tomkins of Chicago, however, as they proved to be so reputable. When a large International Printing Machine Exhibition was to be held at the MacCormack Centre in Chicago I decided it would be a good idea to attend. There was quite a group of Brits travelling together for the 'British Printer' had organised the trip.

It was a long, tedious journey, however, and I couldn't help feeling I had the most uncomfortable seat on the aircraft. We checked into our hotel and I went for a shower. I had arranged to meet two American friends, Larry Tomkins and Dick Patterson for dinner later and decided to rest on

the bed for a while. I had a lot of pain in my back though. As dinner time approached I got up and started to get dressed. Then I collapsed by the side of the bed. I could hardly move. Just as in a movie when someone has been shot, I crawled to the telephone table and pulled the phone down by the wire - I was in such agony. The receptionist eventually answered and I asked if there was a doctor in the hotel or if she could arrange for one to visit me. She explained that no doctors went out on call in Chicago except to known patients. It seemed a few years earlier a group of people were calling doctors out, mugging them and taking their money, credit cards and cars. I tried to explain exactly how I was but she would not send anyone to help me. Finally I managed to persuade her to page Mr Tomkins and Mr Patterson. Thankfully they were in the hotel and she directed them to my room. When they arrived they took one look at me and burst out laughing - until they realised I was not joking and could not move. They were a tremendous help. They managed to help me put on a shirt and some trousers and borrowed a wheelchair from the hotel. They took me down in the lift and into Larry's car - but not without a lot of trouble and excruciating pain. We decided to go to Chicago Central Hospital where yet another wheelchair was organised for me. At the reception my friends said I needed to see a doctor. The clerk simply replied: 'How do you propose to pay?' Larry emphasised it was an emergency but the clerk explained that as it wasn't Chicago Free Hospital he would have to take a rubbing of my credit card and my signature against one of their

standard forms before I could see anyone.

Dick had picked up my watch and wallet from the hotel room and so I offered my Barclaycard which they duly processed. I was then wheeled into the actual hospital and within five minutes was visited by a young doctor. He prodded and poked me and suggested I should have an X-ray. I was left alone in the room for about two hours until two people came and took me for an X-ray. After that I was returned to my solitary room and waited another hour until a doctor came in and said there was nothing they could do for me. He suggested I should go to a friend's home and rest for three or four days or otherwise book into a hospital. He again emphasised they could do nothing for me. By that time I had been in hospital for about five hours and it was 11pm. I was wondering what had happened to Dick and Larry, but as luck would have it they had left a telephone number so I could contact them. I phoned them and they came back to the hospital around midnight. Larry had a long talk with the doctor and returned looking very sad. 'Roy, let's go back to my house,' he said. 'You can rest there for a while and then we'll see what we can do.' When I left the hospital the doctor had given me the X-rays in a very large brown envelope. With a great deal of struggling they got me off the hospital bed, into a wheelchair and out to Larry's car. I was quite happy to go to Larry's house for both Shirley and I had met his wife, Joan, when they had visited England and we had all become good friends.

They had a beautiful house and made me very comfortable. They gave me a room to myself with TV and shower and told me to rest as much as possible. Once on the bed, however, I couldn't move. I even had to use a bedpan - never had I felt so depressed. They were both wonderful caring people and I shall remain eternally grateful to them. It was seven days before I could just about make it to the toilet on my own. I tried to have a shower that day but became paralysed while there and they had to help me back to the bed. Larry had given me free licence to use his telephone and had put it at the side of my bed. So I was able to keep in contact with my family. I told them simply that my back was playing up again. After ten days Larry said he would like me to visit his chiropractor - a doctor who specialised in using the manipulation remedy. Larry and another couple of guys helped me into the wheelchair and took me to the doctor's clinic. I took the X-rays with me. The doctor welcomed me, shook my hand and got me onto the bed. After a few minutes of prodding and poking me he took the X-rays to another room. He came back about half an hour later and said: 'I'm afraid there is nothing I can do for you. Have they informed you at Chicago Central what the X-rays show?' I said 'No' for as far as I was concerned it was a recurrence of my old back problem. He got me back into the wheelchair and took me into the next room with Larry. He put the X-rays onto the illuminated cabinet and pointed to the two big grey areas at the bottom of my spine. He circled them with a red felt tip and said: 'I'm afraid it is

the big "C" - those areas are malignant.' I couldn't
believe it. Larry looked shocked to the core. I was
absolutely devastated. 'Are you sure?' I asked. 'As
near to sure as I can be,' he replied. 'They marked
it in blue at Chicago Central.' I looked at the X-
rays and there was no doubt there was a very big
shadow there. 'There was nothing they could do,'
he said again. Larry took me back to his house
where I asked if he could book me on the next
available flight home. I had a little more
manoeuvrability than I had ten days earlier and I
felt I could stand the trip home. Larry and Joan
left me to phone Shirley in private. I told her the
doctor had diagnosed cancer, but I wasn't sure and
would want a second opinion. We were both in a
state of shock. The journey home seemed endless.
The cabin staff were marvellous. They arranged
for a wheelchair to be available at Heathrow and
another one at Leeds-Bradford. When I arrived
there all my family had come to meet me - that
gave me a big lift. Once home and I was alone
with Shirley we talked it over and felt we should
book an urgent appointment with my own doctor,
Mr Carr. He was the man who had performed a
laminectomy operation on my spine about eight
years previously and had treated me on other
occasions when my back had given me trouble. He
was happy to see me immediately and asked me to
bring along those X-rays. By the time I went I was
feeling much better and didn't even need a
wheelchair. Shirley drove me to his surgery and
when he saw me he exclaimed: 'What a load of
nonsense. You've got cancer! Ridiculous! You
look too well to have cancer.' I gave him the X-

rays. He put them onto his illuminated cabinet, peered closely at those areas marked in blue and red and announced: 'That's scar tissue from your operation - nothing more.'

Shirley and I were now feeling a lot better to say the least. 'I'll tell you what we will do,' he said. 'I will arrange for a scan for you immediately.' Which he did, at the Yorkshire Clinic. I only had to wait a day for the results and although I already felt so much better there was still that nagging doubt in my mind so that day seemed to take years to pass. Pass it did though, and we went to see Mr Carr again. He said he had just received the scan results and suggested we look at them together. He went through everything with me. He explained I had some arthritis in my shoulder which showed on the scan but otherwise everything was completely clear. I felt 10ft tall. Shirley's relief was also visible to see. We went out that night and celebrated. It was great telling the kids and all our friends. In fact, I seemed to be cured overnight. My back was virtually back to normal. So much for the American doctors! We agreed I should try and avoid long plane rides for as long as possible. There was one trip, planned for three months later, which we could not continue to put off, however, and that was to California where my cousin Nancy and her husband Mac lived. They had already visited us twice and we had promised to reciprocate. It was to prove an extremely eventful visit.

CHAPTER 21 (A)

I LEFT MY HUSBAND IN SAN FRANCISCO

It was the 21st birthday present Carol was unlikely to ever forget. The holiday in California with Nancy and Mac was marvellous. We took Chris, of course, who was eight by then. With Shirley and I still enjoying life together it was hard to believe how fast the family had grown up. The day of our return to England dawned hot and sunny in San Francisco so I went to the airport in open-toe sandals, T-shirt and shorts. I intended to change into trousers and jacket just before we got to Heathrow. We bade our farewells to Nancy and Mac and boarded the plane. Departure time was 12.55pm and we were on board with our seat belts fastened by 12.20pm. There was an announcement on the plane's Tannoy saying that as there were no Duty-Free facilities on board passengers would be allowed to leave the aircraft to buy some at the shop by the boarding gate. Although I didn't smoke, I said I would get some cigarettes for Carol's boyfriend, Steven. Along with another six

passengers I left the plane. As we had quite a long time before departure I browsed around in the shop for a while, bought the cigarettes and went down the long corridor towards the plane. To my shock, as I reached the end of the corridor, the plane was being slowly towed away by a small lorry. There it was - I could virtually touch it - but I couldn't get on. The groundstaff man with his walkie-talkie was frantically calling the captain saying he had left two passengers behind. I learned later that Shirley and Carol were also frantic, begging the cabin staff to inform the captain. The plane, however, reversed another 25 yards, the engines started up and that was that. The groundstaff man said there was no way I would be able to board the plane. I was completely devastated.

A senior officer from British Airways (BA) came along and made profound apologies. He said there was a PAN-AM flight leaving within 20 minutes and he would get me on that as I would then reach Heathrow half an hour after my family's arrival. Unfortunately when he checked with PAN-AM he found it had already left. I don't know what was happening that day but all the flights seemed to be taking off earlier than scheduled. My state of nerves had reached fever pitch by then. I let out such a tirade at that BA officer who was beginning to panic himself. It seemed there was no way they could get me to England until the next day. So there I was in San Francisco with no change of clothes and Shirley, Christopher and Carol would arrive in England with no money or passports.

What a ridiculous situation! I seemed to be walking around in a blind panic and I played hell with anyone in a British Airways uniform. I felt I had to sit down for a few minutes and meditate - or I would go mad.

It was then I noticed a door with a cross on it. I pushed it open and, there in the middle of San Francisco Airport, was a small place of worship - a beautiful little chapel. It was empty. I sat down at a pew, put my hands together, said a short prayer and immediately felt better and calmer. For maybe 20 minutes I sat there and decided to look on the positive side with no more dashing about like a headless chicken! A BA officer had been searching for me and when I found him I asked him how they were going to get me home. He explained he had managed to book me on a flight to New York in three hours time and from there I could go on to Heathrow. He expected I would arrive at Heathrow ten hours after Shirley and the kids. It was the best he could offer he said and he stood back expecting another tirade. It didn't come. I accepted the flight with thanks and he proceeded to get me the ticket. When I eventually boarded the flight to New York - in my sandals, shorts and T-shirt - I was given a seat next to an enormous woman. I wasn't slim but she spread over into my seat. I went fishing about trying to fasten my seat belt and while I was doing this her smile became broader and broader. I don't know which part of her anatomy I was touching but it was obviously to her liking. Although I had calmed down considerably the last thing I wanted was a fling

with a large American lady who must have thought, after my antics with the seat belt, that I had designs on her. When I touched her again I apologised and explained what I was trying to do. She immediately replied: 'You are English - what a wonderful accent. Gee am I lucky sitting next to an Englishman on my first visit to England.' Was I trapped!

The plane took off and I think my lady passenger was prepared to take off as well. My groping about for the seat belt had really landed me in it. She said she was visiting England alone and had relatives in Scotland. I'm sure she felt she had just acquired a taxi driver, tourist guide and lover rolled into one. The plane was full and I understood the flight would take five and a half hours. I made an excuse to go to the toilet, walked to the front of the aircraft, drew back a curtain and found the equivalent of a Club Class with about 20 empty seats. I sat in the nearest to the curtain and heaved a sigh of relief. Within a few minutes one of the cabin staff came up to me and said I must return to the tourist section. I explained about being left in San Francisco and BA had booked the seat on my behalf. I had been told by BA it would be Club Class and she should take it up with them. I emphasised there was no way I was moving. After a deep consultation with a senior male member of the cabin staff she told me I could stay, providing I told BA that the crew had permitted this. The rest of the journey proved quite uneventful until we were about half an hour from New York. Then suddenly the curtain was

pulled back and my long-lost lady friend appeared: 'Gee I was worried about you - are you okay?'
'No,' I replied.
'I began to feel very ill and didn't want to inflict my illness on you so thought it best to leave you.'
'Can we travel together to London?' she asked.
'No,' I answered.
'I have to stop over in New York.'
She suspected she was getting the 'bums rush', turned around and left. She looked even fatter out of the seat.

When we arrived in New York, everyone started to put on fur coats, overcoats, hats and scarves. I still had shorts, T-shirt and sandals. We got out of the plane, up the gangway and it was then I noticed ... it was snowing. At Kennedy Airport I had to leave one building and take a bus to another terminal. It was absolutely freezing. My teeth were chattering. I must have looked a sorry sight dressed as I was and with my plastic bag containing 200 cigarettes. People on the bus looked at me as though I had just escaped from the local lunatic asylum. We eventually arrived at the terminal I required. A couple of taxi drivers saw me and burst out laughing. I was furious by that time. At the BA enquiry desk there was a rather cocky looking woman speaking on the telephone. She gave me the sort of look you reserve for despicable old tramps begging for food. She finished her telephone call, put the receiver down and completely ignored me. She went to make another telephone call so I hit the large, loud brass bell on the counter. She put down the receiver,

walked over to the counter and lifted her eyebrows - she didn't say a word. I immediately launched into the full story of being left in San Francisco and asked her what was the quickest way home. She seemed completely disinterested in everything I had said, turned round and walked back to her desk. She picked up the telephone and dialled a number. I thought she was trying to sort out my flight times. Not a bit of it. She had listened to my full story, taken another look at this bald-headed man in shorts and T-shirt and dialled the security number. Within a few minutes a man in BA uniform approached me and asked if he could help. The cocky bitch had telephoned someone to have this idiot thrown out! He did listen to my story and asked me to accompany him. Thankfully he believed me, for he took me to a BA counter and they processed a ticket for me so I could go on to Heathrow after a three hour wait. About 300 yards away I could see a beautiful lounge behind glass windows. It had a sign stating 'Concorde Departure Lounge'. All the passengers seemed to have pin-striped suits, white shirts, red ties and bowler hats, with the usual crumpled overcoat slung over one arm. It was then I started campaigning to go on Concorde. It was BA's fault I was in that predicament! Obviously I would have looked a little out of place on Concorde the way I was dressed but if I didn't mind why should they? It wasn't any good - BA wouldn't hear of it. So eventually I got on that later plane and reached Heathrow, ten hours after Shirley. We greeted each other as though we had been apart for ten years. It was such a relief to be back together again. On

her flight Shirley had received a handwritten apology from the captain and had been offered free drinks and free headphones. They were obviously trying to make up for what had happened but Shirley was so annoyed she didn't accept anything. Chris, however, didn't turn down the invitation to go forward to the flight deck. The captain did radio ahead to say our family had got split up in San Francisco, so Shirley, Chris and Carol were allowed to enter the UK without passports. BA also gave them £25 with which to buy some food. Shirley was asked to sign for the money as BA stressed it should be paid back as soon as the family was reunited. To be honest once we were back together the last thing on my mind was that £25. They did send me a reminder about a week later but in reply I stated that, as it had been their fault I had been left behind in San Francisco, they would have to send me an official invoice if they wanted me to repay them. I decided to press BA for some compensation. It's a very good amusing story to relate now - but at the time it was a terrible ordeal.

After many Fax and Telex exchanges they gave me a BA credit note for £450. This enabled Shirley and I to spend a wonderful long-weekend in Paris. Thank you British Airways!

— CHAPTER 22 —

WHO WANTS TO BE A MILLIONAIRE?

Soon after I returned to work I concluded a very nice deal with a Nigerian client who became very friendly. He wanted to see my home, my family - everything. Once he had checked us out thoroughly he made me the most amazing proposition I have ever had. He wanted to transfer US$11,000,000 into my personal account. Yes 11 million dollars! He said he knew three Government Ministers in Nigeria who wanted to transfer their savings, pension funds and family inheritances to England. They all wished to bring up their children here and settle. There was no way they could transfer the money to their personal accounts and the ideal situation would be for them to move the funds into an account of someone they could trust. They would leave the money in my account for three months and I could have the huge amount of interest that would accrue in that period. After that I was to withdraw the full amount except about US$100,000 interest. Each

man would visit me personally and I would give him a third of the original amount.

Shirley and I discussed it at great length. While the financial benefit would have been acceptable we both felt very uneasy about the whole situation. The first question was - why me? The Nigerian explained they required someone they could trust - a man of integrity, credibility and with strong family traditions and connections. In other words, someone who would not take the money and run. 'Surely you could find a Nigerian national living in this country who could act as the go-between?' I asked. He explained that the same three men had set up a similar operation four years earlier through a Nigerian permanently settled in London. They transferred US$9 million to his account. He drew it out and they never saw him again! We nudged closer to going ahead. We received a telex message from a US bank asking me to confirm that I was indeed Roy W. Tinsley and they gave my home address, my bank account number and where I banked. I even had discussions with my bank manager about the possibility of receiving such a huge transfer. He said he would personally visit me to advise me if such a sum arrived in my bank account! Still Shirley and I debated the issue. We feared it might be drugs money or even grand theft from some Nigerian government institution. Finally we decided to say 'No'. Our Nigerian friend had especially flown back to be in England when the cash was transferred to my account. He was shaken rigid when I telephoned him and told him

we had decided not to go ahead with the arrangement. He had already instructed my bank regarding the transfer and expected it to be made the following day. He pleaded with me to change my mind but I refused. I asked him to stop the transfer immediately. I don't know who they found to make the transfer to, but I felt a sense of relief once I had backed out of the transaction. The Nigerian and I remained good friends and he continued to buy printing machines from me.

SHAKE HANDS ON IT!
About that time a very nice Indian gentleman by the name of Mr Patel paid us a few visits. He resided just outside Bombay and as I had spent a long time there in the 1940s we became good friends. He ordered £28,000 worth of various types of older machines from me and I said we could have them all ready for shipment in about three weeks. When we agreed the deal I informed him we would require a deposit and the balance before shipment. He agreed and said he would come again the next day. The next morning he duly arrived and gave me a large thick envelope and announced, 'Here is the 25 per cent deposit Mr Tinsley. Please count it.' Sure enough there was £7,000 in cash. I thanked him and said I would get him a receipt. 'No receipt Mr Tinsley. No receipt is necessary. Just shake my hand.' He held out his hand. I shook it and said: 'I insist on giving you a receipt Mr Patel,' and I duly had one made and gave it to him. Three weeks later we had completed the machines and they were ready for despatch. We contacted him at a London

address where he was staying with relatives and he came to see us, bringing the £21,000 in cash as settlement. He also gave me another order worth about £30,000 for a delivery about three months later. He told me he planned to be in England again within a couple of months as he had placed an order with another company for some machinery and they expected it to be ready for inspection then.

Two months later I arrived at the office around 8.30am to find a very anxious Mr Patel waiting outside. He urgently wanted to meet with me as he needed help. The day before, he had returned to that other company only to be told they knew nothing about his order. I gathered that following his initial transaction with us he had gone there, given them an order and paid a £10,000 cash deposit. I immediately asked him if he got a receipt. He said he hadn't but they had shaken hands on the deal. Mr Patel was such a nice man who had probably been taught that an Englishman's word was his bond and a handshake sealed any deal. So he had handed over the £10,000 and had simply shaken hands, and as he had done with me, he told them, 'No receipt is necessary'. When he returned to inspect the machinery they denied any knowledge of his order. They said they didn't know him or anything about his £10,000. Poor Mr Patel - I couldn't help at all although I believed every word he said as the whole story was exactly the same as our transaction. About three months later that other company disappeared from the printing trade and has not been sighted since.

— CHAPTER 23 —

THE STING

Just as the business was doing well (1985/86), with a good customer base and plentiful orders on the home market we were almost entrapped in something similar to that shown in the film "The Sting".

The hardest part of our business was acquiring the right machines at the right price. One day we received a telex from a company in Germany offering us a four-colour Heidelberg Speedmaster Model 102VP (1981) and a Heidelberg GTOZP 46 (1982). A good purchase price for us on those presses would have been about £140,000 and £32,000. They offered them both for a total of £110,000. I immediately made a telephone call to the company, Smith Graphics (name changed), to confirm the prices. The owner, who spoke very good English, assured me the prices were correct and said they would be available in four weeks. He suggested we should move very quickly as

many others had shown interest in the presses. So they should have done at that price! I arranged to fly to Germany the next day and for him to collect and take me to inspect the machines - about an hour's drive from the nearest airport. As I entered the Airport Arrivals Lounge I spotted a well dressed gentleman holding aloft a printing journal with 'Mr Tinsley' written on a card underneath. After shaking hands he took me to the car park and ushered me into his magnificent new Mercedes 500. We exchanged a few pleasantries and he said he had been in the business about eight years. He had dealt mainly with companies in Italy and France, he explained, selling many types of Heidelberg equipment. The printer who had these present machines was a close friend of his and although they were being offered at a bargain price he had to make a big proportion of the payment in black money (cash). With that in mind he would do all the talking at the print factory especially as the printer didn't speak English. We went into the works and Mr Smith was very well received by the printer. They chatted a long time in German and eventually Mr Smith introduced me. We went to see the machines and they were both interested in tying up a deal as soon as possible.

The printer went into the office and brought out the original Heidelberg invoice that he got when he purchased the machines. It outlined all the extras and gave proof of ownership. Mr Smith then suggested I should go with him to his office as the printer had another appointment. It was a long drive to his factory which was on a small industrial

estate.   He drove up to what appeared to be a recently constructed unit which had their new nameplate very obviously stuck over an old one. As we passed through the reception I saw a man working at a desk. It struck me as strange that he never lifted his eyes or said 'Goot Morgen'. We then went into a plush office with a beautiful black leather suite and a very expensive table in the middle.   Bidding me to sit down he said he would prepare a contract that I could take back with me and in the meantime would arrange for a cup of coffee. He left the room and an extremely attractive blonde lady entered. She was wearing a very short leather skirt and a blouse with a deep cleavage.   She leaned over and asked in broken English if I took sugar.   I replied 'Just black' and within minutes she returned with a pot of coffee and two cups. She sat down at the side of me and poured the coffee. With the short skirt and low-cut blouse she had a difficult job covering anything up at all.   I asked her how long the company had been in those premises (Mr Smith had told me eight years). She replied 'About seven days I think'.   So I asked her how long she had worked for them and she responded 'Three days'. She did say she really liked the position as it gave her the opportunity to meet so many people. I felt uneasy. It just didn't gel somehow - what with the sign on the door, the guy at the desk ignoring us and now the office girl saying they had only been there seven days. I smelt a rat! Mr Smith came back about half an hour later with a document outlining all the details of the machines taken from the original invoices at a total deal of £110,000. It

required an immediate transfer of a 25 per cent deposit - £27,500 - and the balance when the machines were taken out. He went through the contract with me, paragraph by paragraph. He then requested the name of our bank. He asked if I would like to make a telephone call from his office and arrange an immediate bank transfer. I explained that a bank transfer would require two signatures and I would organise that on my return to Shipley. I should have felt elated at pulling off such a good deal. Both machines were highly marketable and we could expect a net profit on the pair of about £50,000. Yet I was still very uncomfortable and decided to sleep on it. He took me back to the airport where I said I would contact him the next day. Travelling back on the aircraft gave me time to think the deal through and I kept coming up with the wrong answers. I was sure there was a fiddle going on - but where? The printer had welcomed us both and had the original invoice. But to me Mr Smith did not ring true somehow. By the time I got back home I had decided not to go ahead.

When I arrived at the office at 8.30 the next morning, Mr Smith had already rung for me. I immediately called him back and informed him I was not going ahead with the deal. He became quite abusive, accusing me of wasting his time and complained that he had put off four other dealers because I had agreed to the purchase. I just spelt out my worries and said that as far as I was concerned that was the end of the matter. He replied he would make sure no other dealers in

Germany would do business with me. What's more he knew another British company who had said they would purchase the machines. With that he slammed down the telephone. I knew the two men who ran the company he had mentioned and we had been friends for years. I decided to telephone them and let them know what I felt about the deal. One of them agreed that Mr Smith was asking 'Mickey Mouse prices' for the machines but as the other spoke German fluently they would go and see if they could set up a watertight deal. He thanked me for showing an interest and my friendship. They went with Mr Smith to visit the printer who confirmed, in German, that Mr Smith had the sole rights to sell and would arrange some black money for him. My friends paid the deposit and, on the day they were to remove the presses, met Mr Smith at the same German airport. There Mr Smith asked for the banker's draft and explained he would have to go the bank and change a large proportion of it into cash in order to pay the printer. As this had been confirmed by the printer they didn't question Mr Smith but agreed they would all meet at the factory. My friends went ahead with a large lorry, crane, an electrician and two engineers. At the factory the printer said he would just like to wait until Mr Smith came with the cash and then they could go ahead and remove the machines. They waited and waited but there was no sign of Mr Smith. Slowly the awful truth dawned upon them - they had all been conned. The printer was as appalled as they were but he at least had not handed over any money. When they checked they found Mr Smith

had withdrawn all the money against the bankers' draft they had given him. They had been taken for around £100,000, plus the original deposit!

At S.Tinsley's we were bringing in some very good orders but we were having difficulty with processing them. I had to face reality. The main Board of Directors were constantly on my back saying profits were just not good enough. They insisted I should trim staff and create better profits. Although I knew it would be a difficult job I decided I would make my Technical Director redundant. There wasn't a nicer man in the world than Billy Clubb. He came into my office one Monday morning in 1985 as cheerful as ever. 'Good morning Roy - had a nice weekend?' he said. And there I was about to sack him! We discussed everything about the company and our failure to produce the sort of profits required. Finally I told Billy I had to cut corners somewhere and unfortunately he was going to lose his job. He was devastated - and so was I. Then I had to try and fix up a good redundancy package for him. I blamed myself for promoting him to a position he couldn't handle and so I advised him he had best forget being a Technical Director as he did not have the necessary organising ability. Rather he should do what he did best - being a printing engineer. I suggested he should team up with my son-in-law, Steven Fella, and start their own business. Carol and Steven were married in 1981. Steven had set up his own company renovating secondhand printing machinery. Together Billy and Steven created a thriving, superbly profitable

business which is still going strong.

I promoted the Works Foreman, John Brown, who had already shown considerable ability and proved most successful. He was very supportive and conscientious. We produced a good set of figures the following year and I managed to appoint a personal friend of 30 years standing, John Wood, to the position of Sales Manager. This move was resisted by John Rose and Barry Walford (a Group Director) as John Wood was 55-years-old. They said it was ridiculous to take someone on at that age. I stuck to my guns however and John was magic - he brought in a million pounds worth of business on the home market in the first three months. We brought in another salesman, John Goodwin, and the whole company seemed to take off. The next year's profits were excellent and I was beginning to feel a little more relaxed. Then we hit a quiet patch and the head office decided to appoint Barry Walford as Senior Group Director on to the Board of S. Tinsley & Co. and give him sole responsibility for profits.

Over the past nine years I had got on well with Barry. Both he and his wife had made me very welcome when I had stayed at their home. I felt we had a very close relationship. At that time we had progressed a long way in our negotiations with the Japanese firm, Akiyama, to become their exclusive agents in the UK for their exceptional new offset press. After seeing that press at a printing exhibition in Chicago I had chased the company all over the States to try and organise

such a deal but I made little headway at first. At a show in Philadelphia, after much effort, I managed to book an appointment to see Mr Ryujin, the President, and his interpreter Mr Morii. We hit on a perfect relationship and after our initial enquiries in the States, the deal was brought to completion at a show in Paris. Barry was also a very big help at this time and I personally felt that such an arrangement with Akiyama would lead to great things for our company. Unfortunately that agency arrangement led to a lot of friction between Barry and me - some of it very petty with some nasty, bitter exchanges which left no one with any credit whatsoever. We sold a couple of four-colour Akiyamas and that side of the business looked good, but the sales on the secondhand machines were going down and Barry must have felt the best way to improve things was to play hell with me. I can take pressure - but not to the degree that Barry exerted on me. Several things happened to foul our relationship until one day he telephoned me and said: 'Have you seen this month's figures?' 'No,' I said. 'You have an advantage over me - they haven't come up yet.' He began swearing at me - and he knew I would never use such language myself. He called the figures a disgrace and inferred that I was no longer capable of the job. He probably thought that would make me produce higher profits. It certainly did have a profound effect upon me. It actually rattled me. Especially when he said the company would 'go down the river' if I didn't 'pull my finger out'. That telephone conversation will live with me for the rest of my life.

A couple of weeks previously we had a major argument at a board meeting when he had accused me of being a liar. The whole relationship was deteriorating very badly. I will never know if there was any motive in those outbursts - perhaps not. If he did it to make me resign it did eventually have the desired effect. Barry came to our offices two days later to hold a meeting about lack of profits. When he entered he looked straight at me - no handshake, nothing. He announced that John Rose was on his way and was bringing a man called Geoff Lane who he felt had something to offer and was coming to 'look around'. John duly arrived, introduced Geoff Lane to me and then asked my deputy, John Brown, to show him around the works and take him to lunch.

We then started our meeting and tried to get a formula together to utilise our talents in the best possible way to increase profits. We were not making a loss. We did have enormous overheads, but we were still making a profit and were not too far off the set budget. I pointed out that our profitability would be further improved by the very good Nigerian orders I had just obtained. We had a fairly good meeting and had lunch at the office.

John Brown eventually arrived back with Geoff Lane and asked me to see him immediately. We met privately in my office where John told me: 'Roy, this guy is here to take your job.' 'Don't be ridiculous,' I replied. 'No Roy, I'm not exaggerating. He even said, 'This Roy Tinsley is going to be a hard act to follow'. It was then I decided to put the question to John Rose and Barry Walford.

They denied that Geoff Lane had been earmarked for my position but felt that I could do with a little help in making the company more profitable. Geoff Lane was known to me. I didn't particularly like him. I made it very clear that in no way did I want that man on my staff at Shipley. They seemed to accept that and his name was not mentioned again for sometime. My relationship with Barry, however, was becoming worse and to be honest it was getting me down. Work was now a complete pain. There was no fun any more and I was beginning to hate it. The Managing Directors' next quarterly meeting at head office in Chichester was due so I discussed the whole matter with Shirley who was already fully aware of how I felt. I told her I didn't feel I could continue and I might as well hand in my resignation. This was a big decision for I had no capital to fall back on and we had a very high mortgage repayment to make each month. As I drove to Chichester I had ample time to consider all the relevant facts which had led to me considering resigning. Whichever way I decided to do it didn't really matter to me. The only consideration was should I leave or not and my mind was made up - I would leave. I am sure John Rose, the Chairman, had no idea how strongly I felt.

We had discussed my position with the company on many occasions and we always came up with the same result - that I should stay with them until my retirement. John had been a true friend as well as a good employer and there was no way I wished to upset him. In fact if there had been any

other man at the helm, I would have gone for 'constructive dismissal' as that was exactly how I believed things stood. However with all my respect for John I couldn't do that. When I arrived at Chichester I exchanged all the usual pleasantries with the head office staff and the other Managing Directors. As the meeting progressed I felt very uncomfortable giving my usual report when it was my intention to resign afterwards. When the meeting did end and the other Managing Directors had said goodbye I stayed back hoping to see John Rose alone. Unfortunately he was deep in discussion with Barry. After waiting about 20 minutes I decided to intervene. 'John, Barry - I must speak to you before I set off back home.' 'What is it Roy?' asked John. 'I feel the pressure has finally got through to me and I must resign my position as Managing Director of Tinsley's. I'm afraid I've had enough.' Barry looked more visibly shaken than John who said, 'Resign - Roy what's wrong?' 'Oh just about everything John,' I replied. 'There's no point in carrying on in my present state of mind.' 'Well, what are you going to do - have you planned anything?' John asked. Barry then came in 'Don't resign, that achieves nothing. For God's sake don't resign.' John asked again: 'Have you made any plans as to what you will do?' 'I don't know, probably join another company. One thing's for certain I can't afford to retire.' 'Join another company. Who?' queried Barry. 'Kenmart probably,' I said. 'Their MD is a personal friend so I'm sure they will give me a job.' John then stepped in and took charge of our small meeting. 'Take some time off Roy. Go home - do

not go into the Works at all. Keep completely away. We will have another discussion in a couple of weeks.' So although I wanted to resign, I found myself on leave instead. I did not feel any better but realised that if I stayed away from the Works for a while it would give me the opportunity to seriously consider everything and to be sure I had made the right decision.

After two weeks leave I saw John at the Shipley Works. I told him it was still my intention to leave and probably join a competitor. To be very fair to John he offered me a contract to stay with Tinsley's for the next three years with the same salary, same car and same conditions. He said he would arrange early retirement for me and gave me some figures. Unfortunately they were not good enough for me to contemplate retirement. He also offered me a retainer to act as a consultant. He was more than fair but I just felt I could not continue. 'Take another month off,' John said. 'Do not go into the Works at all and I will be in touch with you by letter soon. You do realise Roy that if you resign you leave with absolutely nothing.' I said that was understood. To be honest I cannot think of another man of my age at that time who would have turned down the contract I had just been offered. But 'we are what we are' and I could not face the prospect of continuing my career with S. Tinsley's. There was no point in giving a character assassination of Barry Walford, but so far as I was concerned if he had not come into the equation I would still be there.

John wrote to me after a couple of weeks and asked me to go down to Chichester to discuss the ramifications of my leaving the company and to set up a date. He told me he would ask Barry to be in on the meeting as well. Two weeks later I duly took myself off to Chichester and arrived about 15 minutes prior to the appointment. When I entered Lee Newbon (the Managing Director of the Group) met me and invited me into his office. As we faced each other across his desk he asked: 'Well Roy, what's your decision?' 'I'm leaving Lee - that's it.' 'I don't want you to leave for two reasons,' he responded. 'You are a f... good salesman and a f... good mate and we do not want to lose men of your calibre. You know Geoff Lane don't you? Why don't you accept the three year contract and train him. He could be a good man for the Group and you could take things easy. Jobs don't come that easy Roy. Look at your age - it achieves nothing leaving. We all want you to stay.' To be fair to Lee he did everything within his power to talk me out of leaving, but my mind was made up. Some may have believed I had something lined up but I didn't although I had enough confidence to believe someone would give me a job. Then I went into John's office for the expected meeting with him and Barry. But as I entered John was alone. He got up, held out his hand and said: 'I felt it would be better if Barry wasn't present. It is only a matter for you and me to discuss.' He then excused himself and went out - he obviously had a word with Lee before he returned five minutes later. 'It seems you have made up your mind Roy. You realise that if you leave here today

to join a competitor you leave with nothing - no car, no salary - nothing. You realise that?' I assented but made a point of saying that I had not, at that time, made a decision to join anyone else. 'Oh - you have no arrangements made then?' asked John. 'No. I may even do my own thing for a while. I might even join my sons' business. But I do not wish to go back to Tinsley's.' 'Why on earth not Roy?' 'You don't know the half of it John, I replied.' 'Well, it does put a different complexion on things if you don't join a competitor. Can we talk about that?' 'Yes,' I replied. And we went into a deep discussion about my future away from the company. I hadn't realised how strongly he felt about me immediately working for a competitor. After lengthy deliberations I decided against joining another company and said I would work with my sons for at least six months. We reached the agreement, therefore, that I would receive six months' salary and could keep the car for six months. With that a contract was drawn up which I signed. John shook hands with me and said it had been a great pleasure working together for the past ten years and he would have preferred that I had stayed with the group until I had retired. 'In spite of your decision Roy I do really wish you well,' he said.

— CHAPTER 24 —

WHAT THE HELL HAVE I DONE?

The next few weeks were a torment. I knew I had made the greatest mistake of my life. What a fool I was! In retrospect I realised I should have knuckled down and seen out my time at S.Tinsley Ltd. Shirley (as usual) was marvellous. She fully understood the problems I had been experiencing. Sadly, at home, I was a changed man - on edge, argumentative and miserable. I kept my agreement with John Rose and did not go and join a competitor. For the first couple of months I worked in a consultative capacity with my sons' company and felt that what I contributed was of value. That wasn't the answer though and I decided to start 'The Roy Tinsley Company'. There was some spare office space in my sons' factory and I set up there. With the contacts I had in the trade it made sense and I soon managed to bring in many orders. One of the girls who worked at S. Tinsley's, Sally, had left there and was looking for a job. She was always very competent and amiable

so I invited her to join me as my secretary. It was to prove a very good move for both of us. She knew the trade and was a good and accomplished typist. Together we circulated a very nice letter and leaflet advertising my new company. It was pleasant to find out how many friends I still had in the industry (including overseas) and I received loyal support from quite a few. The three months' salary John had paid me proved a good basis for me to start my business. He had let me keep the car and so I didn't have to use any capital in that direction. Although my position at S. Tinsley's had been very well paid and provided security, starting my own business again was proving a great challenge and I was soon feeling in a much better frame of mind. Even so every day I was hoping John Rose would ring and say, 'Please come back Roy - we need you.' One major regret was that I was unable to continue working with Akiyama, the Japanese agency. I had become close friends with their chairman, Mr Ryujin and two of his other senior executives and I felt a sense of guilt for leaving. I knew they were upset when I left S. Tinsley's. We did remain in contact and Mr Ryujin invited me to meet him in New York to discuss various ideas he had for the agency over there. He sent me Club Class air tickets and we spent two very pleasant days together considering various objectives he had for the market. I felt my contributions were worth the fee he paid me.

My own small business was doing well and I was making quite a reasonable living out of it, what with paying Sally and meeting all my overheads

comfortably. In a 15-month period the turnover was in the region of £1,000,000 but I did feel frustrated occasionally at not having the necessary capital to go ahead with a few very profitable deals I knew I could convert. It was at that time I met up with some old friends, Ron Walker and Steve Bull. They had always struck me as being a couple of honest traders in our industry and they had achieved a lot of success over the past few years with their company, Rapide. We discussed our companies and I put the suggestion forward that a merger of the two could be very beneficial for all of us, especially as they were established in the South and my name was equally well known in the North. We had various discussions about ways of opening a Northern office and on November 26, 1988 I received a formal offer, which I accepted by letter on December 5, 1988. Throughout these discussions they had mentioned another company (Summit Leasing) in the background and in their November letter wrote:

"As we outlined to you we are already talking to a very large institution regarding funding, talks have been going on for six months and we are nearly completed. This would mean large sums of money at our disposal for the expansion of Rapide putting us, within two years, at the 'top of the league'. So the Northern factory is fundamental to the whole programme.

They offered a cash up-front payment, a salary of approximately £30,000 a year, company car and a percentage of the net profit. In return I voluntarily liquidated The Roy Tinsley Company. They employed Sally, took on my firm's assets

(office furniture etc) and the machines I had in stock. They made a net profit on my stock of £32,000. Once the company was established I managed to obtain the services of a top class engineer who had been a personal friend of mine for over 20 years. He was ready for a change and was glad to join me. A very knowledgeable man was needed as Works Manager and Karl Simpson fitted the bill perfectly. So we had the basis of a sound company. We then required a factory at a reasonable rent with facilities for installing our equipment so we could rebuild printing machinery.

I had been a local councillor and had many friends at the Town Hall. So I turned to Bradford Council for assistance. They were extremely helpful and managed to locate a single-storey warehouse with double-door loading, central heating and piped compressed air, good offices and all facilities. They could only guarantee it being available for two years but it was the perfect vehicle for our start. After lengthy negotiations I managed to rent it for only £10,500 per annum. Once we had settled in, Ron and Steve shipped quite a lot of equipment from their Southern works and I proceeded to sell it very, very quickly at good margins. In fact, I sold one machine to a good friend at Deansgate Press within four days of receiving it, whereas the Southern office had it in stock for six months. Karl was doing an excellent job installing the presses and we eventually appointed a further four staff. Within the next 14 months we had sold £2,583,250 worth of stock at a net profit of £391,075.

We were flying. I loved every minute. I recognised the fact that we were proving to be a very, very successful company which had been set up from scratch in the North of England. The only problem in the first four months was the negotiations between Summit and Rapide to conclude a deal or amalgamation. Ron and Steve were obviously holding out for a sound financial package for themselves and I am sure the huge success of the new Northern Division would have enhanced their position. In the meantime, however, they had not been able to open a bank account in Shipley and I had to pay out of my own account all the wages and other running costs of the company until May 1989. Each month I submitted an account to a wonderful old character - accountant Bill Bishop at Rapide. He would then send me a cheque in full settlement. Bill Bishop was very scathing in his remarks about the new Summit regime and said he was being badly hampered 'by men who just didn't understand the industry'. One day he phoned to tell me he had had enough and was resigning. He warned me, 'Watch your back'. How right he proved to be. Our sales continued at a very high rate and the profits on them were exceptional. The administration at the head office, however, was proving to be a complete shambles. They eventually opened a bank account in Shipley in May. They had previously promised me, one would be opened in February but instead seemed quite happy for me to use my own bank account to run the business. I was fortunate that Bradford Council knew me well and were willing to wait six months

before receiving any rent. My official start-up date with Rapide was March 1, 1989 and in February, I sent them the direct debit forms necessary for them to pay money into my pension/insurance scheme. It was also agreed they would include me in the company BUPA scheme. By May I wrote to them emphasising my surprise that neither had been paid even though I had been corresponding with them on those issues for over a month. That month they did enrol me in their BUPA scheme and by July increased my salary to cover my pension/insurance payments. My good standing and high reputation within the industry had a considerable knock-on effect in launching the new company. We pulled off some outstanding deals with enormous profits. To be fair to Ron and Steve they just let me get on with the job with little or no interference. All decisions for the Northern office were made by me. With a net profit of £261,000 between March and December 1989 I had to take on further staff to keep up with the workload. Sally needed assistance so I appointed Caroline who proved to be a superb secretary. As I required some back-up on the sales side I appointed Peter Kershaw - a loyal worker and friend who had the ability to adapt to any type of work given to him. Both had been with me at S. Tinsley's and had been asking me for a job for sometime. Karl appointed a paint sprayer and a very good printer/demonstrator called Mark Simmen. We had a very good loyal staff and built up a reputation in the North of England for the standard of our reconditioned equipment and back-up service.

Early in 1990 (without any consultation with me) two young men were appointed from our chief competitors - Steve Abbot and Mark Parsons. I thought then that Steve Bull and Ron Walker made the appointments. Abbot and Parsons were given very high salaries and new Jaguar cars. A few days later I had a telephone call to say these two young men were on their way and could I be available to see them. Of course I could - but what did they wish to see me about? They arrived in one of those new Jaguar cars, walked straight through to my personal office, exchanged a few pleasantries and then Steve Abbot opened his brief case, brought out some forms and said he would like me to fill them in regarding all future sales. He informed me I also had to fill in enquiry forms and submit them to him on a daily basis. What's more I should submit to him personally a full list of all my overseas contacts as he and Mark had been put in charge of the export side of the business. I was far from impressed. Not only had I not been consulted about these appointments but these young men with only a few years experience of the industry appeared in my office acting as if they had been appointed over me and that I was accountable to them. If I am employed by a company they can expect my total commitment and 100 per cent loyalty. However, I have always believed in discussing important matters with all my staff and keeping everyone informed. Yet head office hadn't the decency or courtesy to discuss any of this with me before these two men walked into my office. I wasn't the only one upset.

The head office already had two exceptional, successful salesmen with many years of experience - Tony Hunt and Chris Hayo, and yet Steve Abbot and Mark Parsons had been put in charge of Tony and Chris. I couldn't believe it - neither could Chris. We were then told there was to be a sales meeting at head office and I along with Ron Walker, Steve Bull, Tony, Chris and all Summit Leasing salesmen were to attend. And who was to address this meeting? Steve Abbot and Mark Parsons. It was not easy for a group of such experienced men to sit there and be lectured on the best way of obtaining sales. I found it especially difficult as I believed I only answered to Ron Walker and Steve Bull. I most certainly had had enough when Abbot and Parsons told us that the company intended to open factories in Singapore, Hong Kong and on the Continent. I got up and left. Ron Walker and Steve Bull followed me. Outside I turned to them and said: 'You might have told me we were considering opening factories all over the world.' To my amazement Steve implied this was the first he knew of it. So who was calling the shots? It seemed to me by then that Ray Keane had appointed Abbot and Parsons. I went back North and knuckled down to running the company as before. There was no way, however, that I would complete those new forms as requested by Abbot and Parsons. Nor did I intend to pass on all my overseas contacts which had taken me 30 years to compile - whatever Abbot thought. In a memorandum he circulated in February he stated: 'Roy Tinsley will send his export contact list to SA and MP as soon as

possible identifying his personal contacts (these are not expected to be no more than a handful)'.

Those at head office exerted considerable pressure, however, arguing that we needed to share our resources to achieve our goals and I was eventually persuaded to send a list. As business in the Northern office continued to increase I found it hard to cope with all the sales and administration. I needed an assistant with his own contacts. So when I met Pam Dawson one day at the bank, I was very interested to hear that her husband, Max, was no longer working for Westmyer and was searching for a job. I told her he could contact me - which he did. I discussed the situation with Ron Walker and Steve Bull, who also knew Max, and we made him an offer. Shirley very rarely interfered with anything to do with my work but she remembered Max from the days when I worked at Westmyer. She warned me it would be a great mistake to employ him. When I said Max would be a big help she replied: 'Alright, you go ahead but promise me you will keep an eye on him - or you will be out of a job.' Shirley was far more perceptive than me. Throughout our married life she was invariably right with such assessments and I should have listened to her. Initially Max did prove a big help and we made a successful team. He brought in a lot of additional export business.

There were times when the Sunbury office did not invoice clients once machinery had been installed. Max and I knew of two such deals totalling £269,500. On both occasions, Rapide

would never have received payment if friends within those companies had not informed us personally that they had not been invoiced.

For myself I pulled off two very big deals that showed a collective net profit in the region of £100,000. While at S. Tinsley's, Tony Smith (the Financial Director), John Rose and I had worked out a very good costing system that although not infallible was accurate. I had introduced this system to Rapide and it was always used by Rapide North. Then one of the ladies in the Sunbury accounts department called me personally to inform me that she believed the sales figures at the head office were being logged incorrectly so that Rapide North showed a loss of £6,000. That £100,000 had, it seemed, been credited to the head office sales staff. Was all this just incompetence - or worse? I found it hard to believe the stories I heard from the Sunbury accounts department that our profits were being apportioned to the head office to bolster their poor sales. I really didn't know who I could turn to at the head office to sort out this inaccurate reporting of the Northern offices' sales and profits.

I had a visit several weeks earlier by the Group Accountant, Alan Harrold. He had initially expressed his disappointment that our sales figures from March to October 1990 stood at only £440,000. I provided him with evidence that our sales in that period amounted to £2,548,250 and asked him if those had been placed somewhere else. With the figures he had quoted, I could

understand the Directors of Summit Leasing at St. Katherine's Way in the Docklands of London arguing that they could not justify retaining the Northern office. With all the confusion over the new premises I wrote on October 22, 1990 to the Board of Directors clearly detailing our sales (£5,131,250) and half a million pounds worth of profits in 1989 and 1990. So I was stunned by the memorandum I received a few days later saying they intended closing down the Northern Factory.

I was devastated. I had to tell most of my loyal staff that they were being made redundant. Even worse I had to inform Karl that instead of getting a promotion he was to be out of work! Only the two girls for the new sales office, Max and myself would be retained. I had to tell my friend at the turbine company that we were unable to go ahead regarding their premises. It had never been my intention to let him down - but there I was doing exactly that. I felt awful. He accepted the situation but in my opinion he felt we had taken advantage of him. It was a very sad time, but I tried to conclude it as diplomatically as possible. After Christmas we were established in our new premises in Shipley. Business still continued at a good rate and Max was handling some excellent export sales. By then all advertisements gave both addresses and not surprisingly many prospective clients wrote direct to 'headquarters' in the south. It bothered me, however, that all enquiries were followed up by Abbot and Parsons even if these were only a one hour drive from our office in Shipley. In February I wrote to Ron Walker and

Steve Bull requesting clarification of their policy on home market sales and stated, 'Personally, it makes little sense to have Sunbury following up sales leads just down the road from here.' I received no reply. In early March, however, they and Ray Keane announced they were coming to see me on a rather important matter. I watched them as they got out of the car by my office - they were all smiling and seemed to be in a good mood.

They said they wanted to speak to me privately and once we were alone they came straight to the point. They were going to reduce my salary from £35,000 to £10,000 a year and pay me a commission on sales. As a Managing Director I had never been paid on a commission basis before and never wanted to be! I was utterly shocked. 'Why?' I asked. Ray said the group was under great pressure. When I asked what would happen if I didn't accept he gave me to understand that I would be made redundant. When I went home and discussed it all with Shirley she was absolutely disgusted. I felt like telling them to 'stuff the job' - my mind was in such turmoil. That same evening Ron Walker rang me at home and said he felt sure I could still maintain my existing salary with the commission offered. To me he sounded so patronising that I felt quite sick. I found it difficult to recognise the man I had known two years earlier. Nor did I feel I received much support from Max even though he did say the right things (like it all being grossly unfair).

I felt sure that the Senior Directors at St. Katherine's Way had no idea about our sales

figures in the North or the other problems within the group. I decided to write to Kit Hunter-Gordon, the head of the Summit Group, and request a meeting. I realised that such a move was liable to cost me my job but to me I was living a lie and I didn't wish to continue that way. I had not intended to tell anyone about the letter but at the last minute I did show it to Max Dawson. A few days later I received a telephone call from Kit Hunter-Gordon requesting me to meet with him. St. Katherine's Way is miles away from Sunbury so no one should have known I was making that visit.

When I arrived I was taken straight through to the board room to meet Kit Hunter-Gordon, Phillip Ralph and John Hancock. We had a long and detailed discussion and Kit Hunter-Gordon was very understanding. I told him I would stake my reputation on the truth of the entire contents of the letter I had sent him. The meeting lasted about an hour at the end of which I was queried concerning the wisdom of telling Max Dawson about my contacting Kit Hunter-Gordon. Upon my return home I received a cryptic telephone call from Pam Dawson who said, 'Ron and Steve know you have been to St. Katherine's Way - forewarned is forearmed.' But who could have told them? Sadly - only her husband.

Next morning Kit Hunter-Gordon confirmed that the leadership of Rapide had been informed about my meeting with him and so it was no longer possible to carry out a private investigation. Sure enough Ray Keane phoned to ask me why I had made such a move. Max Dawson admitted to me

that he had told Ron and Steve. He wanted to put the matter right but this proved impossible to do. I was keen by then to leave Rapide but Shirley and I had booked another visit to my cousin in the States and were due to go within a few weeks. I didn't really want to hand in my notice before then. I therefore agreed (very reluctantly) to accept their proposal to cut my salary and pay me commission. They immediately sent me a contract to sign. I said I would sign it on my return from holiday. They insisted I signed it before I went, and actually drove to Bradford to collect it. I was to learn the significance of that later. When I returned after our three-week holiday in Canada and the States I found a letter on my desk marked 'Private and Confidential'. It was my redundancy notice. It had been typed the day after I signed the new contract. They had also informed 'Printing World' about my departure. In their article of June 12, 1991 the magazine stated: 'Mr Tinsley, who returns from holidaying in the US on Friday, will resume talks with colleagues about the timing of his departure which is termed an "amicable agreement" by Ron Walker, joint Managing Director of the secondhand machinery firm. "He wants to pursue other activities. He's very close to retirement," says Mr Walker. "The Northern office is very strong and will continue. Max Dawson is the sales manager and will keep the title. There will be no replacement of Roy Tinsley directly."' Printing World added: 'Mr Tinsley told us earlier this year, "I can't retire. If I'm not doing a bit of dealing .. oh, I don't know what I'd do." It seemed to me that all the major players at the head office

had closed ranks and I would have to go. As I had been a member of the Printers' Union for so long I did qualify for free legal advice and I believed I had sufficient evidence to prove a claim of constructive dismissal. If I could prove I had been put in such an intolerable situation by my employers that there had been no alternative but to leave rather than working on in such circumstances there was the possibility of being awarded at least two years' salary. The solicitor obviously wanted to know what position I had held and how much I had been paid. I explained that I was the Managing Director and had been receiving £35,000 per year, plus pension, private health insurance and a company car. However there was no contract for that. The only contract I had signed was the one they were so keen to collect the day before they made me redundant. The solicitor was dumbstruck. She explained that if I hadn't signed that contract she felt confident they would have had to pay me a minimum of £40,000 plus the car. With that contract, however, they could get away with one month's notice! I most certainly was not impressed by the type of people I had to deal with. Both my solicitor and I felt we had a good case for constructive dismissal. I was prepared to fight. Shirley, however, was dead against all the trauma of a court case and begged me not to go down that road.

— CHAPTER 25 —

"THE FINAL CHAPTER"

Whilst on holiday Shirley had begun to experience severe pain in her shoulders. It must have been bad for her to complain. Our local doctor diagnosed it as 'a little rheumatism or arthritis' and prescribed some cream for her to rub into her shoulders. However, the pain continued and Shirley was suffering so badly. I decided to instruct my solicitor to negotiate for better terms with Rapide. She did this and obtained an agreement between myself and Rapide which referred to my departure as retirement. As for Max Dawson, he received an increase in salary and took over running the Northern office in my place. I was 63, out of work and not old enough to cash in my pensions. I had to try and start up all over again. It wasn't going to be easy but I felt I could offer something to the companies run by my sons and son-in-law. It was such a refreshing change after the past year to be, so far as I was concerned, involved in just honest-to-goodness business again.

At home though, Shirley was having a bad time. Six months had past and the cream prescribed by her doctor was having no impact on the pain. We decided she must see a specialist as we were concerned her complaint could be serious. We booked an appointment at the Yorkshire Clinic. They carried out some tests and told us the same day that Shirley had Multiple Myeloma (cancer of the bones). We were devastated. Why couldn't that have been diagnosed earlier? In January 1992 we were introduced to Dr Parapia, a leading specialist of this type of cancer, who said Shirley had to have immediate chemotheraphy and radiotherapy. We came to understand that the life expectancy of someone suffering from such cancer four years earlier would only have been about 24 months. With the advances made through medical research it was possible that a patient could now live for a further ten years, but six precious months had been wasted. She had chemotherapy every third week and radiotherapy every six weeks. I could see it was knocking hell out of her but she never complained. She was so brave - she even kept me going. Then one day, when Carol came to do her hair, Shirley unfortunately slipped off a chair. She broke her arm and her leg in two places and had to stay in hospital for six weeks. It was a real down-point in my life yet my beloved wife never said, 'Why me? It's not fair.' Nothing like that at all. She was so courageous through all that extreme pain.

When she did come out of hospital I decided to work from home so I could be there all the time

and take care of her. I had an extra telephone line and a fax installed and did manage to maintain a steady little income. Shirley was wonderful. When I was out shopping for instance she would take all the calls and act as my unpaid secretary. She insisted on getting out of bed each morning and struggling to the shower. I had handles installed right round the shower and up the stairs so she could pull herself along and support herself. She was going through hell with the pain. I would help her shower, washing her hair and help her dry herself. Shirley had wonderful auburn hair. It was so beautiful - it was her crowning glory. Sadly each day, due to the chemotherapy, it fell out in handfuls. I found that especially heart-rending. Surely it was enough to know you had cancer and had to go through the continuous trauma of chemotherapy and radiotherapy without having to lose your hair as well.

Our daughter Carol, and Shirley were always very close. Carol said she didn't look on Shirley as her mum but more as her best friend. She talked Shirley into having a wig. Between them they bought an excellent one but when you consider the beautiful hair Shirley had prior to the cancer you could understand her being reluctant to wear a hair-piece. She did, however, and I helped her battle through the pain to get to the car so I could take her out into the Yorkshire Dales and visit a few country pubs together. She had to use a stick and a walking frame to get about but in the end even that was too difficult. Even so she would not accept using a wheelchair. I can think of no

person on this earth who would have tolerated that extreme pain and yet, whenever visitors came, would be so cheerful and encourage everyone. A dear couple, Joyce and Jimmy Slack, visited regularly. We had all been close friends for over 30 years and Joyce became very upset at seeing Shirley so ill. Yet it was Shirley who put them at their ease. One day Shirley was resting on the bed filing and putting polish on her nails. Jimmy said: 'Shirley, how do you find the patience to do that? It looks agony for you.' She just replied: 'I must always maintain my standards Jimmy - always.' After three or four months of cajoling - and with Christmas 1992 just around the corner - we persuaded her to accept using a wheelchair. I even took her to Marks and Spencers in it and bought a new coat. Sadly she never got to wear it. Little did I know that our days together were numbered. Somehow I always felt that with my daily prayers and the prayers of so many friends, along with the chemotherapy and radiotherapy, she would live to see a couple more summers. I never really lost hope that Shirley's health might improve so we would enjoy a few more happy months together. We had Christmas lunch with Carol and her husband Steven. Steven and I helped Shirley into the house and then had put her in the wheelchair. I'm sure children are more perceptive than adults for Nicola and Richard seemed to quickly understand how ill their grandmother was. It was such a pleasant day. Gary came with his wife Sandra and their children, Thomas and Charlotte. So did Steven, his wife Debbie and their children, Donna and Matthew. I was very proud of my

lovely grandchildren (and still am). Shirley said afterwards she was so relieved Christmas was over.

She was determined to get through to the New Year for all of our sakes - which, when she was suffering so much, was very typical of her wonderful attitude. She managed one more visit to the Yorkshire Clinic for another dose of chemotherapy but I knew then she would not be able to make the trip again. Once she returned home and collapsed on the bed I knew that my beloved Shirley was near to the end.

At this time we received a letter from Nancy in the U.S.A. to say her beloved husband Mac had died from cancer. She had been too upset to talk to me and knew Shirley was very ill, so had decided to write and tell us. We had all been so close and enjoyed many wonderful times together. Shirley knew the letter had arrived from Nancy and became very upset after reading the contents. Yet she still managed to put on such a brave face and speak to Nancy and comfort her. How on earth I ever managed to meet, love and marry such a wonderful person I don't know.

I had never requested any help from the doctor or any other source. All I wanted to do was nurse Shirley myself. She had given me so much. Everything I had achieved in life was down to her. My love for her was deeper than at any time in our marriage - and I had loved her ever since the first day I had met her. My yearning to see a few more summers with her couldn't stop me seeing that she was becoming worse towards the end of

January 1993. The pain became unbearable - I knew that by the look of agony on her face. But still she never complained. It was then I decided to ask Dr Parapia how long we had together. He replied that Shirley was very, very ill and had but a few weeks to live. She had been so brave in covering up, that we all felt we had a couple of years at least. On January 31st I contacted the family and gave them the sad news. We were all devastated. The whole family stayed throughout the night. The next day Shirley slipped into a coma. When the doctor saw her he said it was a matter of hours. We all gathered around Shirley's bed and talked and talked and talked about those happy years together. I will never know if Shirley heard us or not. She eventually died in my arms at 7am February 2nd, 1993. It was the saddest day of my entire life. All her family were there to share the great loss we had experienced.

We had many houses, many joys and many wonderful years together.

A few days before Shirley died, she told me she would not have liked to have missed living in any one of our homes, each one had something special to offer. She said "I have no hobbies just my family who mean everything to me".

Whatever we as a family have achieved is down to my beloved wife Shirley. We and many others are better people for just the knowing of her.

OUR HOMES, OUR LOVE, OUR CHILDREN, OUR LIFE

FROM LINDLEY, GOLCAR, AND LEYMOOR TOO,
TO STAFFORDSHIRE, THAT HOUSE WAS NEW,
THEN ON TO FARSLEY, PART OF LEEDS,
INDEED WE'RE BUYING LOTS OF DEEDS.

THE KIDS ARE HAPPY, SO IS SHIRL,
OH HOW I'M GLAD I WED THAT GIRL,
FIVE HOUSES, THREE KIDS AND SALLY TOO,
THEN THE SEMI ON BELLE VUE.

NICE HOUSE, NICE GARDEN, BUT STOP THERE? NO,
IT'S THEN BACK LANE AND OUR BUNGALOW,
LOVELY HOME WE'VE MADE OUR MARK,
AND OF COURSE IT'S NEAR THE PARK.

SEVENTH HOME, THREE KIDS, NOW DAD IS HERE,
HE SHARES OUR HOME, OUR HOPES OUR TEARS,
HIS HEALTH IS POOR, HE GETS ON WITH LIFE,
HE OFTEN BROODS, THINKS OF HIS WIFE.

DAD LEAVES THIS WORLD, HIS LIFE COMPLETE,
AND ANOTHER CHILD THERE IS TO GREET,
WE ARE BLESSED WITH CHRIS A BABY BOY,
OUR GRIEF IS TURNED AROUND TO JOY.

THE HOUSE IS NICE, WE LIKE LIVING THERE,
BUT MY BUSINESS LIFE IS HARD TO BEAR,
THE BANK CALLS IN MY GUARANTEES,
WE HAVE TO SELL AND BUY KIRKLEES.

WE PAY THE BANK, BUT THE MORTGAGE KILLS,
SO WE LOOK AROUND AT ECCLESHILL,
WE SEE THIS LOVELY OLD ABODE,
IT'S FULL ADDRESS IS 12 LEEDS ROAD.

IT NEEDS A LOT OF LOVING CARE,
IT'S IN A STATE OF BAD REPAIR,
WE LOOK AROUND AND FEEL IT'S FINE,
SO SELL OUR EIGHTH, MAKE THIS OUR NINTH,

WE SPEND A LOT ON MANY THINGS,
AND HAPPINESS IT SURELY BRINGS,
IT HAD THAT CHARACTER AND POISE,
AND COMPLETELY FREE FROM OUTSIDE NOISE.

IT'S WALLS WE'RE SURE ARE FOUR FOOT THICK,
CONSTRUCTED WITH BEST STONE AND BRICK,
ALAS SOME PARTS WERE VERY DAMP,
THE GARDEN THE SIZE OF A POSTAGE STAMP.

SO WE LOOKED AROUND FOR ANOTHER DEN,
AND MOVED TO BAILDON, HOUSE NUMBER TEN,
A LOVELY SEMI , FOUR BEDROOMS TOO!
A SUN BALCONY WITH A LOVELY VIEW.

MY JOB WAS GOOD, MY PAY QUITE HIGH,
TO SAVE SOME TAX A DETACHED WE'D TRY,
WE LOOKED AROUND ON TRANMERE PARK,
NOW THERE'S A PLACE TO MAKE YOUR MARK!

3 BROADWAY WAS THE ONE IN MIND,
A BETTER ONE WE COULDN'T FIND,
LARGE GARDENS, TREES AND PRIVATE TOO,
AND FROM THE LOUNGE, A LOVELY VIEW.

AND VERY NEAR TO CHRIS'S SCHOOL,
AND ALSO GUISELEY SWIMMING POOL,
A DINING ROOM A LOUNGE AND BAR,
THE MOST EXPENSIVE THIS BY FAR.

AS ALL OUR HOMES, A HAPPY PLACE,
IT HAD MUM'S TOUCH AND STYLE AND GRACE,
SHE LOVED IT THERE, IT HAD GREAT STYLE,
AND FOR THREE YEARS, WE BIDE A WHILE.

THE MORTGAGE PAYMENTS ARE VERY HIGH,
AND AT OUR AGE WE WONDER WHY?
MY LOVELY WIFE SHE NEVER MOANS,
AT ALL THESE CHANGES IN OUR HOMES.

SO INTO THE MARKET WE NOW DELVE,
TO TRY AND FIND OUR NUMBER TWELVE,
WHICHEVER HOUSE WE WENT AND BOUGHT,
SHIRLEY FILLED IT WITH HER LOVE AND THOUGHT.

WE TALK IT OVER AND THEN DECIDE,
THIS WILL BE THE LAST THAT WE RESIDE,
WE LOOK, WE VIEW, SO MANY WE SOUGHT,
UNTIL WE'VE FOUND OUR FAIRFIELD COURT.

IT HAD A FEEL ABOUT IT THERE,
I KNEW WITH SHIRLEY'S LOVE AND CARE,
THIS WAS THE PLACE OUR LAST ABODE,
WHERE WE COULD LIVE AND REST OUR LOAD.

WE'D BEEN SO HAPPY LIVING THERE,
IT'S FULL OF SHIRLEY'S LOVE AND CARE,
WE'VE SHARED OUR JOYS HERE AND OUR LOVE,
IT WAS SURELY FASHIONED FROM ABOVE.

Roy Tinsley

Born in 1927, Roy spent his early years living on
council estates with his parents Bill & Trudy Tinsley
and his two brothers. Life was anything but easy
and he left school one month short of his 14th
birthday to enter the Engineering Trade. He
disliked it from day one and with the help of his
Sunday School Teacher entered the Printing
Industry six weeks later - He loved every minute.
When he was seventeen he volunteered for the
Royal Navy and after only six weeks training he was
drafted out to the Far East where he saw service in
Burma, Singapore and the Persian Gulf, spending
his 18th, 19th and 20th birthdays out there. His
account of his time in the Navy is both humorous
and thought provoking and makes one wonder
how on earth we won the war! On 'Demob' he
re-entered the Printing Industry and eventually
achieved his ambition in becoming a salesman in
the Printing Machinery Trade. He may describe his
industry as "one that has more shady corners than
a maze on an October evening"

thriving on the buzz he gets fr

equipment all over the world, I

majority of dealers in many co

account of them and their vari

honest and dishonest) make ca

Having contributed greatly to the Printing industry,
Roy's main outlet has always been his family, his
Cricket, his Rugby League and his bedrock
throughout - his wonderful wife Shirley, to whom
this book is dedicated.

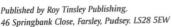

9780952854807

Published by Roy Tinsley Publishing.
46 Springbank Close, Farsley, Pudsey. LS28 5EW